EXCHANGING BIBLIOGRAPHIC DATA

MARC and other international formats

EXCHANGING BIBLIOGRAPHIC DATA

MARC and other international formats

Ellen Gredley
Alan Hopkinson

CANADIAN LIBRARY ASSOCIATION / Ottawa
THE LIBRARY ASSOCIATION / London
AMERICAN LIBRARY ASSOCIATION / Chicago

© Ellen Gredley, Alan Hopkinson 1990

Published by Library Association Publishing Ltd
7 Ridgmount Street, London WC1E 7AE
ISBN 0-85365-899-4

Simultaneously published in the USA by the American Library Association,
50 East Huron Street, Chicago, Illinois 60611
ISBN 0-8389-2151-5

Simultaneously published in Canada by the Canadian Library Association,
200 Elgin Street, Ottawa, Ontario K2P 1L5
ISBN 0-88802-258-1

First published 1990

British Library Cataloguing-in-Publication Data

Gredley, Ellen
  Exchanging bibliographic data : MARC and other international formats.
  1. Documents. Cataloguing. Machine-readable files: MINICS records. Manuals
  I. Title II. Hopkinson, Alan
  025.3'028'5574

  ISBN 0-85365-899-4

Library of Congress Cataloging-in-Publication Data

Gredley, Ellen
    Exchanging bibliographic data : MARC and other international formats / Ellen Gredley,
  Alan Hopkinson.
        p.   cm.
    Includes bibliographical references.
    ISBN 0-8389-2151-5
    1. Exchange of bibliographic information. 2. Machine-readable bibliographic data--Format.
  3. Bibliography. International--Data processing. 4. MARC System. I. Hopkinson, A. (Alan)
  II. Canadian Library Association. III. Library Association. IV. American Library Association.
  V. Title
  Z699.35.E94G74   1990
  025.3'16--dc20   90-104

Canadian Cataloguing in Publication Data

Gredley, Ellen
  Exchanging bibliographic data : MARC and other international formats

  Co-published by: Canadian Library Association and the Library Association.
  ISBN 0-8389-2151-5 (American Library Association)
    ISBN 0-88802-258-1 (Canadian Library Association)
    ISBN 0-85365-899-4 (Library Association)

    1. Exchange of bibliographic information. 2. Machine-readable bibliographic data.
  3. Bibliography, International. 4. MARC System--Format. I. Hopkinson, A. (Alan)
  II. American Library Association. III. Canadian Library Association.
  IV. Library Association. V. Title

  Z699.4.M2G74 1990   025.3'0285'572   C90-090112-8

Typeset in 11/12pt Baskerville by Library Association Publishing Ltd
Printed and made in Great Britain by Bookcraft (Bath) Ltd

To the memory of Anthony Long

Contents

Contents

List of illustrations

Preface

Exchanging bibliographic data is intended to provide students, librarians, information scientists and systems analysts with an introduction to the nature of bibliographic records and machine-readable bibliographic data formats, an outline of the major international exchange formats developed for transfer of bibliographic data and some indication of the problems raised by attempts to exchange data between agencies in different countries.

Where possible, information is presented in a manner suited to readers without expertise in computing technology or in cataloguing for machine-based systems.

Each chapter contains its own list of notes and references, supplemented, where appropriate, by additional readings.

Acknowledgements

We are indebted to all authors, publishers and other organizations for permission to use extracts from their publications and to reproduce examples and other material. We wish also to thank: Ross Bourne and Brian Holt, of the British Library National Bibliographic Service, for kindly allowing access to documentation and supplying information on the progress of the UKMARC format revision; Winston Roberts of the IFLA UBCIM Programme; Sally McCallum and Susan Tarr of the Library of Congress; Stephen Massil for help with formats in S. E. Asia; Sandra Brookes of OCLC Europe; Isabel Dungate, for checking foreign text; and Luz Marina Quiroga and Mirna Willer for detailed help with their respective national formats. We are grateful to all institutions and organizations which have generously supplied the information and documentation which have made this study possible (any errors or omissions are, of course, our own); and to numerous friends and colleagues, in particular Anthony Long, for encouragement and constructive criticism. Thanks also go to Margaret Duane and June York, for skilful handling of the manuscript and for calmness in the face of much MARC tagging; to Library Association Publishing Ltd, for their kindness and forbearance; and to our respective families, for patience and support during the preparation of the book.

Introduction: Bibliographic control and the exchange of bibliographic data

Bibliographic control has been most memorably defined as 'the mastery over written and published records which is provided by and for the purposes of bibliography'.[1] This definition appeared in 1950; in the intervening years computers have had an irreversible effect on the library and information community and technological progress has not only provided sophisticated means of bibliographic control but has made possible the worldwide exchange of bibliographic information in ways which to many people 40 years ago would have seemed scarcely credible.

The problems to be overcome and the methods, actual and potential, for achieving bibliographic control have been the subject of much discussion and research, in which recurrent themes are the significant increase in production of books and other materials and the need to organize this vast output for effective use. National libraries and bibliographic agencies are no longer expected to carry alone the whole burden of controlling a nation's bibliographic output and cooperation in record creation and the exchange of bibliographic data are more essential than ever before.

The goal of Universal Bibliographic Control (UBC) is the creation of an international system for the controlled exchange of bibliographic information. This ambitious enterprise depends upon the full cooperation of every nation and requires national libraries or national bibliographic agencies to assume responsibility for creating, or for coordinating the creation of, authoritative bibliographic records of all newly published items and for speedily producing and distributing those records in an appropriate standardized form. UBC was adopted as a major programme by the International Federation of Library Associations and Institutions (IFLA) in 1974.[2] Since then, IFLA has developed two further and related core programmes: Universal Availability of Publications (UAP) and the International MARC Programme (IMP).[3] UAP attempts to improve access to publications nationally and internationally and a major aim of IMP is the promotion of an international network for the exchange of bibliographic data. In 1987 UBC was fused with IMP to become UBCIM (Universal Bibliographic Control and International MARC Programme), thus merging two aspects of the control of bibliographic records: their creation in standardized form and their dissemination in standard MARC (machine-readable catalogue) format.[4] UBC, it is hoped, will be realized by an international MARC network, based on a universal MARC format, UNIMARC. The unrestricted flow of machine-readable records is thus seen as a crucial part of both national and international bibliographic control.

UBC embraces all publications, although the greatest advances have been made in the control of printed books. In many countries, audiovisual and other non-print materials are not recorded by national agencies; many specialist publications, including documents emanating from intergovernmental and international organizations, are also poorly controlled. Anderson, while stressing the importance of bibliographic control of newer and less conventional information products, notes the problems raised by their elusiveness and rapidly changing character.[5] UBC extends by implication to parts of documents and individual items within collections. National bibliography and the bibliographic control of books as complete units have traditionally been the preserve of libraries, while the recording and indexing of the contents of documents, specifically articles in journals, have in general been undertaken by the abstracting and indexing services. The two sectors of the information community have adopted different conventions and practices, which pose problems for cooperation and exchange. In the past, the activities of IFLA's UBC Programme have reflected more the interests of national bibliographic agencies and national libraries, whereas Unesco, through its UNISIST Programme, has largely been responsible for coordinating developments in the control of documents normally handled by the secondary services, such as articles in journals, patents, reports and conference papers. Over the last decade, however, determined efforts have been made to bridge the alleged gap and to bring the two groups closer together in terms of form and content of bibliographic records.

Easy interchange of bibliographic records requires agreement on standards governing the medium of exchange, the organization and representation of data and record definition and content. That so many successful exchanges take place is a tribute to the commitment of the library and information community to bibliographic cooperation, but acceptance of international standards may create, as well as solve, problems. A global exchange programme of the kind envisaged by IFLA, capable of drawing on the most sophisticated communications technology, inevitably raises a number of serious issues, of which the technical, in the view of many writers, are subordinate to the political, economic and social. New concerns have emerged, such as copyright and legal ownership of data and the economic impact of redistribution of bibliographic records from national agencies to third parties, especially commercial organizations. Technological developments have made it difficult for record producers, particularly those who also provide online services, to regulate the use of their records. The ideal of UBC – exchange, free and unrestricted, yet at the same time cooperative, coordinated, controlled – is perhaps implicitly contradictory; if so, it is a contradiction glaringly exposed by the informational cornucopia which has directly resulted from the explosive growth in the use of microcomputers.

This book is primarily concerned with exchange formats, i.e. formats that are designed specifically for the transfer of machine-readable bibliographic data between systems. There have been relatively few comprehensive analyses of the extent and nature of variation in record structure, although Renaud has provided a useful model which facilitates discussion of the difficulties for data exchange caused by the existence of different formats.[6] He identifies five levels at which data generation and exchange take place: international, national, intranational, regional and local. Data exchange is by definition a two-way process, normally between record-producing centres such as national libraries or bibliographic agencies, and may be distinguished from simple data transfer or distribution, which need be only one-way, perhaps from national library or bibliographic agency to individual organizations within a country. But improved technology has helped break down traditional patterns and multi-directional data movements are now more frequent. Our particular concern is national MARC exchange formats and international formats designed to enable bibliographic data to be communicated between agencies in different countries. Formats used for local/internal processing are therefore outside our scope, although it is recognized that some national MARC formats, for example USMARC, are often used for this purpose. While acknowledging also that current exchange formats may be affected by rapidly changing technology, in particular the development of Open Systems Interconnection procedures for data transfer and the growth of CD-ROM as a medium for data storage and distribution, our main objective is to present a technical and historical account of existing formats, rather than to speculate on the future.

Notes and references

1   *Bibliographical services, their present state and possibilities of improvement*, Washington, Library of Congress, 1950 (Unesco/Library of Congress bibliographical survey).
2   Anderson, D., *Universal Bibliographic Control: a long-term policy, plan for action*, Pullach bei München, Verlag Dokumentation Saur, 1974.
3   IFLA's core programmes are described in *IFLA journal*, **12**, (4), 1986, 296 – 342.
4   *IMP newsletter*, **6**, December 1986.
5   Anderson, D., *UBC: a survey of Universal Bibliographic Control*, London, IFLA International Office for UBC, 1982, (Occasional paper no.10), 28. This also appears as 'Universal Bibliographic Control', *in Encyclopedia of library and information science*, Vol. 37, Supplement 2, New York, Dekker, 1984, 366 – 401.
6   Renaud, R., 'Resolving conflicts in MARC exchange: the

structure and impact of local options', *Information technology and libraries*, **3**, 1984, 255 – 61.

Additional readings

Davinson, D., *Bibliographic control*, 2nd ed., London, Bingley, 1981.
Line, M. and Vickers, S., *Universal availability of publications (UAP)*, Munich, K. G. Saur, 1983, (IFLA publications 25).

1

Bibliographic data and bibliographic records

Bibliographic data

Bibliographic data are generated, for the most part, by bibliographers, cataloguers, abstractors and indexers, publishers and booksellers. The data appear in a range of products, including publishers' and booksellers' lists, online databases, abstracting and indexing services, reading lists, library catalogues and bibliographies of all kinds. The nature of bibliographic data is governed partly by usage: the library catalogue is different in kind from the bookseller's list, and some variation in the selection and presentation of different elements of data must be expected. Cataloguing traditions and practices, however, have exerted a powerful influence on our view of bibliographic data and although the creation of catalogues is only one of many applications, any discussion of the topic is inevitably coloured by this special relationship. To many people, bibliographic and cataloguing data appear to be identical, but bibliographic data have an independent existence and need separate consideration.

What, then, are bibliographic data? The literal answer is information pertaining to the listing or recording of books, but this definition is unsatisfactory on several counts. It does not specify the kind of information involved; it fails to recognize the numerous materials apart from books which are collected in libraries and information units and recorded in bibliographies; and it assumes that the accepted bibliographic unit is a single, physical entity, whereas there is often a need to record parts or groups of documents, for example articles in journals, chapters in books, a series of sheet maps. For want of a more suitable alternative, 'bibliographic item' is here used to mean any document, book, publication or other record of human commun-

1

ication, and any group of documents, or part of a document, which is treated as an entity for bibliographic purposes. Clarification of the type of data entailed is revealed by an examination of several suggested analyses. Hagler and Simmons define bibliographic data as 'elements of information which help to identify a piece of recorded communication *as a physical object*' (their italics) and identify three types of data, distinguished by broad function:

> (1) data which uniquely identify a particular document to distinguish it from others (for example a date of publication or a count of the number of pages in a printed book), (2) data which reveal an association of two or more documents (for example common authorship or the fact that one is a continuation or reprint of the other), and (3) data which describe some characteristic of the intellectual content of a document (for example a statement of its subject or the fact that it is a *Festschrift*).[1]

This analysis is helpful in pinpointing essential characteristics of bibliographic data, although it is expressed in terms best suited to books and book-like material and appears on the surface not to take into account bibliographic entities which do not exist as separate, physical objects. The linking of bibliographic data with the physical object also raises the question of intellectual product vs. physical manifestation, the work vs. book issue which for many years has troubled cataloguers and makers of cataloguing codes. This is discussed in the following section.

Analysis of data in connection with the development of machine-readable formats for the exchange of cataloguing and bibliographic information has led to recognition of three categories: authority, bibliographic and holdings/locations, which are perceived as performing distinct though related functions and which together comprise a complete set of information relating to a bibliographic item held in a specific collection. Authority data are bibliographic data representing uniform, 'official' forms of name and subject headings chosen for use within a system. The distinction between these types of data is discussed further in the section on bibliographic records.

Dempsey, in his comparative study of bibliographic data elements used in libraries and the book trade, identifies three loosely defined and overlapping groups: bibliographic description and control (broadly equated with data describing, identifying and providing controlled access to items), subject data and 'content description'.[2] The last category is used mainly for promotion and selection of materials and includes information such as readership level, category of work, author information and brief description. These elements, he maintains, have not traditionally appeared in library catalogues and bibliographies.

The following is offered as a generally applicable, though by no means exhaustive, list of data functions:

- data naming an item (e.g. title, alternative title)
- data naming persons or bodies connected with the creation of an item (e.g. author, artist, cartographic agency)
- data describing hierarchical, lateral or lineal relationships between items (e.g. component part, host item, numbering in series, companion item, name of earlier edition or version)
- data indicating intellectual content (e.g. subject heading, abstract)
- data naming persons or bodies connected with the production of an item as a physical object (e.g. publisher, designer)
- data indicating form or nature of item (e.g. bibliography, documentary, novel)
- data indicating mode of expression or communication (e.g. verbal, pictorial)
- data describing the physical appearance, characteristics and constituents of an item (e.g. map, film, dimensions, number of volumes or parts, technical information needed for use)
- data assigned by a bibliographic or other agency for purposes of identification or control (e.g. ISBN, key title)

These functions are obviously not mutually exclusive: the title *A history of printing in Britain* not only names a work, but also indicates its intellectual content; 'novel' implies both mode of communication and literary form.

A distinction may in theory be drawn between data which belong inherently to an item (e.g. author, title) and data which are assigned or supplied for a variety of purposes by different organizations. In practice, the distinction is difficult to sustain, as some assigned data, such as key title and ISSN (International Standard Serial Number) can act as unique identifiers, becom-

3

ing permanently linked with the publication. Much bibliographic data has in any case to be derived by intellectual effort from the items themselves, as not all carry the explicit data 'labels' (e.g. title, publisher, date) which are characteristic of books and serials. The main area of disagreement over what constitutes bibliographic data involves locally assigned data (e.g. accession numbers, shelf marks, loan numbers, stock numbers, holdings and location notes), which are assigned purely as a means of controlling or locating items within a particular collection or bibliographic listing. Hagler and Simmons would not regard such data, strictly speaking, as bibliographic data, as they describe not the item itself, but its status within a specific system.[3] This seems reasonable, because it places the emphasis on item-linked, rather than system- or application-linked information. Data used solely for commercial or marketing purposes are normally also excluded, although elements such as price and availability status are frequently accepted as 'bibliographic'. Whichever analysis of bibliographic data is preferred, it is clear that they perform differing but complementary key functions of identification, association and description of bibliographic items. Before considering the organization and major applications of bibliographic data, further examination of some of the stated functions and characteristics is needed.

The role of bibliographic data in the identification of items

Considerable importance is attached to the role of bibliographic data in the identification of items, i.e. in distinguishing one item, or group of items, from others. It is necessary, however, to clarify the precise degree of identification involved, and at this stage the notions of work, edition or version, and individual copy or item can be introduced. These are best illustrated by an example. In 1816, the publisher John Murray brought out the first edition of Jane Austen's novel, *Emma*. The work *Emma* has since appeared in numerous editions and versions, including many translations into languages other than the original English, and a television drama series. One of the many editions of *Emma* was published by Penguin Books in 1966, and copies from this edition can be found in numerous libraries and private collections. From this brief, but by no means untypical, publishing history can be seen the need to distinguish between the work *Emma*, the groups of documents or items which constitute editions or versions of this work, and the individual copies in library and other collections. Identification of the work *Emma* is achieved by citing the title alone, or, in the event of another work having been given the same title, by citing both author and title. Identification of particular editions or versions of *Emma* requires the specification of further details, for example publisher (Penguin Books) and date (1966). To identify a specific copy it is necessary to supply data peculiar to that copy, e.g. missing pages, type of binding, provenance. The case of *Emma* is relatively straightforward. Unravelling the complex histories of many items, for example a computer program that has been reworked through many versions, can present severe problems. Difficulties notwithstanding, the fundamental distinction between a work as intellectual or artistic product, and its physical manifestation in different editions or versions, including physical forms, should always be kept in mind, since it affects the analysis of bibliographic data and subsequent retrieval of items. In practical terms the degree of identification required can be decided by the answers to three questions:

(i) is the user interested only in the work, regardless of edition or version?
(ii) is the user interested in one particular edition, version or form of the work?
(iii) is the user interested only in one specific copy or item?

Unique identification
Can a single element of data uniquely identify an item? The title, or name, of an item is frequently cited as its major identifying feature; but, as we have seen, its powers of identification in most cases extend only to the work, as distinct from its physical manifestation in editions or versions. The need for unique identification of documents, especially important in automated systems, led to the development of standard identifying numbers such as ISBN (International Standard Book Number), ISSN (International Standard Serial Number) and CODEN (a unique six-character code assigned to serial titles). In all three, the identification extends not to individual copies but only to

members of editions or versions in the case of books, and to titles in the case of serials. In theory an ISBN should distinguish all documents which are members of a specific edition of a work, and paperback as opposed to hard-cover books. In practice, however, there is not always agreement whether the ISBN should relate to an edition or an impression, some publishers choosing whichever suits their stock control system. The purpose of the ISBN is occasionally misunderstood; at least one publisher in the United Kingdom has been known to use the same ISBN for all his publications! Further, in some countries, ISBNs are assigned only to commercially published items; in others the ISBN is not used at all. USBC (Universal Standard Book Code) has been suggested as a more reliable alternative to ISBN, particularly in identifying and eliminating duplicate records in shared databases.[4] It consists of a fixed-length machine-generated code, derived from the bibliographic data for each item. There are other systems, in varying stages of development and use, for standard numbering of other materials, e.g. Standard Technical Report Numbers (STRN) and International Standard Recording Codes (ISRC). Numbers assigned to items by national bibliographic or legal deposit agencies can also act as identifiers: the BNB serial number identifies a bibliographic record created by British Library Bibliographic Services; the Library of Congress card/control number performs a similar function. Catalogue numbers, stock numbers and accession numbers may act as copy-specific identifiers, although their use and value in general depends on the nature of the items concerned.

Essential and secondary bibliographic data

Are some data of more help in identifying documents and therefore more significant than others? Since bibliographic data are of different types and serve different purposes it is difficult to compile a generally applicable list of essential data; but high on any list of this kind would be elements such as name of author, title and subject information. The lowest rankings would probably be reserved for data elements such as number of pages, size of container, material of binding. On the other hand, these may be important to certain users. In some contexts, author, title and subject data may not be as significant as data sometimes believed to be generally less important in document identification; in art libraries, for example, the names of illustrators of books may be more significant than the authors of the books; in a collection of antiquarian material the year of printing and the printer's name may be of greater interest than the subject matter. Within each system, documents must be analysed in the light of user needs in order to pinpoint their most significant characteristics. For the successful identification and retrieval of items, a combination of data elements is in most cases necessary, although the exact nature of that combination may vary, depending on the amount and kind of data known to the user seeking the item.

Common data

Are the same bibliographic data elements present in all documents? Some, for example authors, titles, names of publishers, are common to many items. Some are unique to certain kinds of items, for example ISSN to serials, scale to cartographic materials. The same bibliographic data element may vary in length from one work to another, titles being an obvious example:

Hamlet
Requiem for the card catalog
A philosophical enquiry into the origin of our ideas of the sublime and beautiful.

An item may lack a customary data element, e.g.

a book without an ISBN
a computer program without a title
a painting by an unknown artist.

A specific data element may appear in some items and not in others in the same category, e.g.

coloured illustrations
named edition.

The irregularity and unpredictability of bibliographic data may be seen as an initial problem in automated systems by many computer programmers and systems analysts who are more accustomed to working with regular, predictable data. Conversely, bibliographical systems have been developed in complete ignorance of the need for variable-length data and of the need to repeat certain data elements, such as places of publication or series titles.

Accuracy and objectivity

Accuracy, especially in those data necessary to distinguish an item from others, is a *sine qua non* of effective retrieval. Although users may approach catalogues and bibliographies with inaccurate or imperfect bibliographic details, and some online systems can compensate for this, accuracy on the part of the cataloguer and bibliographer is expected. For many years cataloguers and bibliographers have also taken pride in their neutrality and objectivity towards bibliographic data. Judgements may have to be made in analysing data and in determining difficult questions, e.g. which is the correct title of a work for which there is more than one possible title? The general principle, however, is that any data supplied, e.g. the title in the case of an untitled item, must accurately and objectively reflect the nature of the item. Total objectivity is difficult – some would say impossible – to achieve when subject data are being considered. Even if experts agree on the subject content of an item, they may have different ideas on how this should be represented as subject headings or descriptors. In some contexts subjective and evaluative information may actually be desirable, an obvious example being critical abstracts geared to the known requirements of a particular set of users.

Bibliographic 'language'

The task of bibliographers and cataloguers is to make a complete and accurate analysis of bibliographic items, based on an understanding of their bibliographic problems. The results of this analysis are recorded and transmitted to users in the formal language of bibliography. The vocabulary of this language is a combination of common and specialized terminology (frequently in the form of abbreviations) and its syntactical rules are designed to allow communication of large amounts of information within succinct statements. As with any language, it must be learned by both the creators and users of bibliographic records and in the process is capable of being misunderstood and misinterpreted.[5] Indeed, for some library users, bibliographic language often appears to be little short of unintelligible jargon – the hieroglyphs of a priestly élite. One experienced designer of online catalogues has coined the term 'Biblish' to describe this specialized vocabulary.[6] Arguably the worst examples of incomprehensible terminology are a product of the union of 'Biblish' and 'Computerese'; fortunately for users, more effort is now being made to present bibliographic data in an understandable and less intimidating manner.

Bibliographic records

For effective retrieval and use bibliographic data must be organized. The first step in this process is the creation of bibliographic records. The essential character of a bibliographic record is expressed in the following:

> The master set of data elements relating to a bibliographic item, grouped into a logical structure. When data is stored in machine-readable form, the record refers to the master record from which all output is derived. A record generally relates to only one title, of which there may be several copies.[7]

'Bibliographic record' has also been defined as 'the sum of all the areas and elements ... which may be used to describe, identify or retrieve any physical item (publication, document) of information content'.[8]

In this book, the following definitions are used:

Bibliographic record = a collection of data elements, organized in a logical way, which represent a bibliographic item.

Bibliographic item = any document, book, publication or other record of human communication; any group of documents, or part of a document, treated as an entity.

'Bibliographic record' is a relatively new term, having entered the information vocabulary mainly as a result of automation. Much of the terminology in this area is a legacy from cataloguing practice, reflecting the preoccupation with bibliographic records as catalogue records: 'entry' and 'bibliographic record' are often used by cataloguers with the same meaning. *Anglo-American cataloguing rules*, 2nd edition (*AACR2*) does not include

9

in its glossary a definition of 'bibliographic record', but defines 'entry' as 'a record of an item in a catalogue'.[9] 'Entry' is best explained in the context of a printed catalogue or bibliography, where it refers to the listing or recording of selected bibliographic data relating to an item under one possible access point or heading. The data are drawn from the bibliographic record and more than one entry may be made for each item. 'Document surrogate' is also used in the same sense. Entries are usually identified by the kind of access they provide, hence 'author entry', 'subject entry'. 'Access point' (also an import from computing terminology) is any name or term used for searching and retrieval of items; when access points appear formally at the head of entries in printed catalogues and bibliographies they are known as headings. Formally constructed headings may of course be stored as part of machine-held records. 'Description' or 'bibliographic description' is the assemblage of data elements sufficient to identify a bibliographic item and to distinguish it from others. It normally follows or is placed beneath the heading in a printed catalogue. The amount of bibliographic description varies according to different applications.

The distinction between bibliographic record and entry is most clear-cut in automated systems where the master bibliographic record is held in the machine and entries are generated from it by one or more computer programs (see Figure 1.1). The entries might appear in printed bibliographies, or they may be intended for screen display in online public-access catalogues.

In manual systems the distinction between bibliographic record and entry is far less obvious. The bibliographic record may be prepared in the form of a main entry, i.e. a collection of bibliographic data elements grouped under the main access point or heading, as determined by the code of cataloguing rules used, with tracings notes to indicate the additional access points or headings needed for a multiple-entry catalogue or bibliography (see Figure 1.2). Although automated cataloguing is widespread, we are not yet at the point where it can be said with any confidence that the manually produced catalogue is dead.

```
Master Record

ISN=11408
L070 BIBLEV  : m
A000 PROCDA  : 19881007d1988      ¦¦¦y0ENGy01030000b
A010 LAN     : 0 $aENG
A020 COCODE  : $aGB
B000 TITLE   : 1 $aAsking the right questions$ecase studies in library
               development consultancy$fJ. Stephen Parker
B100 IMPR    : $aLondon$cMansell$d1988
G010 PERALT  :  1$aParker$bJ. Stephen
G110 CORALT  :
B150 PAGES   : $a239 p
B250 SERIES  : 2 $aInformation adviser series
C000 NOTE    :
W900 STATUS  : FCAT
W910 SCDATE  : 1988-10-07
T100 DESC    : /Jordan/ /Qatar/ /Libyan Arab Jamahiriya/ /Portugal/ /Saint
               Christopher and Nevis/ /British Virgin Islands/ /Brazil/
               /consultants/ /library science/ /information management/ - /case
               studies/
T980 SCATC   : ST
T990 SHELF   : 9:25 PARKER, J. Stephen. Asking the right questions ...
Z190 ISBNCH  : 0-7201-1898-0
W100 CATALR  : HE
W120 CATDAT  : 1988-10-07
W090 ACCNUM  : 183651
```

```
Master record in UNIMARC

Status code:FCAT
Label biblev:m
00111408
010   $a0-7201-1898-0
100   $a19881007d1988      ¦¦¦y0ENGy01030000b
1010  $aENG
2001  $aAsking the right questions$ecase studies in library development
                consultancy$fJ. Stephen Parker
210   $aLondon$cMansell$d1988
215   $a239 p
2252  $aInformation adviser series
700   1$aParker$bJ. Stephen
900   $a/Jordan/ /Qatar/ /Libyan Arab Jamahiriya/ /Portugal/ /Saint Christopher
                and Nevis/ /British Virgin Islands/ /Brazil/ /consultants/
                /library science/ /information management/ - /case studies/
998   $a9:25 PARKER, J. Stephen. Asking the right questions ...
999   $aHE$b1988-10-07
```

Fig. 1.1   Example of master record and entries generated from it

11

```
Parker, J. Stephen
     Asking the right questions : case studies in library development
consultancy / J. Stephen Parker. -- London : Mansell, 1988. -- 239 p. --
(Information adviser series). -- ISBN 0-7201-1898-0

DESCRIPTORS: /Jordan/ /Qatar/ /Libyan Arab Jamahiriya/ /Portugal/
                /Saint Christopher and Nevis/ /British Virgin Islands/ /Brazil/
                /consultants/ /library science/ /information management/ -
        .       /case studies/

SHELF CATEGORY: [STORE]
SHELVED AT: 9:25 PARKER, J. Stephen. Asking the right questions ...
                                                Record no: 11408
```

```
Information adviser series
     Asking the right questions : case studies in library development
consultancy / J. Stephen Parker. -- London : Mansell, 1988. -- 239 p. --
(Information adviser series). -- ISBN 0-7201-1898-0
```

```
Order record

                        Sussex University Bookshop    Order date:1988-08-10
                             Refectory Building

                                                      Order number: 11408
        Parker, J. Stephen
          Asking the right questions : case studies in library development
        consultancy / J. Stephen Parker
        London : Mansell, 1988
         Number of copies ordered: 1
```

Fig. 1.1 (continued)

(Reproduced by courtesy of the Library of the Institute of Development Studies at the University of Sussex)

```
Lovecy, Ian                              025.002854/LOV
  Automating library procedures : a survivor's
  handbook. – London : Library Association,
  1984. – 247 p. : ill. ; 22 cm. – Includes
  bibliographies. – ISBN 0-85365-516-2

  1. Title   2. Libraries – Automation
  3. Library administration
```

Fig. 1.2   Example of main entry with tracings notes

Authority and holdings records

Earlier in this chapter we mentioned the identification, for
bibliographic control purposes, of authority and
holdings/locations data. For many years librarians have maintained authority files, as a record of names and subjects chosen
for use as headings in a particular system. Any data element
used to gain access to a document can in theory be brought
within authority control, although the most commonly
appearing terms in authority files are names of persons and
corporate bodies (especially those involving difficult decisions
and/or with more than one form of name) and subject headings,
which can be associated with large numbers of items. Authoritative uniform headings are recorded, together with a list of
other forms of name or subject to and from which cross-
references are to be made. An authority file thus acts as a record
of decisions made in the past, and as a means of displaying
relationships between preferred and rejected forms of
headings.[10] Two simple examples, using symbols traditional to
library cataloguing practice, will illustrate the basic principle.
Each example shows the preferred form of heading to be used
in bibliographic records, other terms from which cross-
references are to be made, and the relationships that exist
between terms:

1) Cats   Preferred subject heading
    x   Felis domestica   Synonym
    xx   Felidae   Related heading

13

The references generated from this record are:

Felis domestica *see* Cats
Felidae *see also* Cats

2) Brontë, Charlotte   Preferred author heading
   x Bell, Currer   Pseudonym, rejected in
                                 favour of heading under
                                 real and better-known
                                 name.

The reference generated from this record is:

Bell, Currer *see* Brontë, Charlotte

(In a real catalogue, the reference could be expanded to explain the relationship between the two name forms.)

In the context of specific bibliographic items, 'Cats' and 'Brontë, Charlotte' are elements of bibliographic data. Their existence as authority data arises from an independent consideration of their role as potential access points in bibliographic records, and from the need to consider alternative forms of names and subjects by which users might seek information. Authority records facilitate the integration into existing catalogues and bibliographies of newly created records and provide users with consistent, controlled access points. Many authority files are now held online, which makes it possible to incorporate authority control in both record-creation and retrieval processes. Not all systems hold authority data in separate records – some store the data within appropriate bibliographic records. Although there is some controversy over the need in online catalogues for authority control, its value for exchange is undeniable.

Holdings and locations records are specific to the items held in a particular system or collection. They may contain information relating to the items themselves (e.g. location, call number, shelf mark, accession number), and information relating to the holding organization and its procedures (e.g. department or section which requested the item, order and claims procedures). Such data may be regarded as 'bibliographic' in that they pertain to bibliographic items, but they have meaning only within specific systems or collections. In automated systems, holdings and locations data are sometimes recorded within bibliographic records, sometimes in separate records, linked with appropriate bibliographic records. To the user, viewing the record in the online catalogue, the source of various data elements, whether from one master bibliographic record, or assembled from more than one, is invisible and irrelevant.

Bibliographic levels

The documents which are represented by bibliographic records may not always be single physical entities. They may be collections of items treated as entities (e.g. series, multi-volume monographs) or parts of items (e.g. example single tracks on sound recordings, articles in journals, chapters in books). It is possible to identify different bibliographic levels which may be recognized when creating bibliographic records. Certain systems require their recognition.

Examples of bibliographic levels:

Series level	Library and information research reports
Book level	No. 32: Technology and communication in the humanities
Chapter level	Ch.5: Online searching for humanities users by British academic libraries
Whole journal level	Journal of librarianship
Single issue level	Vol.12, no.2, April 1980
Article level	Pages 71–83: Archival responsibilities of university libraries.

It is clear from the above that chapters from books and articles from journals are not bibliographically independent and can be described only in terms of the larger items of which they are a component part. Records for such items are usually described as existing at 'analytical level'. The analytical level is usually regarded as the lowest bibliographically useful level, but there are occasions when even deeper analysis may be considered significant, for example to pinpoint a section within a chapter of a book. Few systems can cope in practice with this degree of detail.

Guidelines for the application of the ISBDs to the description of component parts specifically addresses the problem of describing such items and offers the following definition:

> Component part = a part of a publication ... that for purposes of bibliographic identification or access is dependent upon the identification of the publication in which it is contained.[11]

Bibliographic records can therefore be made for collections of items, for whole items, or for parts of items. Records for parts of items may be constructed in two ways: *either* by constructing a record for the whole item which additionally contains subrecords for the parts, *or* by constructing entirely separate records for the parts. A record describing a part, when viewed by the end-user, must contain data locating the part within the whole item.

Abstracting and indexing services, which record individual articles from journals, operate at the analytical level. National bibliographies and most libraries construct their records, mainly for economic reasons, for whole items only, usually at book level. Financial considerations aside, a good case can be made for analytical treatment of all library items: it is increasingly being demanded by users and is clearly necessary if collections are to be exploited to the full.

Standards for the content of bibliographic records

The bibliographic record may be viewed as a package of data, the precise content of which varies according to the different purposes for which it is intended. When it is not possible to base the selection of data elements for the bibliographic record on known user needs, general guidelines must be drawn up, preferably based on experience, research and common sense. The 'bibliographic package' should contain data which record the distinctive features of the item, thereby assisting identification, and data which facilitate access to the document for retrieval purposes.

For each designated item, a bibliographic record is constructed according to the agreed rules and standards of the system. There are many widely used standards for constructing bibliographic records. Most have been prepared to meet the requirements of library catalogues and national bibliographies, but they can be adapted for other purposes. The most comprehensive are national and multi-national cataloguing codes, such as Anglo-American cataloguing rules, 2nd edition. Applied in full, these result in detailed bibliographic description best suited to national bibliographies or the catalogues of large research collections; most, however, provide for briefer descriptions, if wanted, and the rules can be modified or reduced for other applications. In contrast, there are standards for brief citations of items, suitable for use as footnotes, or in bibliographies and lists of references. These are intended to supply the minimum data elements needed for identification and retrieval of the cited work. Some standards deal with particular kinds of material; some with specific data elements such as headings for names of persons or corporate bodies, subject headings, bibliographic description, classification and indexing.[12] Many organizations prefer to create their own in-house rules and standards: book publishers normally expect authors to conform to a 'house style' when citing works; specialist libraries often establish their own lists of subject headings, tailored to the needs of users. For automated systems the application of further rules and standards is necessary. Strictly speaking these concern the structure of the record for machine processing, but in many cases they also affect its content. As with standards for bibliographic data, they may be widely used (e.g. MARC formats) or locally restricted.

The most striking contribution to the standardization of bibliographic records has been made by IFLA, with its programme of ISBDs. These are not cataloguing rules, but are meant to act as a common basis for the construction of national and multi-national cataloguing codes. *ISBD(G): General International Standard Bibliographic Description* offers a generalized structure for the description of bibliographic items and is 'intended to provide the maximum amount of descriptive information required in a range of different bibliographic activities'.[13] The elements which are required for this purpose are set out in eight areas:

1 Title and statement of responsibility
2 Edition
3 Material (or type of publication) specific data (used, for

example, in the case of cartographic items and serials)
4 Publication, distribution data, including place and date of publication
5 Physical description
6 Series
7 Notes
8 Standard number and terms of availability.

Each of these areas is further divided into discrete elements and strict adherence to the standard requires that the areas/elements are cited in the order given and separated by the punctuation prescribed. ISBD thus shapes the form, as well as the content, of the description. Reliance on transcription of data directly from the item, especially in Area 1, ensures accuracy and consistency. Here is an example of an ISBD description (monograph).

The allergy connection / Barbara Paterson. – Wellingborough, Northamptonshire : Thorsons, 1985. – 255 p. ; 22 cm. – Includes index. – ISBN 0-7225-0984-7 (pbk) : £5.95

ISBD(G) deals primarily with whole items, but also offers guidance on the description of separately published parts of multipart items, separate parts of multi-media items and items which supplement or accompany others. Multi-level description, which can be used to cope with the problem of bibliographic level, involves the analysis and presentation of data in different levels, ranging from the whole item to the specific part, e.g.

A pictorial review of old Woodford
1900 – 1930 / compiled by Graham Essl
and Peter Lawrence. – London : Old
Woodford and District Times, 1986
    Vol.1. – 24 p. of ill.; 21 cm. –
      ISBN 0-9511529-0-4
    Vol.2. – 24 p. of ill.; 21 cm. –
      ISBN 0-9511529-2-0

This method is particularly suited to national bibliographies, which need to record separately each part of an ongoing work. It is also offered in AACR2, where it is suggested as an alternative in some cases to the more traditional type of analytical entry.[14]

ISBD(G) appears to have been constructed more with the requirements of whole items or groups of items in mind, and within the traditions of library cataloguing practice. *Guidelines for the application of the ISBDs to the description of component parts* represents a more radical approach, designed to bridge the alleged gap between the cataloguing tradition of the library community and the citation practices of the abstracting and indexing community,[15] while remaining consistent with ISBD principles. The description comprises four segments:

1 the description of the component part (patterned on ISBD(G)
2 a linking element (involves the use of formal punctuation (or paragraphing) and an optional term indicating physical containment)
3 an identification of the host item
4 details of the location of the part within the host item (patterned on ISBD(G)), e.g.

Playmates / A.M. Burrage.		Playmates / A.M. Burrage // Roald Dahl's book of ghost stories. – Harmondsworth: Penguin, 1985. – p.94 – 120.
In: Roald Dahl's book of ghost stories. – Harmondsworth : Penguin, 1985. – p.94 – 120.	*or*	

An appendix shows examples in compact form, especially appropriate for citations of journal articles. The technique of multi-level description can also be combined with the method of describing component parts set out in the *Guidelines*.

The distinctive and at times criticized punctuation of ISBD is designed to facilitate visual recognition of the various elements in the description (a help when records from different languages are exchanged) and also to assist mechanization by providing a standard method of distinguishing between fields and subfields within the descriptive part of a record. The punctuation symbols used were heavily influenced by those found on typewriters for Roman script, and their applicability for non-Roman scripts has sometimes been called into question.[16] The early optimism of writers such as Sumner Spalding,[17] who saw in the ISBD punctuation the means for achieving automatic conversion of bibliographic records to machine format by 'simplified format recognition programs' which would eliminate all language

19

problems, has not been justified by subsequent experience.

The complete set of ISBD data is undoubtedly sufficient to ensure identification of an item, and would in many applications be excessive. National bibliographic agencies are expected to apply the standard in full when creating authoritative national records; other agencies are invited to select those elements they wish to include in their descriptions; in effect, they may create subsets of the parent standard. Many codes, including AACR2, have adopted ISBD(G) as a basis for their own rules for description, with the result that the standardization of bibliographic description is further advanced than any other area of bibliographic record construction. Although the family of ISBDs (which includes standards for cartographic materials, non-book materials, printed music, antiquarian books, monographs and serials) includes in its description all the elements which might be used as access points for retrieval purposes, it does not address the problem of choice and form of access points. This is left to the compilers of national and international codes of cataloguing rules. The Paris principles (the Statement of Principles adopted at the International Conference on Cataloguing Principles held in Paris in 1961)[18] have been accepted as a basis for the choice and form of headings and entry words in national cataloguing rules, but their generality and, in some places, ambiguity, leave them open to interpretation. The widespread adoption of AACR in English-speaking countries, its influence on the development of other national codes, and the work sponsored by IFLA on catalogue headings for personal and corporate names, have all helped to foster the growth of standardization in this area; but considerable divergences in practice remain.

There is even less scope for standardization in subject data. The Dewey Decimal Classification, the Library of Congress classification and Library of Congress Subject Headings are perhaps the most widely used standards for subject input; but they will never be suitable or acceptable to all libraries and information units, especially to those in the specialist sector. The British Library's PRECIS (Preserved Context Index System), developed for use in constructing a subject index to a classified listing, but applicable also to the construction of headings in alphabetical subject catalogues, has attracted much interest from

20

students of indexing theory and from practitioners, but has not been widely adopted and is at present undergoing modification. Bibliographic records are likely to contain subject data from other sources, for example classification numbers from other general and special schemes; subject headings and/or subject descriptors from other subject headings lists and thesauri.

This brief discussion of standards rests on the assumption that standardization in record construction is desirable and necessary for successful exchange of bibliographic data. It would be misleading, however, to give the impression that standardization is universally accepted as a bibliographic panacea. Lancaster and Smith offer a perceptive review of the advantages and disadvantages of standardization, noting the uneven development of standards across the entire library and information community, and questioning the relevance of some currently used standards for modern bibliographic and cataloguing practice.[19]

Languages and scripts

The multiplicity of languages and scripts is a longstanding problem affecting all parts of the bibliographic record and with serious implications for exchange. In records created by and for speakers of Western languages the problem is mainly the language used in headings. Should this be that of the item? Or the language of the country where the record is prepared? Also affected are areas of the record not directly transcribed from the item itself: the physical description, notes and subject data areas. National requirements, for example the anglicizing of headings for use in English-speaking countries, may conflict with the best interests of other users and the requirements of international exchange. The establishment and widespread use of comprehensive national authority files for names of persons and bodies would certainly alleviate, but not entirely eliminate, the difficulties. The problem of language is compounded when different scripts are involved. Items containing a mix of scripts, e.g. a bilingual Greek-English dictionary with titles in both languages, can be handled easily in traditional card catalogues or printed bibliographies by the use of special typewriters or typefaces. In computerized systems transliteration has been the norm, thus avoiding the problem of multiple scripts. Biblio-

21

graphic records entirely in non-Roman (e.g. Russian) or ideographic scripts (e.g. Chinese) pose an even greater problem. Much effort has been expended in recent years on the development of international standards for romanization, i.e. the conversion into the Roman or Latin alphabet of data in other scripts. Work in this area has been hindered by the unfortunate proliferation of non-standard schemes, but many romanized records are now being exchanged and integrated into single databases and catalogues. The emphasis on romanization has not been wholly welcomed: Har-Nicolescu believes that there is a greater need for standards for transliteration between non-Roman scripts, and in particular for an agreed Asian character set which would assist interchange and control of Asian materials.[20] Further, she sees little value in romanizing large numbers of records mainly for the benefit of Western library users.

Automation, ironically, has not always facilitated the processing of records in non-Roman scripts, even within the host countries, since most computers were designed primarily for Roman alphabet languages. Catalogues and bibliographies produced by traditional printing methods are superior in this respect, although they have other disadvantages. Even if bibliographic records can be handled without difficulty in national systems (here the situation is uneven, with some countries more advanced than others) the same is not necessarily true when the records are to be exchanged and used in systems designed primarily for Roman alphabet languages. Some machine formats are now able to store data in both Roman and non-Roman scripts, although not all systems allow the non-Roman parts of the record to be displayed to the user. For the sake of easier exchange of records, in itself an impeccable objective, Western interests appear to have been better served than those of other countries. Despite differences of opinion over the value of romanized records, the consensus is that users prefer records in the vernacular and for this to be achieved a much greater investment must be made in systems such as MINISIS which can cope with multiple languages and scripts.

Accessing bibliographic records in catalogues and bibliographies

A multiple-access catalogue or bibliography in which each item is entered or listed more than once, under different access points or headings, greatly improves the user's chances of finding a document, in comparison with the limited access afforded by a single entry list (i.e. where only one entry per item is permitted). Card and printed catalogues, including microform, have traditionally offered access via authors, titles and subject data (in verbal form as subject headings, or in symbolic form as class numbers). Additional access points may be provided where appropriate under names of other persons associated with the document (e.g. editors, translators, illustrators), under names of corporate bodies (e.g. sponsors) and under titles of series. Economic and physical constraints have precluded the provision in printed lists of more access points than these, but there is a case to be made for increasing the traditional number, even if this is done at the expense of bibliographic description. There is a demand, in particular, for increased subject access.

Bibliographic data destined for use in catalogue production have traditionally been divided into two categories: data providing access and data describing items. This simple classification has some merit, but it also begs many questions and is somewhat outdated for today's online catalogues. Improved technology makes it possible for bibliographic records held in a computer to be accessed by a much wider range of data elements than has been possible in printed catalogues and bibliographies. Depending on the sophistication of the system, records may be accessed by any data element present in the record, for example word in corporate name, year of publication, language of item, physical form of item, kind of illustrative matter. The importance of 'correct' forms of headings has declined, as precise formulations of names of authors and corporate bodies may no longer be demanded of users. Additionally, retrieval by keywords and phrases taken from titles, abstracts or even whole texts has become possible, thus further decreasing, in some circumstances, the need for full and detailed bibliographic description of the kind specified in ISBD(G) and in AACR2, level three. Comprehensive bibliographic description is appropriate for some catalogues, but is not always necessary, as was shown in a

23

report from the Centre for Catalogue Research (now the Centre for Bibliographic Management) in 1982.[21] Other applications are equally well served by brief descriptive detail.

Applications of bibliographic records

The differences, actual and potential, in the content of bibliographic records can be understood by considering some of their major applications. It is convenient to consider them separately, but it should be noted that there is considerable overlap between applications.

1 *Production of authoritative national records and the national bibliography*
Authoritative national records are created by the national bibliographic agency, which in some countries is also the national library. They may be intended for production of the national bibliography (with associated archival and historical significance), for international exchange purposes, for use by libraries and other organizations in the host country, for production of the national library's own catalogue, and for use in online databases. Comprehensiveness has been considered essential in a multi-purpose record such as this, and authoritative national records are usually very full, containing data which may be needed for acquisition of an item (e.g. address of publisher, price) as well as data which may be needed for catalogue production (see Figure 1.3).

Creation of records of this degree of detail is a heavy burden for national bibliographic agencies. The British Library's decision in 1987 to trim the content of records for certain categories of items from the second level of description, as defined by AACR2, to the first (minimum) level of description, caused some controversy.[22] AACR2 standard access points continue to be provided for items described at level one, and price and availability data are also given. Reduced level description was seen as the only viable means of reducing unit cataloguing costs, and it has had the desired effect of increasing output in record creation from British Library Bibliographic Services.[23]

The content of national records is further discussed in Chapter 6.

24

942.9 — HISTORY. WALES

942.9'98'009734 — Gwent. Monmouth (District). Lower Wye Valley. Villages, to 1984

Howell, Raymond
Fedw villages : a Lower Wye Valley history / Raymond Howell. — Old Cwmbran : Village Publishing, 1985. — 100p : ill,map,facsims,ports ; 21cm
Includes index
ISBN 0-946043-10-8 (pbk) : £2.95
1.Ti   B87-41550

943.8 — HISTORY. POLAND

943.8'04 — Poland, 1900-1986

Ascherson, Neal
The struggles for Poland / Neal Ascherson. — London : Joseph, 1987. — [288]p : ill ; 25cm
Includes bibliography and index
ISBN 0-7181-2812-5 : £12.95 : CIP confirmed
1.Ti   B87-07185

944 — HISTORY. FRANCE

944'.026'0924 — France. Joan, of Arc, Saint — Biographies — For children

*Nottridge, Harold
Joan of Arc / Harold Nottridge. — Hove : Wayland, 1987. — [32]p : ill(some col.) ; 23cm. — (Great lives)
Includes bibliography and index
ISBN 1-85210-176-9 : £4.95 : CIP entry (Oct.)
1.Ti 2.Sr   B87-27737

945 — HISTORY. ITALY

945'.07 — Italy, 1687-1790

Carpanetto, Dino
Italy in the age of reason : 1685-1789 / Dino Carpanetto and Giuseppe Ricuperati ; translated by Caroline Higgitt. — London : Longman, 1987. — x,357p : 2maps ; 24cm. — (Longman history of Italy ; v.5)
Translated from the Italian. — Includes index
ISBN 0-582-48338-7 (cased) : £18.95 : CIP rev.
ISBN 0-582-49145-2 (pbk) : £9.95
1.Ti 2.Ricuperati, Giuseppe   B87-00307

946 — HISTORY. IBERIAN PENINSULA, SPAIN

946'.04 — Spain, 1517-1598

Lovett, A. W.
Early Habsburg Spain 1517-1598 / A.W. Lovett. — Oxford : Oxford University Press, 1986. — maps ; 22cm
Includes bibliography and index
ISBN 0-19-822136-8 (cased) : £25.00 : CIP confirmed
ISBN 0-19-822138-x (pbk) : £8.95
1.Ti   B86-08144

946.083 — Spain. Social life

Waters, Ivor
Fragments of Spain / by Ivor and Mercedes Waters. — Chepstow : Moss Rose, c1987. — vii,123p,[15]leaves of plates : ill,1map,ports ; 22cm
Limited ed. of 150 copies. — Includes index
ISBN 0-906134-34-x : £12.50
1.Ti 2.Waters, Mercedes   B87-41725

947 — HISTORY. EASTERN EUROPE, SOVIET UNION

947.084 — Soviet Union, 1917-1984

Geller, Mikhail
Utopia in power : the history of the Soviet Union from 1917 to the present / by Mikhail Heller and Aleksandr Nekrich ; translated from the Russian by Phyllis B. Carlos. — London : Hutchinson, 1986, c1985. — 877p ; 25cm
On t.p. the letter 'o' in "power" is represented by a hammer and sickle. — Translated from the Russian. — Originally published as L'utopie au pouvoir. Paris : Calam-Levy, 1982. — Bibliography: p820-845. — Includes index
ISBN 0-09-155620-1 (cased) : £25.00 : CIP rev.
ISBN 0-09-155621-X (pbk) : No price
1.[L'Utopie au pouvoir. English] 2.Ti 3.Nekrich, Aleksandr 4.L'Utopie au pouvoir   B86-03394

949.65 — HISTORY. ALBANIA

949.65'02'0924 — Albania. Geraldine, Queen, consort of Zog, King of Albania — Biographies

Robyns, Gwen
Geraldine of the Albanians : the authorised biography / Gwen Robyns. — London : Muller, Blond & White, 1987. — 220p,[8]p l of plates : ill,ports ; 25cm
ISBN 0-584-11133-9 : £14.95 : CIP rev.
1.Ti   B86-30605

951 — HISTORY. CHINA AND ADJACENT AREAS

951.9'042'0924 — Korea. British prisoners of war, 1951-1953 — Personal observations

Farrar-Hockley, Sir Anthony
The edge of the sword / Anthony Farrar-Hockley. — Leicester : Ulverscroft, 1987, c1954. — 536p(large print) ; 24cm
Originally published: London : Muller, 1954
ISBN 0-7089-1680-5 : £7.25 : CIP rev.
1.Ti   B87-16867

953 — HISTORY. ARABIAN PENINSULA AND ADJACENT AREAS

953'.65 — Bahrain, to 1983

Vine, Peter
Pearls in Arabian waters : the heritage of Bahrain / Peter Vine. — London : Immel, c1986. — 159p : ill(some col.),col.charts,col.maps,plans ; 31cm
Bibliography: p157. — Includes index
ISBN 0-907151-28-0 : £27.00 : CIP rev.
1.Ti   B86-29305

954 — HISTORY. SOUTH ASIA, INDIA

954.02'54 — India. Royal courts. Social life, 1556-1605 — For schools

Wigner, Annabel
Elizabeth & Akbar : portraits of power / Annabel Wigner. — Cheltenham : Thornes, 1987. — 52p : ill(some col.),1map,ports (some col.) ; 24cm. — (A World of change)
Includes index
ISBN 0-85950-541-3 : No price : CIP rev.
Also classified at 942.05'5
1.Ti 2.Sr   B86-30286

956 — HISTORY. MIDDLE EAST

956.94'001 — Zionism, to 1958

Reed, Douglas
The controversy of Zion / Douglas Reed. — Sudbury : Bloomfield, 1978. — vii,587p ; 22cm
Bibliography: p574-580. — Includes index
£10.00
1.Ti   B87-41918

956.94'04 — Palestine, 1945-1985. Public opinion in Western world

Public opinion and the Palestine question / edited by Elia Zureik and Fouad Moughrabi. — London : Croom Helm, c1987. — 206p ; 23cm
Includes index
ISBN 0-7099-3007-0 : £27.50 : CIP rev.
1.Zureik, Elia 2.Moughrabi, Fouad   B87-04700

959.7 — HISTORY. VIETNAM

959.704'342 — Vietnamese wars. Army operations by United States. Army, to 1973

Krepinevich, Andrew F.
The army and Vietnam / Andrew F. Krepinevich, Jr.. — Baltimore ; London : Johns Hopkins University Press, c1986. — xviii,318p : ill,ports ; 24cm
Includes index
ISBN 0-8018-2863-5 : £21.60
1.Ti   B87-41949

963 — HISTORY. ETHIOPIA

963'.004963 — Ethiopia. Murai

*Woodhead, Leslie
A box full of spirits / Leslie Woodhead. — London : Heinemann, 1987. — 1v. : ill
ISBN 0-434-87788-3 : £10.95 : CIP entry (Oct.)
1.Ti   B87-27706

Fig. 1.3 Example of page from BNB

(Reproduced from the *British national bibliography* with the permission of the British Library Board)

UBC requires an authoritative and comprehensive record, constructed according to internationally accepted standards and including all data needed for use in libraries and other information and documentation services.[24] It should support bibliographic research and scholarship, the selection of materials, and the production of catalogues and other products. Groups of data elements stipulated are those relating to authorship, bibliographic description, unique identification, and subject content.[25] As national records are the majority of those made available for international exchange, the constraints to which many national agencies are subject will in turn have an impact on the UBC Programme. Other matters which affect international exchanges of national records are standardization and compatibility of bibliographic data, potential conflict between internal and external commitments of national agencies, and machine-readable formats. Records designed specifically for international exchange inevitably assume a more neutral character than national records. They normally make provision for a core of common data elements, a variety of optional elements, and the accommodation of non-standard elements resulting from the diverse applications and requirements of originating and receiving agencies. At this stage, a brief note on the bibliographic data elements identified by current major international exchange systems will indicate some of the requirements and problems. The UNIMARC[26] and UNISIST RM records[27] both distinguish between mandatory and optional data elements, the presence of optional data depending on the nature of the item and the practice of the originating agency. UNIMARC, for example, specifies only seven mandatory fields, including title and statement of responsibility and material specific area. Other fields, such as edition and physical description, may be present if the cataloguing practice of the originating agency requires them. For some recipients of UNIMARC records this could necessitate the insertion of additional data elements to raise them to the desired standard. UNISIST RM includes a table of data elements, many of which are regarded as essential in bibliographic records for all types of documents (e.g. title, date of publication, edition) and some of which are essential only for certain categories of material (e.g.

name, location and date in the case of conference proceedings). A full discussion of these and other international exchange formats will be found in Chapters 4 and 5.

3 Creation of records for cooperative systems

Cooperative systems, known by various names including 'bibliographic utilities', 'bibliographic services' and 'bibliographic networks', exist to share the cost and effort of creating bibliographic records. Most began as shared cataloguing systems, their origins and growth being directly linked with the availability of MARC data from national agencies such as the British Library and the Library of Congress.

```
  Screen 1 of 2        ¶
↦ NO HOLDINGS IN OZZ - FOR HOLDINGS ENTER dh DEPRESS DISPLAY RECD SEND
  OCLC: 10072914      Rec stat: c Entrd: 831014        Used: 860128 ¶
⁚ Type: a Bib lvl: m Govt pub:    Lang:   eng Source:    Illus: af    ·
  Repr:    Enc lvl:    Conf pub: 0 Ctry:   nyu Dat tp: s M/F/B: 10
  Indx: 1 Mod rec:    Festschr: 0 Cont: b
  Desc: a Int lvl:    Dates: 1984,     ¶
⊦ 1 010        83-22206 ¶
⊦ 2 040        DLC ‡c DLC ‡d OCL ‡d FDR ¶
⸱ 3 019        11220033 ‡a 11248973 ‡a 11286709 ¶
⊱ 4 020        0394527771 ¶
⊧ 5 039 0      2 ‡b 3 ‡c 3 ‡d 3 ‡e 3 ¶
⊦ 6 050 0      D210 ‡b .T89 1984 ¶
⸜ 7 082 0      909.08 ‡2 19 ¶
⊮ 8 090           ‡b  ¶
⸕ 9 049        OZZZ ¶
⊩10 100 10     Tuchman, Barbara Wertheim. ¶
⊧11 245 14     The march of folly : ‡b from Troy to Vietnam / ‡c Barbara W.
Tuchman. ¶
⊦12 250        1st ed. ¶
⊦13 260 0      New York : ‡b Knopf : ‡b Distributed by Random House, ‡c 1984. ¶
⸱14 300        xiv, 447 p., [32] p. of plates : ‡b ill. (some col.) ; ‡c 24 cm. ¶
⊮15 504        Includes bibliographies and index. ¶
```

```
  Screen 2 of 2        ¶
⸱16 650  0  History, Modern. ¶
⸱17 650  0  History ‡x Errors, inventions, etc. ¶
⊧18 650  0  Power (Social sciences) ¶
⊦19 650  0  Judgment. ¶
```

Fig. 1.4   Example of record for a book from OCLC

(Reproduced with the permission of OCLC from *Books format*, 3rd ed.)

```
Screen 1 of 2
NO HOLDINGS IN EQA -  FOR HOLDINGS ENTER dh DEPRESS  DISPLAY RECD SEND
OCLC: 8253753      Rec stat: n Entrd: 820318      Used: 820318
Type: g Bib lvl: m Govt pub:    Lang:  eng Source: d Leng: 149
 InLC: u Enc lvl: I Type mat: f Ctry:  ctu Dat tp: s MEBE: 0
Tech: n Mod rec:           Accomp mat:  mz
Desc: a Int lvl: e Dates: 1981,
  1 010       81-730297
  2 040       IBS c IBS
  3 007       g b o c r d c e n f b g f h f
  4 020        c $73.00
  5 090       b
  6 049       EQAA
  7 245 00  Papermaking h filmstrip / c produced by Educational Dimensions
Group, a division of Educational Dimensions Corporation.
  8 260       Stamford, Conn. : b Educational Dimensions Group, c c1981.
  9 300       2 filmstrips ([149 fr.]) : b col. ; c 35 mm. + e 2 sound
cassettes (30 min.) + 1 teacher's guide.
 10 500       Title on container: Papermaking, the art, the craft.
 11 500       Sound accompaniment compatible for manual and automatic operation.

Screen 2 of 2
 12 520       Shows the basic skills in creating handmade paper.
 13 500       Educational Dimensions Group: 696.
 14 650 0  Paper, Handmade.
 15 650 0  Paper making and trade.
 16 650 0  Handicraft.
 17 710 21  Educational Dimensions Group.
 18 740 01  Papermaking, the art, the craft.
```

Fig. 1.5 **Record constructed according to OCLC audiovisual media format**

(Reproduced with the permission of OCLC)

Most have now diversified, providing many other services to members and clients. Members are able to contribute to, and take records from, a shared online database or union catalogue. Cooperative systems normally use the national cataloguing code and a format based on the appropriate national MARC, and have recommended data input standards, permitting more than one 'level' or fullness of record. They also provide access to authority file data, to ensure consistency in names of persons or bodies used in headings, and maintain systems for quality control of bibliographic records. All allow for the input of local data and local processing information. Records may be used not only for catalogue production, but also for acquisitions and circulation systems.

For maximum benefit, organizations which contribute to shared databases should make use of the same standards. Both UK and USMARC format specifications incorporate minimum requirements for bibliographic records intended for exchange via a nationwide network.

4 Records for use in individual libraries

Some libraries create their own records; some obtain records from external sources, such as a national library/bibliographic agency, a cooperative system or a commercial record supplier. A mixture of locally produced and 'bought-in' records is also possible. Unwanted data elements can be removed from records obtained elsewhere, and data added to support local housekeeping and other processes. Most libraries do not require records as comprehensive as authoritative national records, at least insofar as bibliographic description is concerned.

In a fully integrated system, the same bibliographic record may be called on to perform different functions, e.g. acquisitions, cataloguing and catalogue production, circulation, bibliographic compilation. Although certain data are common to all these subsystems, each will require data unique to the subsystem, e.g. order number, bookseller or book supplier, invoice number in the case of acquisitions; borrower number and status in the case of circulation. Each operation will draw from the master bibliographic record only those data needed, and the nature and amount of detail presented to the user may be only a subset of the total data held in the master record. Many libraries have not taken an integrated approach, but maintain separate systems, with appropriately designed bibliographic records, for each operation.

While discussing records for use in individual libraries, it is useful to note the different ways in which the records may be made available to users. An automated cataloguing system may provide an online catalogue and/or a printed catalogue, the medium being paper, microform or card. CD-ROM discs are also in use for storage and distribution of catalogues and have often been set up to simulate online systems. In printed catalogues which offer multiple access, space is normally restricted, and abridged entries may be used for all but the main or principal entry. An online public-access catalogue (OPAC) is a computer database accessible to users via a computer terminal (cf. online information-retrieval systems); the same database may also provide a printed catalogue. Access in an OPAC may in theory be to any part of the record and the user may request the records to be displayed in different formats, i.e. elements of data may be taken from the master record or records and assembled in the user's chosen form. If a printer is attached, hard-copy output is available. In less sophisticated OPACs, the user is presented with pre-determined or 'ready-made' entries, more like those in printed catalogues, but usually briefer. The presentation of data on OPAC screens is itself a topical issue, with many arguing for a break with traditional styles of layout and the development of displays which are more flexible and more easily understood by users.

5 *Records for abstracting and indexing services (secondary services)*
These are created by a variety of organizations, including many commercial firms. Abstracting/indexing services normally cover specified subject areas which can range in scope from broad disciplines (e.g. *Chemical abstracts*, *British humanities index*) to narrower subject fields (e.g. *Helminthological abstracts*, *Library literature*, *Psychological abstracts*). Some cover particular kinds of material, e.g. *Dissertation abstracts international*. In general, secondary services have not adopted the same rules and standards for record construction as those used by libraries. As noted earlier, bibliographic records produced by secondary services are constructed at the analytical level, usually for articles within journals, although many of these services also create records for whole items, e.g. reports, dissertations. Some include monographs and newly published serial titles. Bibliographic records for articles within journals must include bibliographic data relating to the containing journal, as well as to the article. The same applies to articles in collections. Many are available in hard-copy, for example as weekly or monthly listings, or online (cf. online information-retrieval systems).

6 *Records for use in online information-retrieval (I/R) systems*
Online I/R systems are computer-held databases which are accessible via a terminal, in many cases available for use in locations far distant from the computer which houses the database. Examples include Lockheed's DIALOG, ESA-IRS (the information-retrieval service of the European Space Agency) and British Library's BLAISE-LINE. These systems make use

of bibliographic records which are computer-held, and stored and indexed so that whole records and/or specific elements of data are retrievable. Their system architecture may be identical to that of OPACs and some may function as *de facto* catalogues. Indeed, as time goes on, and computers are networked via telecommunications, it will be less clear and less relevant to users where the database they are accessing is actually stored. In general, while the online catalogue reflects the holdings of a collection, the online information-retrieval system is used as a bibliographic tool, to ascertain what exists on a particular subject, or by a particular author. Some allow the user either to see the full record or to select a tailor-made subset of data elements. Others offer a series of pre-selected forms of entry, ranging from accession number (or system control number) and title to comprehensive master record. Great emphasis is placed on subject information and master records in these systems usually include full, informative abstracts and detailed subject data, including keywords and/or pre-coordinate subject headings. Searching may be done by pre-coordinate methods, i.e. on whole phrases or subject headings, or by post-coordinate methods, using Boolean operators. Many online services are now offered on CD-ROM.

7   *Records in the book trade*

The book trade is both producer and user of bibliographic records, generating large quantities of data at different stages of its operations, pre- and post-publication. Promotional material, publishers' catalogues and booksellers' lists, the contents pages and indexes of books, are all valuable sources of information, particularly subject data. Cataloguing-in-Publication (CIP) programmes involve the supply by publishers to national bibliographic agencies of advance information which is used to create records of forthcoming books for inclusion in printed bibliographies, exchange tape services and online databases. The same CIP data is normally printed on the verso of the title page of a book. The information is brief, with emphasis on authoritative headings for persons and bodies, subject headings and class numbers. CIP records can be adjusted, if necessary, after publication, when the book itself arrives at the national bibliographic agency. A seminar held in 1987[28] showed a high degree of coincidence between the needs, in terms of records, of the book trade and the library community, particularly in respect of selection and acquisition of materials. But there are also fundamental differences, as the main purpose of book-trade records is to expedite sales, not to provide a basis for the construction of definitive, bibliographically complete records for use in national bibliographies and library catalogues. Data elements such as price, short standard title, estimated date of publication, availability and target audience assume greater importance than in many other applications (see Figure 1.6).

At present there is considerable variety in data content, fullness and quality of book-trade records. Some suppliers have adopted standards used by their library clients: B. H. Blackwell, for example, supplies full AACR2 records with books despatched (see Figure 1.7). A computer database of records for English-language books and other publications has been created by the British company Book Data (see Figures 1.8 and 1.9).

```
Beaton, Roderick
The medieval Greek romance


PUBLISHED BY:Cambridge U.P.               ORIGIN:UK
ISBN:0-521-33335-0    £35.00     DATE DUE:15-09-89
SUBJECT:Mediaeval lit
        Comparative lit
350pp. Provides basic information for the
non-specialist about Greek fiction 1071-1453 &
considers relations & interconnections with
similar literature in Western Europe.
Substantial bibliography

[format, date & price provisional]        [01703]

NEBS PROFILERS
```

Fig. 1.6 Advance information card

(Reproduced by courtesy of Blackwell's New Title Service)

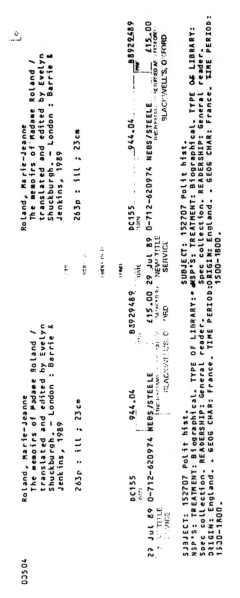

Fig. 1.7 New title announcement service slip

(Reproduced by courtesy of Blackwell's New Title Service)

```
Printed on 26 Jul 1989 at 14:57:18                    Requested by PATRICK


Main ISBN     : 0-333-77657-7
List code     : MACMIL-EDUC
Title         :  Feminist mothers
Complete      : N/ /              Released : Y            Awaiting : PUB/
Master ISBN   :


Sub title     :
Authors       : Gordon, Tuula (Acting Assistant Professor, Sociology
                Department, University of Helsinki)
Corp authors  :
Editors       :
Illustrator   :
Translator    :
Intro by      :
Foreword by   :
Preface by    :


Pub date      : 31 Jul 1989
Announcement  :
Published     :
Edition       :
Total pages   : 168
Page detail   :
Binding       : H    hardback
Page size mm  : 216 x 138
Illus etc     : notes, bibliography
Language      :
Trans from    :

SERIES
  ISSN        :
  Part        :
  Title       : Women in society: a feminist list
  Editors     : Campling, Jo

PUBLISHED WITH
  Name        :

Biblio notes  :


Short descr   : A study of how women influenced by feminism and the Women's
                Liberation Movement perceive and construct their lives as
                mothers. Based on interviews with mothers in England and
                Finland, the interview materials are located within a
                theoretical context of an analysis of patriarchal, racist
                capitalism.

B D class     : E370 women's studies
Geog subj     : Finland
                England
Lang subj     :
Name subj     :
Date subj     : from:      to:
Readership    : G    general
                U    undergraduate

Reading age   :    to                    Interest age:    to
```

Fig. 1.8   Full diagnostic record from the Book Data database

(Reproduced with permission from Book Data)

34

Óther ISBN   :
Dupl ISBN   :

Description:
A study of how women influenced by feminism and the Women's Liberation
Movement perceive and construct their lives as mothers. The book is based on
interviews with feminist mothers in England and Finland. The women include
married, cohabiting, single, lesbian, black women, and women in different
occupations working full-time or part-time, or unemployed. The interview
materials are located within a theoretical context of an analysis of
patriarchal, racist capitalism.

Contents:
Structures, cultures and personal lives; processes and outcomes -
socialization into femininity; feminism - differences and alternatives;
motherhood and subjective experience; work yes - careers no; children and
partners; pleasures and gains - contradictions and difficultues; what is a
feminist mother?.

Available   : NYP
Reprint date :
Weight gms   :

CURRENT PRICES
  UK   : £25.00   Net   Status:
  Other   :
Last changed : 17 Nov 1988

NEW PRICES
  Effective   :
  UK   : £   Status:
  Other   :
Sell in   :
NFS   in :
Trade notes   :

CIP to BL   : 21 Nov 1988
    from BL   : 10 Feb 1989
Dewey   : 306.8743
Mod Dewey   : 306.8
LC Class   :
Bl heading   : Motherhood. Attitudes of feminists
LC heading   :

Pub ref   :
Pub class   :

Comments (BD):

Created: 17 Nov 1988 by KATE   Edited 30 Jun 1989 by DBA

Fig. 1.8 (continued)

Women in Society: a Feminist List
Series edited by Jo Campling.

FEMINIST MOTHERS. By Tuula Gordon (Acting Assistant Professor,
Sociology Department, University of Helsinki).

Macmillan Education, July 1989, 168pp, 216 x 138mm, notes,
bibliography.

| Hardback | UK £25.00 | ISBN 0-333-77657-7 |
| Paperback | UK £7.95 | ISBN 0-333-44658-5 |

A study of how women influenced by feminism and the Women's
Liberation Movement perceive and construct their lives as mothers.
The book is based on interviews with feminist mothers in England
and Finland. The women include married, cohabiting, single,
lesbian, black women, and women in different occupations working
full-time or part-time, or unemployed. The interview materials are
located within a theoretical context of an analysis of
patriarchal, racist capitalism.

CONTENTS
Structures, cultures and personal lives; processes and outcomes –
socialization into femininity; feminism – differences and
alternatives; motherhood and subjective experience; work yes –
careers no; children and partners; pleasures and gains –
contradictions and difficultues; what is a feminist mother?.

Readership: general, undergraduate.

Distributor: Macmillan Distribution Ltd, Houndmills, Basingstoke,
Hampshire, RG21 2XS. Tel: 0256-29242. Telex: 858493. Fax: 0256
842084.

Fig. 1.9   Standard Book Data record

(Reproduced with permission from Book Data)

The records, based on information collected from publishers,
are especially rich in subject data. They are available, by
subscription, in hard-copy or machine-readable form. Book
Data aims to facilitate the buying and selling of books; its
records are not intended as catalogue records, but library
subscribers could, if required, adapt them to conform with
accepted cataloguing rules. There appears to be general
agreement that both book trade and library community would
benefit from adoption of common standards for record content
and from the further development of bibliographic databases
which could be made more widely available. Some of the efforts
being made to establish common standards for record content
and exchange are discussed in Chapter 6.

No archetype of the bibliographic record can be readily suggested; there is too much variation in nature, purpose and use.
Successful communication and exchange certainly require
agreement on common data and acceptance of standards which
ensure compatibility but, in practice, accuracy, fullness of
content and adherence to standards rigorous enough to assist
fluent exchange have to be balanced against cost and time,
arguably the two decisive considerations. As Line has rightly
observed,[29] bibliographic records are merely a means to an end,
namely access to documents by the reader; indeed they have
value only if they attain this goal. Their creators are thus faced
with conflicting demands and the need to compromise.

How might such conflicts be reconciled? The most promising
answers to this question appear to lie in, first, the potential of
new technology for linking disparate systems and, second, the
efforts being made towards establishing common ground among
different sectors of the information world. Bibliographic control
on the scale envisaged by the UBCIM Programme can be
accomplished only by the use of computers, which in turn
require the imposition of varying degrees of standardization in
form and content of bibliographic records. For this purpose
record formats are used, and these are the subject of the
following chapters.

Notes and references

1 Hagler, R. and Simmons, P., *The bibliographic record and information
  technology*, Chicago, American Library Association, 1982, 55. This
  is the most comprehensive work available on bibliographic data
  and bibliographic records. (Reprinted with permission of the
  American Library Association, excerpts from chapter 3 taken
  from 'The Bibliographic Record and Information Technology' by
  R. Hagler and P. Simmons; copyright © 1982 by ALA.)
2 Dempsey, L., *Bibliographic records: use of data elements in the book world*,
  Bath, University Library, 1989, (BNB Research Fund report 40),
  9.
3 Hagler and Simmons, *op. cit.*, 84.
4 Ayres, F. and others, *USBC (Universal Standard Book Code): its use for
  union file creation*, London, British Library Bibliographic Services
  Division, 1984.
5 Hagler and Simmons, *op. cit.*, 56.

6 Mitev, N., Venner, G. M. and Walker, S., *Designing an online public-access catalogue*, London, British Library, 1985, (Library and information research reports 39), 109.

7 Seal, A., Bryant, P. and Hall, C., *Full and short-entry catalogues: library needs and uses*, Bath, Centre for Catalogue Research, Bath University Library, 1982, 8.

8 *Standard practices in the preparation of bibliographic records*, rev. ed., London, IFLA UBCIM Programme, 1989, 3.

9 *Anglo-American cataloguing rules*, 2nd edition, London, Library Association, 1978, 565.

10 Malinconico, S. M., 'Bibliographic data base organization and authority file control', in *Authority control: the key to tomorrow's catalog*, Phoenix, Oryx Press, 1979, 1–18.

11 International Federation of Library Associations and Institutions, *Guidelines for the application of the ISBDs to the description of component parts*, London, IFLA UBCIM Programme, 1988, 2.

12 A full description of standards for bibliographic records can be found in *Standard practices*.

13 International Federation of Library Associations and Institutions, *ISBD(G): General International Standard Bibliographic Description: annotated text*, London, IFLA International Office for UBC, 1977, 1.

14 *AACR*2, Chapter 13.

15 *Guidelines*, v.

16 Anderson, D., 'IFLA's programme of ISBDs', *IFLA journal*, **4**, (1), 1978, 26–33; Har-Nicolescu, S., 'Romanized and transliterated databases of Asian-language materials: history, problems and prospects', in *Automated systems for access to multilingual and multiscript library materials*, ed. by C. Bossmeyer and S. W. Massil, Munich, K. G. Saur, 1987, 13–29.

17 Sumner Spalding, C., 'ISBD, its origin, rationale and implications', *Library journal*, 15 January 1973, 121–3.

18 Verona, E., *Statement of principles: adopted at the International Conference on Cataloguing Principles, Paris, October 1961*, annotated ed., London, IFLA Committee on Cataloguing, 1971.

19 Lancaster, F. W. and Smith, L. C., *Compatibility issues affecting information systems and services*, Paris, Unesco, 1983, (PGI-83/WS/23).

20 Har-Nicolescu, S., *op. cit.*

21 Seal, A., *op. cit.*, 34–6.

22 British Library Bibliographic Services, *Consultative paper: currency with coverage*, London, British Library, July 1987.

23 'BNB MARC currency survey', *Library Association record*, **90**, (11), November 1988, 670; 'Record levels for record creation', *British Library Bibliographic Services newsletter*, **48**, February 1989, 1–2.

24 Anderson, D., *UBC: a survey of Universal Bibliographic Control*, London, IFLA International Office for UBC, 1982, 13.

25 *Ibid.*, 14.

26 International Federation of Library Associations and Institutions, *UNIMARC: Universal MARC format*, 2nd ed. rev., London, IFLA International Office for UBC, 1980.

27 *Reference manual for machine-readable bibliographic descriptions*, 2nd rev. ed., compiled and ed. by H. Dierickx and A. Hopkinson, Unisist International Centre for Bibliographic Descriptions (UNIBID), Paris, Unesco, 1981.

28 *Bibliographic records in the book world: needs and capabilities: proceedings of a seminar held on 27–28 November 1987 at Newbury*, compiled by D. Greenwood, London, British Library, 1988 (BNB Research Fund report 33).

29 Line, M. B., 'Satisfying bibliographic needs in the future – from publisher to user', *Catalogue and index*, **90/91**, Autumn/Winter 1988, 10–14.

Additional readings

Anderson, D., *Universal Bibliographic Control: a long-term policy, a plan for action*, Pullach bei München, Verlag Dokumentation Saur, 1974.

Ayres, F. and Yannakoudakis, E. J., 'The bibliographic record: an analysis of the size of its constituent parts', *Program*, **13**, 1979, 127–42.

Davinson, D., *Bibliographic control*, 2nd ed., London, Bingley, 1981.

Gorman, M., 'Bibliographic description: past, present and future', *International cataloguing*, **16**, (4), October/December 1987, 43–4.

Massil, S., 'Standards for sharing in bibliographic systems', *Catalogue and index*, **65**, Summer 1982, 1–6.

'Technical standards for library and information science', *Library trends*, **31**, (2), Fall 1982.

Tillett, B. B., 'Bibliographic relationships in library catalogues', *International cataloguing and bibliographic control*, **17**, (1), January/March 1987, 3–6.

UNISIST guide to standards for information handling, prepared by the UNISIST Working Group on Bibliographic Data Interchange, compiled by E. Vajda, Paris, Unesco, 1980.

Verona, E., 'A decade of IFLA's work on the standardization of bibliographic description', *International cataloguing*, **9**, (1), January/March 1980, 2–9.

2
Bibliographic data formats

Data organization in general

All data for computer handling must be converted to machine-perceptible or machine-readable form. This process is similar in some respects to that of translation from one language to another, although the analogy with conversion from printed text to Braille is perhaps more accurate. Various approaches are taken to the identification, organization and storage of data, resulting in essentially different systems. Their common aim is rapid and efficient retrieval and manipulation of data. Bibliographic systems have many unique features, but they also have much in common with other data-processing applications, sharing concepts, terminology and methods. What follows is a brief and simplified account of some key concepts necessary for an understanding of bibliographic data formats. This is offered for the benefit of readers who may not be familiar with the subject.[1]

Records, fields and subfields

A record is a group of related data elements treated as a unit by an application program (i.e. a computer program designed to perform a specific procedure). Each record contains data which refer to a separate entity, object or unit recognized by the system; in commercial applications the units might be employees, customers, stock items; in bibliographic and library applications the units are books, journals, articles, library clients, book suppliers, etc. Consider the following:

Bennet, P. *Typewriting dictionary*. London : McGraw-Hill, 1987. ISBN 0-07-084992-7.

Lovecy, I. *Automating library procedures: a survivor's handbook*. London : Library Association, 1984. ISBN 0-85365-516-2.

No highly specialized knowledge on the reader's part is required to recognize these as two book citations, or to be able to locate them in a catalogue or bibliography. (It must be said, however, that those totally unfamiliar with the world of books and libraries might not find them so easy to understand.) The computer, on the other hand, needs further, precise information in order to store, access and manipulate these records. Specifically, it must be told that they are two separate records, each containing certain elements of data. This is normally done by arranging the data in a prescribed way and/or by adding special labels, tags or codes (collectively called content designators) to act as identification marks. In this way the computer can tell the length of each record and is able to locate certain data elements within the records.

Because it may be necessary to access parts of a record, for example to ascertain the price of an item, or to find out whether a particular name or subject term is present, records are usually divided into fields, and also, if needed, into subfields. Computers can, of course, read through whole records in order to detect the presence or absence of specific data, but dividing the records into identifiable fields and subfields speeds up the processes of search and retrieval (see Figure 2.1).

Key field

ISBN	Author	Title
0070849927	Bennet, P.	Typewriting dictionary

Imprint

Place	Publisher	Date
London	McGraw-Hill	1987

|_____ Subfields _____|

Fig. 2.1 A simple record, diagrammatically represented

A field is part of a record which contains data referring to one characteristic, or group of characteristics, of the entity or unit represented by the record. Fields may be fixed in length (i.e. containing a prescribed number of characters) or variable in length (i.e. capable of holding a variable number of characters). As has been shown in Chapter 1, bibliographic items possess various attributes or characteristics which must be recorded. Although some items (e.g. films, computer software) have unique features, there are, generally speaking, a limited number of commonly recurring attributes, for example authorship, title, subject matter, and these same characteristics will be recorded for each bibliographic item. The number and nature of fields is usually determined at the time the record structure is designed and obviously takes into account the requirements of the application. Most systems provide for additional fields to be added at a later date. Choice of fields has not surprisingly (some say regrettably) reflected the traditional areas of a catalogue entry and examples of commonly occurring fields include author field, title field, imprint or publication details field and subject data field.

Subfields are parts of fields which cannot stand completely in isolation from the data in the field, but require individual treatment. Examples of typical subfields in bibliographic records include family name (within author field) which may need capitalizing or emboldening, subtitle (within title field) which may need to be omitted in a title index and volume numbering (within series field) which may need to be sorted as a numeric field rather than as an alphanumeric string. In many data-processing applications subfields are the smallest parts of records that in the normal course of events need to be manipulated or accessed. There is, however, one exception: online information-retrieval systems and many online public-access catalogues (OPACs) offer access to individual words in records. These may be retrieved from anywhere in the record, or from specific fields. The main purpose is to allow the combination of individual words in searching. Many of these systems also offer string searching. The system can find any pattern of characters in the database, even in a field on which searching is not normally permitted (for example in a publication details field). String searching by its very nature requires no preorganization of the data, but it is very slow and makes very heavy use of system resources. Recourse to string searching is had only as a last resort.

A word here may be helpful on the difference between the terms *data element* and *field/subfield*. In some system specifications *data element* is treated as synonymous with field; in others (including the Common Communication Format) as synonymous with subfield. It must be pointed out that data elements (i.e. pieces of data which describe or help to identify an item) exist independently of computer systems and may be defined in different ways when record formats are designed. Fields and subfields may therefore contain one or more data elements, depending on the ways the designers of the system choose to treat the data. An author field, for example, may be defined in one system as containing a single data element comprising surname, forename, affiliation and date of birth. In another system, an author field may be defined as containing separate subfields each containing discrete data elements for surname, forename, affiliation and date of birth. In other words, *data element* is a relative term.

Characters and character sets

Records may also be described as strings of characters. A character is any symbol representing a letter of the alphabet, a digit, or a sign (including punctuation and diacritical marks). A record described as 500 characters in length may be regarded as a string of 500 characters, one following the next, with all characters counted, including spaces between words (blank characters), punctuation marks and any symbols used to identify fields and subfields.

A character set is a group of machine (binary) equivalents of the total number of characters that can be exactly represented within a given computer system. Each character is represented by a number of bits (binary digits) which are present in the computer as electrical charges or magnetic blips. Most computers used in Western countries have standard character sets designed to cope with routine English or other Roman alphabet languages. (The main character set used is ASCII, the American Standard Code for Information Interchange.) Bibliographic records, on the other hand, may necessitate the use of special characters and non-Roman scripts. Problems arising from this are discussed later in this chapter.

Logical and physical records

A record for a bibliographic or other item presented in machine-readable form may be described as a logical record. The logical record is not necessarily stored within the computer system in the same form; it may be broken up and the parts stored in different places on a computer disk; or it may be grouped with other records and stored in one large physical record. Physical here refers to the physical arrangement on the storage medium. Computer programs cope with the task of converting logical records into physical records, and vice versa.

Record format

The terms *record structure*, *record format* and *readable form/format* are all used to refer to the arrangement and identification of data for computer handling. The word *format* conveys the notion of a formalized framework or structure which will hold records of varying content. Also implicit is the idea of a set of rules or conventions controlling the representation of the data; these rules may be unique to a system, or shared with other systems. A machine-readable bibliographic record is arranged according to a particular format. In the UNISIST *Reference Manual*.

> a [machine-readable] bibliographic record is defined as a collection of information which pertains to a single document and which is stored in machine-readable form as a self-contained and unique logical structure.[2]

Bibliographic data format and *bibliographic record format* are used to describe the arrangement or structure of computer-readable records of bibliographic items.

Record structures may be fixed or variable. Fixed records each contain the same number of fields, and the fields are always of a prescribed length. Variable records contain fields whose length can be adjusted to suit the bibliographic data. The records are not the same size, as some will have more fields than others and some fields will contain more data than others. Some record structures make use of a combination of fixed and variable-length fields, using fixed fields for regular, predictable

44

data and for coded data (i.e. symbols or codes representing certain characteristics of the document) and variable-length fields for bibliographic data. A more detailed discussion of record structures will be found in the second section of this chapter.

Files, file storage and access to data

A file is a collection of related or similar records, for example a file of catalogue records, a file of records of library clients and their addresses. The two best-known storage media for computer files are magnetic tape and disk, including the floppy disk associated with microcomputers and the more recent CD-ROM (compact disc – read only memory). In earlier computer systems which relied on magnetic tape storage, similar records were grouped into separate files and computer programs were written to manipulate data from the files for specific purposes. On magnetic tape, records are stored serially (one record after another, as they are added to the file). A file of bibliographic records arranged by ISBN, for example, cannot provide direct access to individual records: these are accessible only by a search through the file until the desired ISBN is located.

With the development of direct- or random-access storage devices, of which the disk is the major example, it became possible for the computer to access or select any record, regardless of where it was stored relative to others. Files of records can be stored on disk in a number of ways: serially, sequentially (arranged by a control or key field) or in random storage locations or addresses, and accessed directly, either by an address key, or by means of one or more indexes. Direct-access systems are the norm in online information retrieval, and make use of inverted files (indexes of key parts of the records) to provide fast access to record content. They allow free-text searching (i.e. the ability to pick up a word or words occurring anywhere in the record), as well as more structured searching (i.e. focusing on specific, named fields within the record and examining their content). Many online public-access catalogues (OPACs) also offer these capabilities.

Database Management Systems (DBMS) are more common in commercial environments, but also have bibliographic applications. They rely on direct-access storage but represent a change in emphasis from separate files, each devoted to a special application, to the data themselves. These are collected and organized in a large central pool or database and their record structure is for the most part defined in such a way as to be independent of the various programs which make use of them. The data elements are connected with each other by a series of linking mechanisms which permit the establishment of relationships required by the users of the system and which eliminate unnecessary redundancy of data (e.g. a commonly occurring author's name, such as Shakespeare, may need to be stored only once). Databases of this nature obviously facilitate the development of integrated library systems.

The ways in which data are physically stored and made accessible, and the ways in which relationships between data are shown are complex matters, beyond the scope of this book. Furthermore, technology in this area is rapidly changing and the development of highly sophisticated systems for data transfer may lead to new methods of data storage. It should be noted, however, that not all sectors of the library and information community choose the same methods of data management: information retrieval, for example, may be best served by methods of data organization and storage different from those suited to catalogue production. The main determinant is use: systems which are called upon to deal with unanticipated demands may require methods of organization and storage differing from those needed in systems which deal only with routine, predictable uses. Most organizations want to use their data for more than one purpose. Conflicting demands can lead to tensions between different potential uses and the need for compromise when the software is selected or designed.

Data organization for bibliographic records
This book is primarily concerned with the exchange of bibliographic data and record formats which have been developed to facilitate this exchange. Because sharing of data is so important in the library and information field, exchange formats have had great influence on internal formats.

Exchange formats
It is important to distinguish between exchange formats, also

46

known as interchange or communication formats and local or internal processing formats. In this book, 'exchange formats' is the preferred term, although the term used in International Standards is 'interchange format' as found in the title of the Standard, *Documentation: format for bibliographic information interchange on magnetic tape.*[3] Another usage is to call the physical record structure a communication format and the format including tags, indicators and subfield identifiers an exchange format. However, this distinction is by no means adhered to, and it is confusing to try to maintain it when it is not applied in practice.

Exchange formats are intended for the exchange of records between systems. They must therefore be acceptable to the exchanging agencies; hospitable to the types of materials which are the subject of the records being exchanged; and sufficiently flexible to cope with the needs of many different software systems. Ideally, they should facilitate the exchange of data which are to be used in a wide range of different bibliographic applications, from the production of the traditional catalogue card to records in databases which are used for online access. A major problem for designers of exchange formats is the lack of international agreement on standards for constructing bibliographic records. As we have seen, although ISBD is available, it is not accepted by many organizations outside the sphere of the national libraries or those libraries in cooperatives based on national library practices and using records from or contributing records to national databases. Nor does it address the problem of choice and form of access points. Set against this, however, are the traditions and established practices of cataloguing (arguably in need of re-examination in the light of changed user needs and technology) which have influenced even those organizations concerned with information which are far removed from the traditional library. The emphasis on author and title access, and the inclusion in records of such details as publisher, date and place of publication are manifestations of such traditions which ensure that bibliographic records from diverse sources share many features in common.

Internal formats

Internal formats are so called because they are internal to a software system. In contrast to the exchange format they can be tailored specifically to the needs of the local system and do not have to conform to any external standards. For the internal format (the identifiers used and their record structure), system designers can adopt any conventions that they wish. Rules for input are more restricted, being constrained by existing cataloguing codes and practices and, in those systems intent on being part of a network, by the need to be compatible with other systems or with a standard exchange format. Their main aim is economy and efficiency in processing while the ability to convert, if necessary, from the local format to an exchange format is an extra. This conversion can be done by computer program. An agency may therefore adopt its own internal processing format, but at the same time retain system compatibility with a national or international exchange format. Since internal formats can be structured in an infinite variety of ways which depend on the software used, this book could not hope to begin to cover all the different possibilities. It will therefore be concentrating on features of exchange formats since these have to be understood to appreciate the problems of sharing data between systems.

Exchange formats: structure and content

Those bibliographic data formats which have been adopted as means to exchange of data tend to consist of three basic components:

1   *A defined physical structure*: rules for the arrangement on a computer storage medium of data to be exchanged. This may be likened to a container or carrier into which data may be placed. The carrier remains constant although the data change from record to record.

2   *Content designators*: codes to identify the different data elements in the record (e.g. author, title, scale of map, starting date of journal, etc.).

3   *Content* of the record governed by rules for the formulation of the different data elements, very closely tied up with 2. The data elements separately identified by the codes in the exchange format have to be defined, not only in terms of content but also in form, if the records are to be suitable for use by another agency.

48

Structure

As mentioned earlier in this chapter, records in automated systems may be of fixed length or variable length. Fixed-length records in a file must each contain the same fields and any given field must always be of the same length from one record to another. If a field is repeatable, it must be repeated the same number of times in each record. Variable-length records may be variable because they do not contain the same number of fields (a given field may not occur in every record) or because a given field is not always of the same length.

Bibliographic records do not fit naturally into the fixed-length pattern. An example of a database whose records can be treated as fixed length is a mailing list for officials within organizations. In each record there can be fields for each of name, job title, organization name, departmental name, street, town, county/province, state, postal code. Few if any of these data elements will always be the same length, but most of them will have a similar length. Each data element is allocated a number of characters and any not used will be filled with spaces. The system designer has to allocate to each data element a suitable number of characters which will not be too small to accommodate the majority of records, but not too large to waste space by having records full of spaces. Most records in a mailing list will include all the fields mentioned above and there will not be too many fields in a mailing list database which are completely filled with spaces. In bibliographic records, the situation is different.

- Many fields occur only from time to time, for example cover title, ISSN, edition. Edition is particularly interesting because traditionally it appears in bibliographic records only when the document contains a specific edition statement or when it is known to be other than a first edition. Beware the systems designer who would argue that logically every item is a member of an edition and would make the edition field mandatory!

- Many fields occur a variable number of times in each record. A document may have one author or it may have any number of joint authors. The same document may be a member of more than one series. A record may be assigned more than one subject descriptor or subject heading.

● Last, but not least, a data element may vary in length between records. This is probably true in most systems which do not code their data but record them in ordinary language. However, the variation is greater in bibliographic systems than in most others. Titles may vary enormously in length and cannot easily be truncated to fit fixed-length fields. Even mailing systems have that problem and filling in a form to enter one's name and address on a mailing list frequently involves substantial use of abbreviation. In the context of bibliographic records, cutting words out of titles and abbreviating title words cannot be regarded as satisfactory ways of solving problems of space caused by the use of fixed-length formats. Abbreviating a word in a corporate body name such as 'Department' to 'Dept' would make subsequent searching more complex. A user could well search for 'department' and on finding the word absent would assume the corporate body containing the word 'department' was not on the database. Although this kind of abbreviation was permissible in the days of catalogue cards, it should be avoided in automated systems.

Therefore because of the large number of different kinds of data elements, their repeatability and the fact that many appear only infrequently in records, bibliographic exchange formats usually avoid fixed-length formats. They employ content designators to denote the identity of each data field instead of identifying data fields by position within a record.

A content designator may immediately precede the data it identifies. Alternatively, content designators may be grouped together at the beginning of the record with 'pointers' to the data they identify. This latter method is the one usually used in bibliographic data processing and has its origin in systems that imported data from tape. Such a system locates the data it is seeking by reading the identifiers and their pointers at the beginning of the record and moving quickly to read the data. The storage on tape of computer files invariably uses this method of indexing the location of files at the beginning of the tape to obviate the need to read a complete tape sequentially. The computer calculates from the given starting character position of each file the likely position of that file on the tape, moves the tape very quickly to a position just before the start of that file at which point the tape moves more slowly in order to locate the data. This index, whether it be to files on a tape or data elements in a record, is known as a directory.

(a) *Variable-length format without content designators*
Here is a simple example of a record in a variable-length format which allows the possibility of up to five fields: Record Number, Author, Title, Publisher, Date. Though it has a directory, it does not employ content designators.

001000006023026@1761Oxford DictionaryOUP1990

The record begins with a directory which is divided into five groups of three characters. The first three characters indicate the position of the record number in the record: 001 means starting at character 1. The next three characters are 000 as the data element 'Author' does not exist. The next three characters are 006 which indicates that the third data element 'Title' starts at character position 6, and '023' that the publisher starts at character position 23. '@' indicates that this is the position where the directory finishes and the data start, so the values mentioned earlier are calculated from this point.

This kind of directory is not very common. The directory entries are fixed in number for every record using this format. If the format has 20 fields, there must be 20 entries in the directory of every record. If a record does not contain a particular field, the entry for that field will be '000'. Even if a field should logically be repeated, there can never be more than one entry in the directory, so repeatability must be indicated in a different way.

(b) *Variable-length format with content designators*
It is more usual to add to each directory entry a content designator. The record above could be treated in this way. Then there needs to be no entry for a missing field. Each entry in the directory consists of one character for the name of the field followed by three for the position. Record number is 1, Author 2, Title 3, Publisher 4, Date 5.

1001300640235026@01761Oxford DictionaryOUP1990

Field 1 starts at character position 001, field 3 starts at 006, field 4 at 023, etc. '@' signifies the end of the directory.

(c) *Simple variable-length format without directory*
To complete the picture, here is the same example without a directory. Each content designator (other than the first) has to be identified as a content designator rather than as text of the record so a character has to be reserved for that purpose. A control character (see p.63) could be used, but in this example we use @.

@0101761@03Oxford Dictionary@04OUP@051989

The system knows that in every case the two characters following immediately after @ constitute a content designator and it will not treat them as part of the data. One character could be used in this example which would give 10 possible fields (labelled 0 to 9) but a system like this would usually employ two characters to allow for expansion up to 99 fields. If the system were asked to print out all the titles in the records, it would search for '@03' in every record and print out all the data after '@03' until it reached the next @. As this method does not include a directory, there is no way of finding any desired data element in a record without searching for it sequentially. Some systems using very fast sequential-searching techniques store records in this way.

From this, it is evident that physical structures affect processing. Although formats based on variable-length fields organized with directories are more suitable for the kind of data that are found in bibliographic records, they are more complicated and expensive to program and processing takes longer than it would with fixed-length record formats.

The International Standard Exchange Format: ISO 2709
Remarkably there is agreement on the structure of an exchange format; ISO 2709 is the international standard *Format for bibliographic information interchange on magnetic tape.* As its title states, it was developed for the exchange of bibliographic records on magnetic tape. It had its origins in the Library of Congress MARC format.

The ISO 2709 structure consists of the following elements: record label, directory, bibliographic data fields and record separator, and follows the structure of the record described in (b) above with the addition of a record label.

The record label includes data that identify to the system the type of record and contains information necessary for the processing of the record such as the total number of characters in the record and the length of various elements of the record.

The directory consists of a content designator for each data field followed by an indication of the position in the record where the data relating to that field start and the length of the field. If a field is repeated, it has two entries in the directory, one for each appearance.

Figure 2.2 is an example of a record. It is the record of a book with an author John Jones and a title *Games*. It is not possible to illustrate an ISO 2709 record without including tags from one of the formats which implement it, unless one makes up a scheme of tags for the sake of the example. This example uses the tags of the Unesco Common Communication Format. This has implemented the 1981 version of ISO 2709, and in the following explanation the additional features of ISO 2709 – 1981 compared with ISO 2709 – 1973 are pointed out.

Record label

The first five characters in the record represent the total number of characters in the record, 101 in the case of this illustrative example. The 'a' that follows indicates that the record is a new record. The next character position is not used and is filled with a space (represented by _). Then follows the bibliographic level, here code 'm', since the record relates to a monograph. The next two are not used and they are followed by '22' (indicating that the data in each field other than 001 begin with a two-character indicator and each subfield begins with a two-character identifier).

The next five characters, here 00067, indicate the length of the label and directory. Since the first character of the record is numbered 0, the first character of the data is number 67.

Label	00101a_m___2200067____452_
Directory	001000700000**200001000023**300001600007**#
Data	A12345#00@AJones@BJohn#00@AGames#%

Fig. 2.2   Label, directory, data and record separator

After three unused character positions, '452' indicates that the second, third and fourth elements of each entry in the directory consist of 4, 5 and 2 characters respectively. The first element, the tag, always consists of three in any implementation of ISO 2709, and is therefore not indicated. The fourth element is implemented only in ISO 2709 – 1981, and in earlier implementations of the standard as followed by MARC formats, the third character ('2' above) indicating the length of the fourth element is always 0.

Directory

The directory consists of an entry for each field present in the record. This record has three fields, which have the tags 001, 200 and 300. The tags in the directory are ordered in numerical order, but the data they relate to need not be in the same order, though usually systems do enter them in the same order. The order of the fields does not matter because their position in the record is indicated in the directory. In this example, the data relating to field 200, the title, occur at the end, the data relating to field 300, the author, preceding it. After each tag comes a group of four characters representing the length of the field (0007, 0010, and 0016 in the example) and then five characters representing the starting character position of each field (00000, 00007 and 00023 in the example). The two asterisks at the end of each entry in the directory have in the example replaced the characters which indicate the occurrences of a field and the number of the segment containing the field. They would be 0 in all cases in this example; the first would be 0 since no field is repeated; and the second also 0 since there is only one segment in the record and segments are numbered from 0 to 9. These two characters replaced by asterisks in the example are not present in MARC formats or in any other format which pre-dates the 1981 version of ISO 2709. The directory ends with a control character, ASCII character value 30.

In order to be able to create the directory, a computer program has to be written. No cataloguer can be expected to enter the directory manually. The program has to count the characters of data in each field and calculate the relative position of each data element from the start of the data.

Data

The data appear as the last element in the record. Each field is terminated by ASCII character value 30, and the complete record is terminated by ASCII character value 29. The '@' in the record and the character following make up a subfield identifier. The '@' is used in this example to represent ASCII value 31.

Content designators

(a) *Tags*

Most exchange formats employ a three-digit identifier known as a tag, but some internal system formats employ a two-digit tag. In order to be compatible with ISO 2709, a three-digit tag must be used. A system which uses two-digit tags may prefix each tag by zero to make it three. Three digits allow 999 data elements, and two digits 99, assuming that 000 is not used. Most formats use numeric tags; the UNISIST *Reference Manual* format uses alphanumeric tags and these have been adopted by the MINISIS software system, with one alphabetic and two numeric characters making up the tag. Some systems have two-digit mnemonic tags, with identifiers like AU for author and TI for title, but there do not appear to be any exchange formats based on ISO 2709 which have adopted this kind of tag.

There is no international standard for the allocation of content designators to data elements. ISO 2709 – 1983 states 'in the absence of an International Standard special agreement has to be reached between the interchange partners'.[4] So different formats have been devised, some with the status of national standards, others *de facto* standards like the Reference manual or the CCF. These are the subject of later chapters.

Although there is no standard philosophy for the allocation of tags, common strands exist through many formats. There are not many formats where the tags are allocated from 001 sequentially to the last tag, so that if there are 25 fields tags 001 to 025 would be used. Most allocate tags to 'areas' based on the hundreds digit. So, fields 200/299 are often used for the title area and other parts of descriptive area. Numbers are allocated to give associated data elements associated tags. 700 to 799 are often allocated to access points, while the 600 fields are used for subject. Outstandingly different is the Reference manual; there a deliberate decision was made not to prejudge the use of the data in the format and the tags were not intended to convey any hierarchy though in practice they were not allocated absolutely at random.

Many exchange formats, in particular those based on the MARC II format and its successors (see Chapter 3) use indicators and subfield identifiers to define further the data into separate categories.

These were used by the MARC II format, which was the first bibliographic exchange format (other than the MARC I experimental format) to be developed, but were not made mandatory in the American Standard ANSI Z.39.2 – 1971 on which ISO 2709 was based. As they are not mandatory, character positions 11 and 12 in the label (see above) indicate whether they are used in the record. It is unusual if not unknown for a format to vary the number of indicators or the length of subfield identifiers between one record and another in the same file; if a format uses subfields and indicators it will use them consistently across all records. This variation is, though, permitted in the standard.

(b) *Indicators*

Indicators, where they are used, appear at the beginning of each field in the data portion of the record. They often qualify the tag. They may identify whether a corporate author is the name of a meeting or the name of a country. They can indicate the number of characters to be ignored in filing when a definite or indefinite article appears at the start of a field. If a format chooses to use indicators in just one field in a record, they have to appear in all fields. If no indicator values are required in a field, the character positions have to be filled, so it is usual to fill them with spaces or zeros.

(c) *Subfield identifiers*

Subfield identifiers, where they are used, are embedded in the data. They are purely codes, even though they are embedded in the text, and should be removed before the records are displayed in a catalogue. In the early days of BLAISE (the British Library Automated Information Service), they were not extracted from the data; this made the output difficult to read for anyone but a student of MARC. They are usually replaced by punctuation or they may indicate a change in typography in output intended for end users.

Fields 001 to 009 do not have subfields and indicators according to the specification of ISO 2709, though internal formats which have been designed for compatibility with ISO 2709 may well have subfields and indicators in these fields as it is easier to be able to treat every field in an internal format in a consistent way.

Fields for fixed-length data

Many exchange formats have a need for fixed-length data, invariably coded data. A limited number of fixed-length data elements may be entered in the record label, but these usually relate to the record as much as to the document being recorded, the most obvious of these being a code to indicate the record status, whether the record is, for example, a new record or replacement record. Other coded data include language of publication, country of publication, whether a document is a conference publication, Festschrift or government publication. The original reason for including this kind of coded data was that codes were easier to find in the early days of data processing and they took up less space on the tape and in any system to which the data on the tape were transferred. The use of codes also facilitates consistency: code 'c' can mean conference publication, proceedings of a meeting or the publication of a seminar; in circumstances where bibliographic items such as these need to be grouped under one small category, it is easier to use a code than to find a term that can represent all members of the category. It is the need to ensure consistency that is the most important of these considerations today when processing is faster. If a data element is worth including for the benefit of the end user, it is often better to use unabbreviated language rather than a code. Many systems use as codes the ISO country codes; not so many use the ISO language codes which are unsatisfactory for bibliographic use, as only the more common languages are included; the Library of Congress developed a set of language codes for MARC which have been adopted by most bibliographic systems except in those countries which prefer the

ISO codes for ideological reasons.

In order to include this kind of fixed-length data, most systems have fixed-length fields which can readily be imposed on the variable-length structure. MARC formats usually use field 008 for this purpose.

Subrecords

In terms of the structure, there is one other feature which has been implemented by a number of formats, the subrecord directory. This has never been implemented by the Library of Congress or USMARC format (though it was mentioned in the 1968 Supplement 1 to LC MARC II and is still reserved though not defined in the 1988 specification). It is found in the UKMARC format and in certain other formats such as the AGRIS (International Information System for the Agricultural Sciences and Technology) format used by the Food and Agriculture Organization. Using this method, bibliographic data fields for analytics can be grouped together in the record following the bibliographic fields containing the data describing the item as a whole. These fields have entries in the directory like any other field. The fields in each set of fields relating to each analytic have to occur next to each other in the directory because of the way the subrecord directory, contained in field 002, works. The 002 field contains information on the starting position and length of each set of directory fields relating to each subrecord. The information for each subrecord is held as a sequence of 12 characters. So the length of field 002 itself will always be one more than a multiple of 12, the extra character being for the end of field marker. Within each group of 12, the first 3 positions are for a relationship code. In UKMARC, this is always 'a__' because these refer always to analyticals (underscore represents space). Character positions 4 to 7 contain the length of the directory entry or entries which refer to each subrecord. This figure will always be a multiple of 12 as each directory entry is 12 characters long. Character positions 8 to 12 contain a five-digit number which indicates the starting character position of the directory entry counting from the start of the record. A record may contain up to nine subrecords. Here is an example of the contents of field 002:

a__002400240a__003600264

This shows that there are two subrecords coded as analytics. The first has directory entries of 24 characters starting at the 240th character from the beginning of the record. The second is 24 characters long starting at the 264th character.

The directory from character 240 to 287 could be as follows:

100002500980 245003201005 100002501037 245004801062

The data to which the directory relates:

10$aShakespeare$hWilliam#01$aHamlet$eWilliam Shakespeare#10$aShakespeare$hWilliam#01$aMerry wives of Windsor$eWilliam Shakespeare#

Author starting at 980 – 25 characters long
Title starting at 1005 – 32 characters long
Author starting at 1037 – 25 characters long
Title starting at 1062 – 48 characters long

This is used by UKMARC to group together fields belonging to one analytic in a record which may (following AACR) consist of the record of a monograph and up to three analytics.

The complex arrangement of a record formatted according to ISO 2709 need not worry the cataloguer. It is invariably the task of a computer program to format records. Worksheets or screen data-entry programs can be designed to be as free from codes as possible to make the system easy to use. That having been said, cataloguers quickly become accustomed to entering subfield identifiers and other codes. Indeed, it becomes easier to use subfield identifiers than to enter spaces and punctuation symbols. This is especially true if the worksheets are then converted to machine-readable form by data-entry personnel who may not be aware of the correct spacing for ISBD or AACR punctuation.

Linking techniques
Other ways exist to show relationships between different biblio-graphic entities. The relationship between analytics and their containing monograph is only one such relationship. One way of showing relationships is by allocating a tag to the relationship. This is often done with serials. In the ISDS format, field 780

indicates the name of a former title of a periodical, and this is used also in some MARC formats.

However, more esoteric techniques have evolved and they tend to be used by only one format or by one format and others based very closely on it. There is the use of segments which are indicated in the fourth element of the directory in the CCF which is used also by FORMEX. UNIMARC employs an embedded-field technique to indicate relationships: the embedded fields can hold actual titles of related works or identifiers like database numbers or ISBN.

These features are not addressed by ISO 2709, and since they relate to individual formats, they will be discussed in the chapters relating to the formats in which they occur.

Content of the record

The content is the data recorded in the fields and subfields of the machine-readable record. It is beyond the scope of ISO 2709: indeed content is likely to vary less between exchange and internal formats than any feature of the record structure.

Content is determined mainly by three factors:

(a) the nature of the bibliographic item recorded
(b) the use to be made of the record
(c) the standards used in the records: the code of cataloguing rules used for author, title and descriptive data; the classification scheme used for classifying the item; the list of subject headings or keywords used for verbal subject data.

Differences in national cataloguing practices have made it difficult to reach agreement on a wholly standardized communication/exchange format at the international level. The greatest advances have been made in bibliographic description, with the widespread acceptance of ISBDs and their incorporation into national codes such as AACR2. ISBDs set out standard data elements, a prescribed order of citing data elements, and distinctive punctuation to separate data elements.

Differences in the use to which records will be put has made it difficult to develop a format accepted across different kinds of institutions, such as national libraries, national and international abstracting and indexing services and smaller libraries in the public or private sector.

Different languages and scripts also pose problems for designers of exchange formats and for the interchange of records between agencies in different countries. Standardization of character sets has been achieved in many individual countries, but the necessity to use more than one of the standard sets for international exchange leads to an undesirable complexity.

Data in all systems have to be defined. Compatibility between systems stands or falls on the compatibility of their data elements. Therefore, for an exchange format to be truly effective, it should have well-defined data elements. Since this is the most difficult area in which to reach agreement, strict definition of data elements has generally been left out of exchange formats. UNIMARC and the CCF each allow data to be defined according to any cataloguing code, though UNIMARC assumes that the code will conform to ISBD in its descriptive area. The Reference Manual format was designed for A & I services which do not have the same long-standing tradition of cataloguing rules as do libraries and are more able to accept something suggested to them. Each national MARC format is usually designed with the national cataloguing code in mind, increasing their effectiveness and ease of use as an exchange format. Other formats, such as AGRIS and INIS (International Nuclear Information System) have cataloguing rules associated with them, but could be regarded as a means of transferring data within a system rather than between different systems.

All specifications of exchange formats include a list of data fields. Some may be designated essential or mandatory; others may be designated optional. Those formats which are intended for carrying data produced according to a particular cataloguing code often refer to the sections in the code which relate to the choice or form of data in each field.

Other standards associated with ISO 2709

Hardware standards

Although standards to be used to define the data elements in formats based on ISO 2709 have not been adopted as international standards, other standards used alongside ISO 2709 are specified in the standard itself. These include standards for magnetic tape labelling and file structure and for the size of tape to be used. The majority of instances of the use of ISO 2709 conform to these standards and use 1600 bpi ½" computer tape. However, recently, exchange of ISO 2709 data has been accomplished in other ways on diskettes and online. ISO 2709 records have also been stored on CD-ROM. The standard has not yet been amended to reflect this and although working groups of standards organizations like ISO have been discussing this for a number of years they have to date still to make any necessary changes. In the meantime, exchanges have taken place on these other media. This has become essential since the time when ISO 2709 records began to be created outside the environment where ½" computer tape has no place. Mainframe and minicomputers like the Hewlett Packard, IBM and VAX ranges are supplied with ½" tape units. Smaller computers rely on cassette for input and output of data on magnetic media. Microcomputers use 5¼", 3½" and sometimes 8" or 3" diskettes. None of these is officially supported by the ISO 2709 standard.

So long as exchanging partners agree on the media and on the character sets used, the lack of official standardization causes few problems. Industrial standardization, the acceptance of standards imposed by manufacturers, has solved the problem of the potential multiplicity of different media.

Character sets

The standardization of character sets is a long-standing problem and the solution to it has been always akin to that being adopted to solve the problem of different exchange media: parties to an exchange usually agree between themselves on the character sets to be used.

In a stand-alone system, it does not matter how a computer represents characters when it is processing them; all that matters is that the characters are converted to the appropriate text at output. However, computer systems in general have not been designed to stand alone since the earliest days of data processing. Manufacturers of computers had to adopt one method or another of representing characters inside the computer. From these practices, they developed various standards, some officially approved by standards organizations such as ISO, ANSI and BSI while others were manufacturers'

62

standards such as those developed by IBM and copied by other manufacturers. Many of these standards were developed from standards used for transmitting data by telex which explains why the standards for character sets were agreed on early in the history of computing.

The main standard that has been developed in this area is the standard known as ASCII, the American Standard Code for Information Interchange.[5] From this was developed the international standard ISO 646: *7-bit coded character set for information processing interchange.*[6] One implementation of this is called the International Reference Version on which national standard character sets should be based. These are all seven-bit character sets. They use combinations of seven binary digits (bits) for identifying the different characters. This allows a range from $2^0 - 1$ to $2^7 - 1$ $(0 - 127)$.

The first 32 characters in character sets are usually reserved for special purposes. They are called control characters as opposed to graphic characters which are the characters that have a pictorial representation when printed out. They are used for such functions as backspace, carriage return, form feed. Of the graphic characters, space always has the value of 32, letters A to Z, 65 to 90 and lower case a to z are 97 to 122. Punctuation is consistent between different national sets, but there are a number of diacritic characters which cannot be included in all national sets in the same way. Each national set includes the characters it requires. Many national sets defined by countries where diacritics are used in the national languages have included combinations of character and diacritic. However, in a character set of 96 graphic characters, there is not enough space for all the combinations required in even the European languages.

These character sets are usually represented in the standard document by a 16 by 8 matrix, an example of which is shown in Figure 2.3.

b7				0	0	0	0	1	1	1	1
b6				0	0	1	1	0	0	1	1
b5				0	1	0	1	0	1	0	1
			column →								
b4	b3	b2	b1	row	0	1	2	3	4	5	6	7
0	0	0	0	0	NUL	TC7 (DLE)	SP	0	@	P	` (2)	p
0	0	0	1	1	TC1 (SOH)	DC1	!	1	A	Q	a	q
0	0	1	0	2	TC2 (STX)	DC2	" (1)	2	B	R	b	r
0	0	1	1	3	TC3 (ETX)	DC3	£	3	C	S	c	s
0	1	0	0	4	TC4 (EOT)	DC4	$	4	D	T	d	t
0	1	0	1	5	TC5 (ENQ)	TC8 (NAK)	%	5	E	U	e	u
0	1	1	0	6	TC6 (ACK)	TC9 (SYN)	&	6	F	V	f	v
0	1	1	1	7	BEL	TC10 (ETB)	' (1)	7	G	W	g	w
1	0	0	0	8	FE0 (BS)	CAN	(	8	H	X	h	x
1	0	0	1	9	FE1 (HT)	EM	)	9	I	Y	i	y
1	0	1	0	10	FE2 (LF)	SUB	*	:	J	Z	j	z
1	0	1	1	11	FE3 (VT)	ESC	+	;	K	[	k	(3)
1	1	0	0	12	FE4 (FF)	IS4 (FS)	, (1)	<	L	(3)	l	(3)
1	1	0	1	13	FE5 (CR)	IS3 (GS)	–	=	M	]	m	(4)
1	1	1	0	14	SO	IS2 (RS)	.	>	N	^ (1)	n	‾ (4)
1	1	1	1	15	SI	IS1 (US)	/	?	O	_	o	DEL

Fig. 2.3 Example of ISO 646

Notes to Table 1: ISO Character set
(1) The graphic characters in positions 2/2, 2/7, 2/12 and 5/14 have respectively the significance of quotation mark, apostrophe, comma and upward arrow head; however, these characters take on the significance of the diacritical signs diaeresis, acute accent, cedilla and circumflex accent when they are preceded or followed by the backspace character in position 0/8.
(2) The symbol in position 6/0 represents grave accent.
(3) Positions 5/12, 7/11, 7/12 and 7/13 are reserved exclusively for specific characters to be explicitly agreed between partners to a particular exchange. These positions are primarily intended for alphabet extensions. If they are not required for that purpose, they may be used for symbols.
(4) Position 7/14 is used for the graphic character overline, the graphic representation of which may vary to represent the tilde or another diacritical sign provided that there is no risk of confusion with another graphic character included in the table.

Another standard used in computer systems is EBCDIC (Extended Binary Coded Data for Interchange) which was originally developed by IBM and has never been adopted as an official standard. It was developed as an eight-bit set and having 256 possible combinations had plenty of space for additional characters, and many national versions were developed. The British Library LOCAS system which was run on an IBM used an extended EBCDIC character set known as BLECS (British Library Extended Character Set). However, additional characters were lost on conversion to MARC exchange tapes which used ASCII-based characters.

As mentioned above, the 96 places in the 8-by-16 matrix are not enough for all the characters including combinations with diacritics to be represented, not to mention other alphabets such as Cyrillic, Greek, Japanese and Chinese, the last two being strictly speaking a syllabary and a set of pictographs rather than alphabets. The Library of Congress designed a character set to deal with extended Roman (Roman with diacritical marks). This was adopted by the American Library Association and later became an unofficial standard within the library automation industry, resulting in the manufacture of typewriter golf-balls, computer print-trains and a number of VDU terminals specially designed to support the character set. This was an eight-bit set and so allowed for 192 graphic characters and 64 control characters.

Because many computer systems cannot use an eight-bit character set, it has been necessary to formulate standard ways of expanding the number of possible characters over the limit of 96, or of avoiding the problem.

International standards can provide a number of techniques for diacritical characters, but one of the most commonly used techniques is not found supported in international standards. That is the one akin to that used in typing, where a diacritic mark does not move the carriage with the result that the next character occupies the same space. The typist types ´ followed by a and the result is á. Certain characters may be assumed not to move the carriage or to produce a backspace immediately after. Alternatively, a backspace may be typed following the diacritic character. This method of producing combinations of diacritic and character may not have the desired effect on a VDU screen.

Sending a diacritic and then a backspace and a letter to the screen will usually result in the backspace or the letter erasing the diacritic. However, some terminals have been developed which display the desired combination.

International standards prefer to allocate individual character codes to each combination of diacritic and letter. Additional characters which are not truly combinations such as Polish dark l (ł) can also be treated in the same way. Most systems use eight-bit bytes, where the last bit is used as a check-bit. Recent systems can support eight-bit without the need for this. There is therefore room for two seven-bit character sets side by side: one extra bit in each character doubles the number of characters that can be represented.

The operating system on which IBM personal computers are based has a number of standard character sets for each of a number of different languages. They work on the eight-bit principle, obviating the need for escapes. These national sets are convenient for supporting the exchange of data, but not easily usable internationally as data would have to be exchanged using one particular set such as the American set to avoid compatibility problems. Moreover, they cannot be adopted as international standards since eight-bit character sets complying with the international standard have to reserve characters 128 to 159 for control purposes whereas the IBM sets use these values for extended Roman characters.

Alternatively, a reserved character (one that is not used for any other purpose) or sequence of characters beginning with a reserved character, embedded into a string of characters can indicate that all characters after that point are to be taken from another character set; or a reserved character can indicate that the following character only is to be taken from another set and subsequent ones will return to the original set. These are known as escapes. The control character with value 27, 'ESC', is often used to start an escape. 'ESC', 'S' could mean 'the next character is to be taken from the Spanish character set' and 'ESC', 'U' would return to the UK character set.

Character sets are an extensive subject in their own right and the reader is referred to Clews[7] as a useful work of reference.

Computer systems influenced by ISO 2709

It has been stressed above that exchange formats are independent of the internal structure of software. ISO 2709 has in fact influenced a number of computer systems in their internal structure, such as MINISIS and CDS/ISIS for microcomputers. Both these are systems which were developed with a view to hosting ISO 2709 data and both have an internal record structure which includes a directory for each record, amounting to a list of fields and pointers to the data. Many library systems have been developed specifically to process records from national MARC tape services. These are dealt with in Chapter 7.

Developments in ISO 2709

ISO 2709 was developed from the record structure of LC MARC which had itself been made into an American Standard ANSI Z39.2, first promulgated in 1971. The first version was dated 1973. It immediately came under review and a second version was published in 1981. This was upward compatible with the first version. The main enhancements to the later version of ISO 2709 are that alphanumeric tags are permitted and each entry in the record directory can be extended by up to nine characters. These characters can be used to extend the tag if 999 different tags are not enough. Note that the tag is restricted to three digits, so that if the tag were extended, the extra digit(s) for the tag would be held separately in the fourth part of the directory and would not be physically adjacent to the existing three-digit tag. They can be used as a subrecord indicator; two characters, say, could be allocated to allow up to 99 subrecords to be identified within one record. They can be used to indicate a repeat number for repeatable fields, which is necessary when formats need to make links between fields, such as between a personal author and a corporate body which represents an affiliation. Another use is to store the indicators instead of placing them at the beginning of each data field.

Of all the national and international exchange formats used by the library community, only the Unesco Common Communication Format (CCF) appears to have made use of the extended directory, and it does so in order to identify repeated fields by an occurrence number and subrecords by a segment number. This is discussed in detail in the section on the CCF in Chapter 5.

Conclusion and summary

Effective exchange of bibliographic data between agencies can be accomplished only if the records of agencies exchanging data conform in respect of three components, the structure, the content designators and the data element definitions.

The universal acceptance of the ISO 2709 record structure as a basis for exchange formats has enormously benefited the information community. It is accepted for the exchange of bibliographic data on magnetic tape, and in its logical aspects it is also being used for the formatting of bibliographic data sent online and stored on other media such as diskette (floppy disk) and CD-ROM. Although it has at times been criticized, it is an interesting example of an instance where the existence of a standard that is recognized as having a few imperfections is better than having no standard at all. It implements other standards such as those for the types of computer media used, and character sets.

The second component is the content designators which are represented in most bibliographic formats by tags, indicators and subfield codes, in short, codes which define the different elements in the record. There is no universally accepted standard for these. One reason why they vary between different implementations is said to be that agencies have different requirements in respect of the type and form of the data they wish to exchange. Hence the existence of different formats such as the MARC formats intended for use by libraries as well as formats developed by or used by abstracting and indexing services like the Chemical Abstracts Tape Format. They all embody different schemes of tags and other identifiers. However, it must be stated that many of the differences between the formats are only superficial. Bibliographic records regardless of source all tend to contain much the same data elements, and it is possible to convert the content designators automatically in order to convert data from one format to another.

The last component, the form and content of the data elements, varies according to the 'cataloguing rules' used as well as according to the way the different data elements prescribed by the rules are divided up and separately identified by the format. All bibliographic information-retrieval systems need cataloguing rules of some sort to ensure consistency of the data they contain. The same is true of exchange formats which need rules to ensure consistency of data exchange between systems. Many exercises which attempt to convert data between systems fail not because of the differences between content designators but because data have been formulated according to different cataloguing codes.

Most MARC formats depend for the definitions of their data elements on the national cataloguing rules. UNIMARC assumes the use of a cataloguing code based on ISBD. The Reference manual contains its own cataloguing rules to define its data elements. The Common Communication Format does not assume any particular cataloguing code because the intention was that it would serve as a vehicle of exchange between systems which held data formulated according to different traditions.

Notes and references

1   Useful general works are Fry, T. F., *Data processing*, London, Butterworths, 1983 *and* Martin, J., *Principles of database management*, New Jersey, Prentice-Hall, 1976, 336.
2   *Reference manual for machine-readable bibliographic descriptions*, 3rd rev. ed., compiled and ed. by H. Dierickx and A. Hopkinson, Unisist International Centre for Bibliographic Descriptions (UNIBID), Paris, Unesco, 1986, 3.2.2.
3   International Organization for Standardization, *Documentation: format for bibliographic information interchange on magnetic tape*, 2nd ed., Geneva, ISO, 1981 (ISO 2709–1981). The first edition was published in 1973.
4   *ibid.*
5   *American national standard code for information interchange*, New York, ANSI, 1977 (ANSI X3.4–1977) (known as ASCII).
6   *Information processing: ISO 7-bit coded character set for information processing interchange*, Geneva, ISO, 1983 (ISO 646–1983).
7   Clews, J., *Special characters in libraries: the development of character set standards*, Boston Spa, British Library Document Supply Centre, 1988 (BL R&D report 5962).

3
MARC: its nature, history and development

This chapter explains the nature of MARC, identifies the characteristics that distinguish MARC from other exchange formats and attempts to explain some popular misconceptions of MARC. The history of MARC in the United States and the United Kingdom is traced, from its origins at the Library of Congress (LC) in the mid-1960s, to the current US and UKMARC formats, which are summarized in an appendix. The leading role throughout this period has been played by the LC, and MARC developments in the United States have always been followed closely in the United Kingdom and elsewhere, often with fruitful collaboration and interaction. A separate section deals with MARC format developments outside the US and the UK. UNIMARC, the Universal MARC format, and related international activities are discussed in Chapter 4.

What is MARC?

MARC is an acronym for MAchine Readable Catalogue or Cataloguing. This general description is in some respects misleading, implying that MARC is a kind of catalogue or method of cataloguing, whereas MARC is more accurately described as a group of formats employing a particular set of conventions for the identification and arrangement of bibliographic data for handling by computer.

The original MARC format, from which all current formats are descended, was developed at the Library of Congress in 1965–6. Since then more than 20 formats have appeared which are known as MARC. Their common characteristics are:

(a) adherence to the ISO 2709 record structure, or its equivalent national standard, including the option which allows use of indicators and subfield identifiers in data fields;

(b) official or quasi-official status: most are national formats based in a national library or national bibliographic agency and are the designated communications formats for exchange of bibliographic records with other similar organizations.

A combination of historical, bibliographic and technical factors has meant that MARC has served the needs of the library community rather than those of the secondary information services. MARC has also been most closely identified with the production of library catalogues and national bibliographies, although MARC records have many other library and non-library related uses.

Although MARC is one of the library and information world's best-known acronyms, it is arguably the least well understood. Much of the confusion arises from imperfect knowledge of the nature of machine-readable records. Bibliographic data formats, explained in Chapter 2, have three main components: a defined structure; content designators identifying the different data elements in the records; and data content. The term 'MARC' is often applied (i) to these three components collectively, (ii) to each component individually and (iii) to the products and services based on MARC formats. The potential misunderstandings inherent in such various and indiscriminate usage can be seen in the following examples: 'MARC' is used

- generically to describe the family of MARC formats, ranging from the international UNIMARC to specific national, regional or local formats;
- with reference to national MARC formats (UKMARC, USMARC, etc.) and to the specifications for these formats (*UKMARC manual, USMARC format for bibliographic data*, etc.). To librarians in the United Kingdom, 'MARC' normally signifies the UKMARC format; to those in the United States, 'MARC' is invariably equated with the USMARC formats;
- to refer to formats developed by specific bibliographic agencies or services, for use within the organization and/or

71

for exchange with other similar organizations. OCLC MARC is an extended version of the USMARC format; BLCMP MARC is based on the official MARC format; the British Library uses several modified UKMARC formats for the production of its own catalogues;

- as equivalent to the ISO 2709 record structure. This is understandable, given the history of MARC and the relationship between the original MARC II format and the ISO standard; but it is confusing, as there are a number of formats (e.g. the UNISIST Reference manual) which adhere to ISO 2709 in physical structure, but which are not generally described as 'MARC'. In other words all MARC formats adhere to ISO 2709, but not all formats based on ISO 2709 are MARC formats;

- with reference to the content designators which are a distinctive feature of MARC formats (MARC tagging, MARC coding). The distinguishing characteristic of otherwise similar implementations of ISO 2709 is the set of content designators and codes used to define the data in the record. MARC was initially designed for magnetic tape exchanges, and MARC records stored on other media (in online databases, on CD-ROM) may be converted to other, more appropriate, structures, while retaining MARC content designation. As this kind of use may predominate in the future, it is possible that 'MARC' may become more closely associated with content designation than with structure.

- to describe records in various MARC formats (UKMARC records, UNIMARC records);

- with reference to the data content of MARC records. A common complaint about certain MARC records is that they are poor in subject data. This is essentially a criticism of the subject cataloguing and indexing practices and policies of the agency which created the records and/or the input standards used. Data content is primarily determined by standards external to the formats. All MARC formats are technically capable of full subject content; whether this occurs is at the discretion of record producers;

- to refer to services supplied by MARC record producers (British Library MARC services, Library of Congress

MARC Distribution Services)
- to describe programmes and projects based on MARC record exchange (International MARC Network, International MARC Programme);
- occasionally and, in our opinion, incorrectly to mean any system of automated catalogue production, not necessarily one which has adopted a MARC format. Many computerized cataloguing systems do not use MARC formats or records.

'MARC', then, is a concept evidently difficult to define, as it is capable of many meanings, encompassing format and format components, record, processing and service. It is therefore not surprising that the British Library found it necessary in 1987 to issue a revised nomenclature for its MARC-related services, which distinguished the official British national MARC format, specified in the *UKMARC manual*, from its manifestations within and outside the Library.[1]

In practice, a unitary definition of MARC's identity is impossible. Of the plural and diverse views taken of it, most, considered individually, are sustainable within their own terms of reference.

MARC authorities and holdings formats

Separate exchange formats have been developed in the US and elsewhere to carry authority data and holdings/locations data. A UNIMARC authorities format has also been issued.[2] Such data may of course be embedded in bibliographic records; UKMARC, for example, contains several fields which are used in exchange records for cross-references. Removing authority data from bibliographic records assists updating; it allows authority records to be exchanged, replaced or amended without the need also to exchange bibliographic records. It means, however, that each appropriate field in the bibliographic record must have a subfield containing the record control number of the authority record containing the relevant authority data. This can complicate record exchange, as it is essential that the authority records are exchanged as well. As noted in Chapter 1, libraries have for many years maintained separate authority files, initially in manual form, more recently online, and the availability of exchange records for authority data is simply an extension of this practice which enables the data to be more widely used.

Inclusion of holdings and locations data in bibliographic records can lead to excessive length and complexity, particularly in the case of detailed holdings statements for serials; nor is such information necessarily required by all receiving agencies. Machine links can be provided to connect holdings/locations records to the relevant bibliographic records.

'MARC-like' formats

Some formats are described as 'MARC-like', 'MARC-related', or even 'MARCoid'. Usage is inconsistent and encompasses a variety of formats which can differ from recognized MARC formats in one or more of the following aspects: physical structure (including restricted record and field lengths), character sets, content designators and data content. Some systems are likewise described as 'MARC-compatible', implying that they can handle full MARC records obtained from agencies such as the British Library, the Library of Congress or major cooperatives. MARC-compatibility is discussed in more detail in Chapter 7.

History and development in the United States and the United Kingdom

Detailed analysis of the events of the past 25 years is beyond the scope of this chapter. We have, therefore, not attempted a comprehensive account of the history and development of MARC, but offer instead a strictly selective overview, confining coverage to what is considered especially significant in the evolution of the American and British formats. Although the main division is by decade, an arrangement both natural and convenient, within these time bands a presentation consistently or even primarily chronological is often made difficult by the complex interrelationships which characterize the various activities and programmes of the period. Where the growth of the MARC formats is contingent on international developments, these are briefly mentioned to provide the necessary, wider context.

The early years: MARC I to MARC II, 1965 – 8

Even for those whose main concern is the current US and UKMARC formats, much useful information can be gained from a brief look at the early history and development of MARC, not least an understanding of the aims and expectations of its creators.[3]

The Library of Congress had considered the possibility of producing catalogue data in machine-readable form as early as the 1950s. Although automation was already in place for many financial and administrative purposes, the main impetus for the development of MARC was the 1963 King Report, *Automation and the Library of Congress*,[4] which suggested that automation of major operations within the LC was feasible and desirable. A further report, *The recording of Library of Congress bibliographical data in machine form*,[5] led to a conference at LC in January 1965, attended by representatives of the library community at large. The mood was optimistic and work went ahead on the creation of a suitable machine record. A team was assembled, headed by Henriette Avram, whose name has become inextricably linked with MARC, and who has been a driving force behind the development of MARC both within the US and internationally. A preliminary draft format, drawn up by LC staff between March and June 1965, was presented to a second conference at LC in November 1965 and was accepted as the basis for the proposed machine record.[6] Financial backing was forthcoming from the Council on Library Resources and in 1966 the MARC Pilot Project was initiated.[7] The aim was twofold: to create and distribute machine-readable data and to ascertain what uses might be made of the data by LC and other libraries. The suitability of the format was also under consideration.

The LC was by no means the first library in the United States or elsewhere to become involved in catalogue automation. Computer-generated library catalogues had been pioneered a decade earlier, but the creation of a centrally produced pool of high-quality, standardized machine-readable data was seen as a vital element in the general thrust towards automation, and LC was the logical choice as creator and distributor of that data.

Sixteen libraries, chosen to represent a cross-section of library types, took part in the project. Between November 1966 and June 1967, they received bibliographic data on magnetic tape for use on an experimental basis.[8] These early MARC records were for English-language monographs with United States imprints. Lack of time between the design and implementation stages of the project meant that the pilot project format, subsequently called MARC I to distinguish it from its successor, was restricted to book materials.

Despite some difficulties the results were encouraging and the distribution of tapes was continued to June 1968; but MARC I was under review even before the project officially ended. The format contained a fixed field of 108 characters, holding a considerable amount of coded data for record length, LC card number, language, date of publication and other data useful for machine searching, but allowed for only 20 variable fields, all designed with the requirements of monographs in mind.[9] There was also a limited character set, and the project indicated that further work was needed to develop an extended character set for Roman-alphabet languages. MARC I was far less significant in itself than in the promising developments it signalled.

In the United Kingdom the Council of the British National Bibliography studied with interest the progress of the MARC Pilot Project and conducted its own feasibility study into the use of machine-readable data for production of the printed *BNB* and for other library-related purposes. Support was obtained from the Office for Scientific and Technical Information (later to become the Research and Development Department of the British Library) and in September 1967 the BNB MARC Project was officially launched.[10] British interest was timely, coinciding with the appraisal by the LC of the MARC I pilot format; and the MARC II format, developed in 1968, was the result of Anglo-American cooperation. The new format was intended to be hospitable to all kinds of library materials; sufficiently flexible for a variety of applications in addition to catalogue production; and usable in a range of different computer systems. It was expected that individual libraries would have their own internal processing formats tailored to meet their own needs. Records would be exchanged in the standardized common format and then translated or reformatted into the local processing format for internal use. Thus, according to A. J. Wells, at the time General Editor of the *BNB*: 'the concept of the communications format was created'.[11]

MARC II is the archetype of all subsequent MARC formats.

Despite Anglo-American cooperation there were two versions of MARC, here described for convenience in identification as LC MARC II and BNB MARC II. LC MARC II was formally published in January 1968 as *The MARC II format: a communications format for bibliographic data*.[12] A preliminary version of BNB MARC II was issued in June 1968 as *MARC record service proposals*.[13] In the intervening period, meetings between LC and BNB staff had been held, a common format agreed and changes made to both versions to enhance compatibility. BNB *MARC II specifications*, published in March 1969,[14] incorporated further changes; by this stage records issued in machine form by BNB and the Library of Congress shared 'an identical structure and an identical character set'.[15] The same underlying philosophy was apparent in both formats, with accompanying documentation stressing the importance of the format as an exchange medium between the two countries and its potential as an international communications vehicle. The physical structure was considered hospitable to a wide variety of bibliographic items; initially, however, analysis of data and definition of content designators was confined to monographs. Both BNB and LC planned to develop the format for use with other kinds of materials, although the precise manner in which this was to be done was not made explicit in the original documentation. Subsequently, different approaches were taken, resulting in separate LC formats for specific materials, whilst the British format remained unitary. The formats used the same extended ASCII character set and were identical in structure, conforming to the pattern:

Leader	Directory	Control fields	Bibliographic data fields	Record separator

This structure was later adopted by the American National Standards Institute (ANSI), the British Standards Institution (BSI) and the International Organization for Standardization (ISO). As ISO 2709,[16] it is explained and illustrated in Chapter 2.

The control fields, which followed the directory, used neither indicators nor subfield codes. Tags 001 – 009 were reserved for control fields, but only three (001, 002, 008) were described in detail.

001 contained the control number, the unique number for each record. In BNB MARC II this was the Standard Book Number or the BNB number in the case of items lacking SBNs. Standard Book Numbers, recently introduced in the UK, were seen as the answer to the problem of finding a universal, unique machine-search code which would allow fast and easy access to individual records and provide the connection between selection, acquisition, cataloguing and circulation procedures. In LC MARC II the Library of Congress card number was used. This number, assigned to each title for which the LC produced printed cards, was an obvious choice, as it was a well-established device for ordering catalogue cards. Because of differing national and local requirements, the 001 field was variable in length.

002, the subrecord directory, was described but not used in LC MARC II. It was present in BNB MARC when the record contained analytical entries and it has remained a feature of the UK MARC format. LC MARC was unable to deal with analytical records.

Field 008 was used to carry information codes in fixed character positions. The original intention was that the length of this field would be determined by the organization creating the records and might vary according to its needs and the type of material. It was fixed in both MARC II formats at 40 characters, for data relevant to books. There were minor differences between the American and British formats in the codes used to represent these data, which served *inter alia* to supply information not made explicit elsewhere in the record (e.g. intellectual level, form of contents) and to make directly and easily accessible information held in the data fields (e.g. nature of illustrations, country of publication).

This redundancy of data was deliberate, but met with criticism from some computer experts because of the allegedly unnecessary storage space it required in the machine. It was defended on the grounds that the record was designed for communication, not for storage and that data redundancy was essential for the success of the format as a communications vehicle, offering various ways of accessing data for different applications.[17] MARC II format designers consistently stressed its role in providing a total, flexible, multi-purpose package of data, far in excess of that needed by any one library system. At the same time it was recognized that some libraries might use the format without restructuring for local processing.[18] Conversion to LC's own internal processing format was achieved by program.

Both formats used similar content designators, although their specific implementations did not always coincide. BNB MARC II in general made more use of subfields than LC MARC II; in the title (245) field, for example, it had five subfields compared with LC's three.

Three-digit tags were used to identify whole fields and the tagging structure had some mnemonic features, e.g.

110 Corporate name main entry
610 Corporate name subject entry
710 Corporate name added entry.

Two-digit indicators were used to give additional information about a field (e.g. the nature of the name in a main-entry heading) and/or to supply information that might be useful in processing (e.g. whether or not a title added entry should be generated in a printed list). The original LC MARC II specifications provided for, but did not use, a second indicator. In the second indicator position in each field, a space (blank) was assumed. Subsequent revisions brought two indicators into play, but LC continued to use spaces in contrast to the zero indicator settings used in BNB MARC II in cases where no values were attributed, e.g. in the bibliographic notes (5--) fields.

Two-character subfield codes, consisting of a delimiter or special symbol (ASCII value 31) followed by a lower-case alphabetic character, were used to separate data within fields. Graphic representations were the double dagger (‡) in LC MARC and the dollar sign ($) in BNB MARC, although for some years the typewriter graphic $ continued to be used in LC specifications for this purpose. In contrast to BNB MARC, which made use of subfield codes to generate punctuation symbols, LC MARC normally supplied end-of-subfield punctuation, e.g.

00$aLondon$bMethuen$c1968   (BNB)
0b$aLondon,$bMethuen,$c1968 (LC)

A one-character field terminator signified the end of a field (ASCII value 30). As the field length was ascertainable from the directory, this terminator was in theory redundant, but had some use as a double-checking device and was helpful for some processing applications. There was no ASCII graphic representation for the field terminator; the hash symbol (#) was adopted by BNB, although never by LC.

A one-character record terminator (ASCII value 29) was the last character in the record. This had no graphic representation in early MARC II.

The variable data fields contained the bibliographic data and the arrangement of data elements in both formats followed that of the traditional catalogue entry, resulting in data grouped by bibliographic function:

Tag 01- / 09-	Bibliographic control numbers and knowledge (i.e. class) numbers.
Tag 1--	Main entry headings.
Tag 2--	Titles. Edition. Imprint.
Tag 3--	Collation, including price.
Tag 4--	Series statements.
Tag 5--	Bibliographic notes.
Tag 6--	Subject entries, including personal and corporate name subject entries.
Tag 7--	Added entries for persons, bodies and titles.
Tag 8--	Series added entries (LC MARC only).
Tag 9--	Cross references (BNB MARC only). Numbers for local use.

Some fields and subfields could be repeated, e.g. to cope with added entries for more than one person, or to allow mention of more than one place of publication.

An alternative grouping of fields, described in the original documentation as 'analytical', was seriously considered but rejected.[19] The essential difference between the 'functional' approach, which was adopted, and the 'analytical' approach can be illustrated with reference to personal and corporate names. The traditional approach resulted, as can be seen above, in designated main and added-entry fields, with tags used to show content (whether personal or corporate); the analytical approach would have resulted in fields for personal names and for corporate names, with tags used to indicate function (main or added entries). Considered in retrospect, an analytical grouping of fields might have been preferable and more suitable for an exchange format, but the LC MARC designers were influenced both by the major use of MARC as a means of producing catalogue entries and by the current state of technology. They saw no advantage, for other potential uses such as information retrieval, in the alternative data structure.

The differences in content designation between the two formats were linked to the differences in data content, which arose mainly from cataloguing. Here, the publication of Anglo-American cataloguing rules (1967) in two texts, British and North American, served to emphasize divergent national practices. The major difference lay in the treatment of forms of heading for corporate bodies, where the North American text departed from the 1961 *Paris principles* (the agreed basis for construction of national codes) and stipulated entry under place for many corporate bodies. Although *MARC record service proposals* stated 'Entries on the BNB MARC tape will be catalogued in accordance with the British text of the Anglo-American cataloguing rules 1967',[20] no such restriction attached to the LC MARC II format, which was designed to accommodate pre-AACR cataloguing as well as that conforming to the new code. Differences in data content, especially in main-entry headings, make exchange of records more difficult, as some intellectual editing must take place before the two sets of records can be merged. On the other hand, a format which can act as carrier of data from different sources and traditions permits a greater number of records to be communicated between potential users.

At this early stage in the life of MARC, the conflict created by internal and external demands and the tension resulting from the desire, on the one hand, for standardization and conformity, and, on the other, for the flexibility essential to a true exchange

81

format, were all too apparent. This was to be a recurring theme in the history of bibliographic data processing.

Expansion and consolidation, 1969-79

Progress during this decade was to be considerable: rapid developments in computer technology, a shift towards automation in the library community and the secondary services and the establishment or significant growth of many of today's major cooperatives and information-retrieval systems.

In 1969 BNB began distribution of MARC tapes for current British books (effectively a machine-readable form of the *British national bibliography*). In the same year LC formally implemented its MARC Distribution Service, initially with tapes of English-language monographs. In 1970 LC set up a MARC Development Office, with responsibility for the development, implementation and promotion of MARC-based systems and records. The response was good: by 1972 LC had 54 MARC subscribers, including OCLC (then named Ohio College Library Center).[21] A report on the BNB MARC Project published in 1973 noted that the 'MARC network' comprised 22 institutions: 12 in the UK, including BLCMP (then named Birmingham Libraries Cooperative Mechanization Project) and the book supplier B. H. Blackwell; and 10 from outside the UK, including institutions from North America, Australia, Europe and Eire.[22] The commitment to MARC by major cooperative systems in the UK and US helped ensure its future, and the relationship was reciprocal, as the success of the cooperatives depended in large part on the availability of centrally produced MARC records from the national agencies.

The British Library was formally established in 1973 and BNB became the focal point of a new Bibliographic Services Division, with continuing responsibility for the production of MARC records and printed BNB. Both LC and BL have issued comprehensive documentation charting the progress of their MARC services and formats, which developed along different lines. Between 1969 and 1979 the original LC MARC II format was reissued as *Books: a MARC format*[23] and separate formats published for serials, maps, films and other pictorial media, manuscripts, music and sound recordings.[24] All followed the basic pattern, with additional fields uniquely defined for specific materials. A preliminary, experimental version of an authorities format appeared in 1976.[25] This shared the MARC II physical structure, but differed in other respects, as it accommodated headings data, not full bibliographic records. In 1973 MARBI (the ALA Committee on Representation in Machine-Readable Form of Bibliographic Information) took responsibility for working with LC on format changes. Long notes that between 1972 and 1980 approximately 20 addenda were issued for the books format;[26] other formats were also amended, with many additions of detail. The materials covered by MARC Distribution Service similarly expanded. By 1979 LC was distributing MARC records for monographs in English and other Roman-alphabet languages, for films, serials and maps, and for some romanized Cyrillic and South-Asian languages. In 1977 LC MARC Editorial Division began online correction and verification of MARC records; in the same year, the one-millionth MARC record was verified.[27]

The 1970s was a period of intense activity for LC, as it developed its own internal automation systems and participated in a number of cooperative ventures. The RECON Pilot Project (1969 – 71) tested a range of techniques and methods for the conversion of retrospective bibliographic records, including microfilming and Automatic Format Recognition (AFR). The latter was considered at the time to be feasible and cost-saving, although many practical difficulties were encountered, particularly in the processing of records for older books and foreign-language works. In the final report on the project, mention was made of the need for standard practices in recording data and in the use of punctuation.[28] Successful development of the ISBD and its implementation by national bibliographies and cataloguing agencies were regarded as essential for effective format-recognition programs. CONSER, the Conversion of Serials Project, began in 1974. Later renamed the Cooperative Online Serials Program, the project involved the cooperation of LC, OCLC and North American research libraries in the establishment of an authoritative serials database in LC MARC serials format.[29] The COMARC (Cooperative MARC) project began in 1975 with funding from the Council on Library Resources.[30] Its aim was to assess the feasibility of adding to the pool of LC MARC records those created by other organizations. The project highlighted some problems in communications between LC and participants over machine input specifications and data content. It was discontinued in 1978.[31] NACO, the Name Authority COoperative (later renamed the National Coordinated Cataloging Operations) was established in 1977–8 to facilitate the development of a nationwide authority file.[32] NACO originated in an agreement with the US Government Printing Office Library for GPO authority data to be included in LC's authority database and now involves over 40 participants. Its aim was to share the burden of producing authority data, believed to be one of the most expensive operations in bibliographic record creation. All data contributed under the scheme are distributed with LC authority records. In 1978, a contract was made between LC and Carrollton Press to convert to machine-readable form around five million records for books in LC's collection not hitherto included in MARC. These REMARC records were used by a number of libraries in the United States and elsewhere (including the UK, where they were available in UKMARC format) for retrospective conversion. Under the terms of the contract, they could not be distributed by LC through its MARC Distribution Services.[33]

In the second half of the 1970s, the growing interest in networking on a nationwide scale and the appearance of AACR2, a fully integrated multimedia code based on ISBD principles, led to a reappraisal of the nature and scope of the MARC formats. In 1976 the MARC Development Office produced a composite MARC format, intended for comparative purposes.[34] It tabulated content designators for seven formats: books, films, manuscripts, maps, music, serials and in-process materials (designed for records of items in process of being catalogued within the LC). The existence of separate formats had made it easier to accommodate the special needs of each type of material, but at the risk of some inconsistency, with the same field tags used in different ways for different materials. The serials format, for example, included many fields which were relevant to, but could not be used for, materials other than printed serials. MARC format development was henceforth to take into account the needs of a shared environment. Agreement on bibliographic content for records destined for a common database, as well as format integration, was considered necessary. In 1977, LC commissioned Helen Schmierer of the University of Chicago to draw up draft proposals for data elements to be included in machine-readable records for a nationwide database. The resulting document, *National level bibliographic record: books*, revised draft, was published in 1978 and circulated to the Association of Research Libraries and other interested bodies for comment.[35] Emphasizing content, rather than content designation, the proposed *NLBR* was based on current standards, particularly AACR2 and MARC formats. By the beginning of 1979, LC and RLIN were working jointly on the construction of a database of content designators in LCMARC records.[36] The initial aim was to assist uniform usage of MARC tags; easier maintenance of the formats was also anticipated. At the same time, MARC revisions proceeded: at the end of the decade LC was involved in discussions on the expansion of the authorities format to include series, and the expansion of all formats to include analytics, the latter necessitating techniques for linking data between records.[37] The draft of a new MARC format for machine-readable data files was completed towards the end of 1979.[38] Concurrently, LC placed a contract with David Weisbrod of Yale University Library to review all existing MARC formats, to evaluate them for suitability for networking and to suggest any necessary changes in content and content designation.[39]

The multiplicity of MARC formats in the US contrasted markedly with the situation in the UK, where a single format persisted at national level, although work had been carried out elsewhere on the development of formats for other materials, especially serials, music and sound recordings.[40] *Description of the BNB/MARC record: a manual of practice* was prepared in November 1970, taking into account suggestions made at a MARC users' seminar held the previous month at the Bodleian Library.[41] The document was an interpretative manual, intended for a wide audience, including BNB/MARC cataloguers and those considering the use of BNB/MARC in their own local systems. Tags, indicators and subfield codes were unchanged from earlier documentation, although level and repeat digits were introduced at the input stage in order to cope with analytical entries and with repetitions of fields. Neither was held in the machine record; repeated fields were identified by the recurrence of the appropriate field tag in the directory and the presence of analytical records was shown by subrecord directories. A significant departure from LC MARC was the exclusion from the British record of the 130 field for main-entry uniform title. Special indicator settings in the 240 field (uniform titles) were used instead. British text AACR was closely followed, with definitions of fields and subfields cross-referenced to appropriate AACR rules. Any BNB departures from AACR were noted, e.g. in field 245 (title area) where more title added entries were generated by BNB than those required by AACR. The format was at this stage still defined only in terms of books. First issues of periodicals, which were listed in BNB, were forced into the format and were indicated by the use of the code 'p' in character position 39 of the 008 (information codes) field. Field 245 also contained subfields for volume or part numbers and titles, which could be used for serials.

The *UKMARC manual*, 1st standard edition, published in 1975,[42] consolidated earlier format documentation with minimal change. It presented the UKMARC format in a comprehensive manner, with information for all types of users: librarians, systems analysts and local cataloguers. The change from BNB to UKMARC was in itself an indication that MARC was firmly established at national as well as local level. The format complied in structure with ISO 2709–1973 and BS 4748:1971:

Record label	Directory	Control fields	Variable data fields	Record mark *

To preserve compatibility with LC MARC, 12 *Types of record* codes were reserved for the record label, implementation codes (character position 7), although only code 'a' (language materials, printed) was used in UKMARC exchange tapes. Class of record (character position 8) always contained 'm' for monographs, although three other codes taken from LC MARC were available for future extensions (a = analytics, s = serial, c = collective). Definition of fields and subfields remained largely unchanged, with three control fields (001, 002, 008) and variable data fields (01- /9--) grouped in the same functional blocks (Figure 3.1).

Tag	Definition
010	Library of Congress card number
015	British National Bibliography number
017	Corrected field message
018	Amended field message
021	Alternative ISBN
041	Language codes
043	Area codes

CLASSIFICATION FIELDS

Tag	Definition
050	Library of Congress classification number
080	Universal Decimal Classification number
082	Dewey Decimal Classification number
083	Verbal feature

MAIN ENTRY HEADING FIELDS

Tag	Definition
100	Personal author
110	Corporate author
111	Conference proceedings

TITLE FIELDS

Tag	Definition
240	Uniform title
243	Collective title
245	Title statement

EDITION FIELD

Tag	Definition
250	Edition statement

IMPRINT FIELD

Tag	Definition
260	Imprint

COLLATION FIELD

Tag	Definition
300	Collation

PRICE FIELD

Tag	Definition
350	Price

SERIES FIELDS (cf 800—840 also)

Tag	Definition
400	Personal author series
410	Corporate author series
411	Conference proceedings series
440	Title series
490	Series not in added entry form

NOTES FIELDS

Tag	Definition
500	General notes
503	Bibliographic history notes

NOTES FIELDS (cont'd)

Tag	Definition
504	Bibliography and index notes
505	Contents notes
511	Alternative ISBN notes
513	Subject notes
518	Change of control number notes
521	Intellectual level notes

SUBJECT HEADING FIELDS

Tag	Definition
600	Personal name subject heading
610	Corporate name subject heading
611	Conference name subject heading
640	Uniform title subject heading
645	Title subject heading
650	Topical subject heading
651	Geographical subject heading

PRECIS FIELDS

Tag	Definition
690	PRECIS descriptor string
691	Subject index number (Not used on exchange tapes)
692	Reference index numbers

ADDED ENTRY HEADING FIELDS

Tag	Definition
700	Personal name added entry
710	Corporate name added entry
711	Conference name added entry
740	Uniform title added entry
745	Other title added entry

TRACING FIELD

Tag	Definition
790	Tracing

SERIES FIELDS
(cf 400—490 also. Used to provide series entry form when not present in 400—490)

Tag	Definition
800	Personal name series added entry
810	Corporate name series added entry
811	Conference name series added entry
840	Series title added entry

REFERENCE FIELDS

Tag	Definition
900	Reference from personal names
910	Reference from corporate names
911	Reference from conference names
945	Reference from titles

Fig. 3.1 Example from *UKMARC manual*, 1st standard edition

(Reproduced from *UKMARC manual*, 1st standard ed., with permission of the British Library Board)

87

No separate authorities format has ever been produced by the British Library. The 9-- fields held references from personal and corporate names and from titles of works. Though useful for generating references in printed catalogues, they were primarily intended for production of printed *BNB*.

Although the ISO 2709 structure is hospitable to different kinds of materials, the 1975 UKMARC format remained chiefly geared to monographs, reflecting the main use of MARC records as the basis for the generation of printed *BNB*, the record of the nation's book-publishing output. UKMARC exchange tapes of the period (see Figure 3.2 for an example record) contained only monographs and first issues of serials; thus the collation field (tag 300) contained subfields only for pagination, illustration, size and binding.

By this stage the LC and UKMARC formats were showing substantial differences, exemplified by two appendices in the *UKMARC manual*. Appendix G lists valid LC MARC (books) and UKMARC fields and shows 20 fields used in UKMARC but not present in LC MARC and 14 fields found only in LC MARC. There were differences also in the use of indicators and subfield codes. In order to distribute LC records to British libraries for handling by the same programs as those used for processing UKMARC records, a conversion program was necessary. (Appendix D outlines differences between LC records reformatted to UKMARC.) Significant changes included the removal of punctuation marks from LC records before subfield, field and record marks, the change from certain LC information codes in the 008 field to BNB equivalents, the conversion of many subfield codes in the main entry fields (100, 110, 111) and the removal of data from the LC 130 field (uniform-title main heading) to the 240 field (uniform title) in the UKMARC record. Some character conversion was also needed, as the character set used for UKMARC was not as extensive as that of LC. Many of the differences between the two formats involved the straightforward substitution of one set of codes or content designators for another, but despite the conversion some British MARC subscribers continued to experience problems in the use of LC MARC records, particularly in cases where there were differences in the degree of detail, for example in the number of subfields in any one field.[43]

Record label								Directory									
01050	n	a	m	ƀƀ	2	2	00301	0ƀƀƀƀƀ	001	0011	00000	008	0041	00011			

{ 010 0014 00052 | 015 0013 00066 | 041 0011 00079 | 050 0010 00090 | 082 }

{ 0013 00100 | 083 0046 00113 | 100 0017 00159 | 240 0035 00176 | 245 0129 }

{ 00211 | 260 0027 00340 | 300 0024 00367 | 350 0010 00391 | 440 0069 00401 }

{ 500 0014 00470 | 503 0091 00484 | 650 0011 00575 | 690 0054 00586 | 692 }

ISBN
{ 0014 00640 | 700 0019 00654 | 700 0030 00673 | 900 0046 00703 # | 0080157 }

Information Codes
{ 424# | 720609 | s1972ƀƀƀƀ | enƀ | aƀƀƀ | ƀ | ƀ | ƀƀƀƀ | 00011 | ƀ | ƀ | eng | ƀ | ƀ | # }

LC card no.   BNB no.   Translation   LC no.
{ 00 | $a78—129853# | 00 | $aB7214573# | 10 | $aengger# | 00 | $aQC176# | 00 | $a }

DC no.   DC feature
{ 530.4$b1# | 00 | $aSolids.ƀPhysicalƀstructureƀandƀproperties# | }

Author   Uniform title   Title
{ 10 | SaHaug$hAlbert# | 00 | $aTheoretischeƀFestk"orperphysik# | 10 | $aTheor }

{ eticalƀsolidƀstateƀphysics$dbyƀAlbertƀHaug$etranslatedƀ[fromƀtheƀ }

Imprint
{ German]ƀbyƀH.S.H.ƀMassey;ƀeditedƀbyƀD.ƀterƀHaar$gVol.1# | 00 | $aOxford }

Collation   Price   Series
{ $bPergamon$c1972# | 00 | $axiv,497p$bill$c26cm# | 00 | $a£5.50# | 10 | $aInter }

{ nationalƀseriesƀofƀmonographsƀinƀnaturalƀphilosophy$vvol.36# }

Note   Note
{ 00 | $aInƀ2ƀvols# | 01 | $aTranslationƀofƀ'TheoretischeƀFestk"orperphysik' }

Subject head   PRECIS
{ .ƀBandƀl.ƀWienƀ[Vienna] :ƀDeuticke,ƀ1964# | 00 | $aSolids# | 00 | $z101$a }

String   RIN
{ solids$z101$aphysicalƀstructureƀ&ƀproperties# | 00 | $a00080513# }

Added entry   Added entry   Reference
{ 11 | $aHaar$hDirkƀter# | 12 | $aMassey$hHughƀSeanƀHolland# | 20 | $aTerƀHaar, }

{ ƀDirk.$xSee$aHaar,ƀDirkƀter$z700* }

Fig. 3.2 Example from *UKMARC manual*, 1st standard edition

Long has summarized the major differences between LC and UKMARC during this period and noted how the different functions of the LC and BL affected format development.[44] In a more general discussion, Avram has also drawn attention to the varying roles of national bibliography and national library, and the functional distinctions between library catalogue and national bibliography which affect both format and content of records.[45]

In 1977 BLAISE, the British Library Automated Information Service, was introduced.[46] In addition to biomedical files originating from the National Library of Medicine in the United States, BLAISE also offered online access to files of MARC records, primarily the UKMARC files containing records from *BNB* and from the Library's Department of Printed Books. CIP records and Extra-MARC Material (EMMA) were also available. (Many EMMA records were created by subscribers to the system, and were thus outside the official process.) LC MARC book records, reformatted, were also offered. The Editor subsystem allowed users to create their own catalogue records and edit them online: UKMARC records were thus being used for online information retrieval and online cataloguing. The availability of a shared database of MARC records led to the provision (after consultation with LC) of extra fields in UKMARC, to carry BLAISE record number and a code for the organization which created the record (024), the national shelf mark giving locations within BL (087) and a field for holdings information, similar to that used by OCLC (948). Character position 24 in field 008 was used in LC MARC to show form of reproduction. It was used in BLAISE to indicate physical form of item, using a series of codes derived from those developed for the EUDISED (European Documentation and Information System for Education) record format.[47] Fields were also added to enable better handling of serials, based on fields present in other formats, including LC MARC Serials, Canadian MARC Serials, ISDS and BLCMP MASS (MARC-based Serials System).[48] An extended UKMARC format for non-book materials was also developed as part of the Learning Materials Recording Study in 1977–8. The format was experimental and not formally presented as a standard, but it was used in the creation of the AV (Audiovisual) MARC files on BLAISE.[49]

The publication of AACR2 in 1978 imposed further demands on the format and highlighted inadequacies, in particular its inability to cope with materials other than books. This had led to 'variations in practice among libraries wishing to produce machine-readable records for materials not covered by the national format' and to 'non-standard use of tags and subfields listed in the UKMARC manual and the use of tags and subfields not listed in the UKMARC manual'.[50] There was clearly a need for further work on the format to make it more suitable for use in shared database systems covering a wider range of materials. In January 1979 the British Library notified users of its intention to modify the format and to issue a second edition of the *UKMARC manual*.[51]

In the early 1970s, soon after MARC had become fully operational, moves were rapidly made towards the establishment of international standards for machine-readable records. The physical structure of MARC II (leader, directory and variable fields) was in 1971 adopted by the American National Standards Institute as ANSI Z39.2 and in 1973 accepted as an international standard by the International Standards Organization, ISO 2709. In 1971 the British Standards Institution published its own standard, BS 4748, *Specification for bibliographic information interchange format for magnetic tape*, setting out a generalized machine format designed specifically for communication between systems, not for use within systems.[52] It comprised three sections: record label (the leader of MARC II), directory and data fields, including reserved fields 001–009. The standard was later revised and reissued in a form identical with that of ISO 2709. There were several reasons for the choice of MARC II as a model for an international communications format: the authority of the Library of Congress and the British National Bibliography; endorsement by bodies such as the American Library Association, the Association of Research Libraries and the major cooperatives; and the highly specific detail achievable in MARC, which could support a wide variety of library and bibliographic operations. Gapen notes that it was considered 'as coherent as any other structure for carrying bibliographic data';[53] quite simply, there was no serious rival.

Other standardizing activities contributed to, and in turn

grew from, the success of MARC. Although designed to help publishers in stock control, the ISBN, introduced in 1971, nevertheless provided a convenient method of identifying books in automated library systems. ISBNs replaced SBNs as control numbers in BNB MARC records, although LC retained the LC card number for this purpose in its own records. Unique identification of serial titles was made possible in 1973 by the development, for the International Serials Data System (ISDS), of the International Standard Serial Number (ISSN) and the key title (a unique, standardized form of the serial title). An important feature in both standard-numbering systems was their independence of language and bibliographic/cataloguing practice.

IFLA's programme of International Standard Bibliographic Descriptions (ISBD) further encouraged the standardization of bibliographic records, both in content and format. Despite some criticism for unnecessary rigidity and conservatism in perpetuating the display format of the card catalogue, ISBD principles were widely adopted.[54] Several ISBDs were published during the period, including, albeit belatedly, the *General International Standard Bibliographic Description, ISBD(G)*,[55] intended to provide a unifying framework for the specialized ISBDs and a basis for the construction, by national and international committees, of fully integrated multi-media cataloguing codes, exemplified by *AACR*2. The primary purpose of ISBD was not, as has sometimes been alleged, to facilitate machine handling of records, although it was considered likely to be of value in this respect. It offered a standardized framework for bibliographic description consisting of agreed data elements, cited in a prescribed order, separated by prescribed punctuation, thereby assisting the translation of manual to machine records and the integration in a single database of different kinds of records. The need, however, for distinctive yet reasonably natural-looking punctuation in records presented to users conflicted with the requirements of computers for totally distinctive separating symbols. Much of the ISBD punctuation, e.g. the full stop or period and the slash or solidus, can occur in text, thus 'confusing' the computer, unless highly complex programs are written to circumvent this.

Following the success of LC and BNB MARC, MARC

formats were developed in other countries. By 1975 it was apparent that an international MARC network was beginning to emerge and that coordinated development was desirable.[56] The work of the International MARC Network Study Steering Committee, appointed by the Directors of the National Libraries, and the studies made by Wells and others into incompatibilities between various MARC formats, together with the proposals for overcoming these, are discussed in Chapter 4. A frequently occurring theme in the literature of the period is the need for agreement on content designators for a common format and for greater uniformity in cataloguing practices.[57] UNIMARC, the Universal MARC format, and CCF, the Common Communication Format, were the eventual outcome of much of this concern.

Format revision and integration: the 1980s

At the beginning of the 1980s MARC, in its various manifestations, was at the heart of an interrelated group of standards for content and transmission of bibliographic records. The widespread acceptance of MARC formats had undoubtedly encouraged the exchange of bibliographic data and increased compatibility in library systems. MARC records, as Avram has noted, had become valuable commodities, involving questions of copyright and the nature of agreements between national bibliographic agencies for their supply, distribution and use.[58] The formerly straightforward tape exchanges between two national agencies were now complicated by issues such as redistribution to third parties and downloading of records to local systems. Rapid technological progress, however, was soon to lead to speculation about the impact on MARC formats of new storage media and networking developments, and to talk of a 'post-MARC' era, made possible by decentralization of computing processes.

Arguably the most exciting and far-reaching technological innovations of the 1980s are the CD-ROM (compact disc – read only memory) and the development of standard procedures for transfer of information between computer systems with diverse hardware and software. The latter, best exemplified by the ISO's Open Systems Interconnection (OSI) protocols, may well be the decisive advance which will make possible networking on a global scale. Much work, however, remains to be done before effective national networking is achieved. CD-ROM, which came into prominence in the mid-1980s, is beginning to revolutionize storage and distribution of bibliographic data. The general advantages of CD-ROM in comparison with other media are well documented,[59] and include capacity (approx. 500 million characters per disc, although larger-capacity discs have been produced), durability, compact size and portability, an especially important feature for record exchange. CD-ROM has opened up to a wide audience large quantities of information at relatively low cost and can offer to users with only a CD-ROM reader sophisticated search capabilities of the kind formerly found only in online information-retrieval systems. This is of great value in countries where telecommunications are difficult.

The first LC CD-ROM product, *CDMARC subjects*, the complete subject authorities file, was issued in 1988.[60] In the same year, a joint Anglo-French effort produced a pilot CD-ROM disc containing 30,000 records on European history from BL's MARC database and 30,000 records representing the French acquisitions for 1986 of the Bibliothèque Nationale.[61] UK records can be downloaded (i.e. transferred and stored in a user's computer system) in UKMARC format and the French records in UNIMARC format. Both databases may be searched in novice or expert mode using English, French, German or Italian search languages, though the records reflect the language in which they were created. Information from the evaluation of the pilot disc will be used in the development of standardized software for use with CD-ROM discs carrying national bibliographies in different languages. Further CD-ROM products are being released, for example *CDMARC names* (LC's name authorities records), *CDMARC bibliographic* (the entire LC files of bibliographic records for books, serials, maps, music and audiovisual materials), the *British national bibliography* backfile (1950–85) and 'current' BNB (from 1986 onwards) and the first disc of the British Library's *General catalogue of printed books to 1975*.[62] Sample printouts from LC's CDMARC products appear in an Appendix at the end of the book.

Both in the US and the UK, positive steps were taken towards the establishment of national bibliographic networks, based on current technology. The Linked Systems Project (LSP) began in 1980, with funding from the Council on Library Resources.[63] Three original participants, LC, RLG and WLN, were joined in the mid-1980s by OCLC. LSP took as its basis the ISO's OSI protocols, aiming to connect different and separate online systems for the purpose of exchanging, initially, authority data, and ultimately, bibliographic records, in USMARC formats. LSP has been more successful than the United Kingdom Library Database System (UKLDS), proposed by the Cooperative Automation Group in 1982.[64] Envisaged as a common database for the entire library community, with records in UKMARC format contributed by the British Library, the cooperatives, and, in due course, by other libraries, the project foundered in 1984, chiefly for economic reasons.[65]

Both projects (discussed further in Chapter 6) highlighted the conflicting demands made on producers of bibliographic records in an increasingly commercial environment and the difficulties of achieving a balance between the economic incentives of record providers and the free flow of bibliographic information considered essential for national and international bibliographic control.

By the mid-1980s LC was distributing MARC records (including CIP records) on magnetic tape for monographs in Roman-alphabet languages, languages in non-Roman scripts that had been romanized and languages in non-Roman scripts providing both romanized and vernacular data (Chinese, Japanese and Korean or 'CJK').[66] Also available were minimal-level records, for monographs in the Library's collection not given full-level cataloguing, including microform monographs and microform collections and brief romanized records for items in non-Roman scripts. Other forms of material for which records could be obtained included serials, maps, music and visual materials. All, except books in CJK and minimal-level records, were available either in USMARC or UNIMARC format. Name authority records, in the USMARC authorities format, were produced for new and revised headings. Records created outside the LC, but made available via its Cataloging Distribution Service, included those for art-exhibition catalogues from the Boston Public Library; from the CONSER project; for items appearing in the GPO monthly catalogue;

from the University of Chicago and Harvard University; from the National Library of Canada (converted to USMARC format) and UKMARC records from the British National Bibliography (also converted to USMARC). A full range of complete or selective retrospective services could be obtained. The complete monographs retrospective file, dating from 1968, in March 1985 comprised approximately 1,940,000 records. Two years later, it stood at around 2,240,000.[67] Subject authority records in the USMARC authorities format, formerly available only in retrospect, valid to 1982, were added to the current distribution service in 1986. More recently, records in Chinese, Japanese and Korean (CJK), created by RLIN and OCLC members, have been incorporated in LC's MARC Distribution Services.[68] Library of Congress records converted from exchange tapes into UKMARC by the British Library are also available to subscribers in the US in UKMARC format.

During the 1980s the British Library substantially augmented its BLAISE-LINE database, which at present contains records for British books (BNB MARC records 1950– and Whitaker's file of brief records for in-print and forthcoming books); for publications of other countries (supplied by LC MARC records, the combined catalogues of the Library's own departments and the University of London catalogue file) and for 'grey' literature, i.e. documents issued informally in limited numbers and not available through normal bookselling outlets.[69] SIGLE (System for Information on Grey Literature in Europe) covers items from 1981 to date. Audiovisual materials are featured in the AVMARC and HELPIS (Higher Education Learning Programmes Information Service) files. Other MARC-format files include ESTC (Eighteenth-Century Short-Title Catalogue), ISTC (Incunable Short-Title Catalogue), and the Library's Music Library catalogue and cartographic materials files. The BLC Preview file contains entries thus far converted in the BLC Catalogue Conversion Project, which, when completed, will add over 3.5 million records from the Library's *General catalogue of printed books to 1975*. Records available via BLAISE are in full UKMARC exchange-tape format, although some files, e.g. BLC Preview file, are in modified or simplified MARC form. A new MARC-record supply service, BLAISE Records, began in 1987.[70] As well as providing access to the online files in BLAISE-LINE, this offers back-up access to the OCLC Online Union Catalogue. Records are available for downloading and use in subscribers' local systems.

Although BL had from the outset distributed LC MARC records in BNB/UKMARC format, it was only in 1985 that an agreement was signed between the two libraries which enabled UKMARC records to be supplied to US subscribers in USMARC format.[71] In the same year BL introduced its 'Licence to use British Library records', a recognition of the rapidly changing nature of record supply and distribution, in particular the increase in 'third-party' use (i.e. the use made of national MARC records obtained via an intermediary, such as a cooperative or commercial supplier).[72] It was also an attempt to encourage cooperation and sharing of bibliographic data without loss of revenue for the Library. By 1987, BL had made similar agreements for the use of UKMARC records with the National Libraries of Canada and Australia and with North American networks including UTLAS, OCLC and RLIN.[73]

In 1980 three significant sets of MARC specifications were published: *UNIMARC*, second edition revised,[74] *MARC formats for bibliographic data (MFBD)*[75] and *UKMARC manual*, second edition.[76] UNIMARC, which is discussed in detail in Chapter 4, was designed purely as an exchange format, to accommodate different standards for bibliographic input although based on ISBD for the descriptive elements of a record. The first edition of *CCF: the Common Communication Format* (discussed in Chapter 5) was published four years later, with even greater flexibility and independence of cataloguing rules and practices.[77] The parallel development of international and national formats well illustrates one of the problems facing IFLA and other international organizations: progress at national and local level cannot be delayed while an international standard is conceived, developed and tested. Throughout the 1980s MARC format development continued both in the US and the UK and, while note was taken of progress made towards common exchange formats, national requirements took priority.

ISO 2709 *Documentation: format for bibliographic information interchange on magnetic tape* was revised in 1981, the major change involving the directory.[78] Corresponding American and British standards, ANSI Z39.2 and BS 4748, now conform with ISO

2709 – 1981. None of the changes to ISO 2709, which are described in detail in Chapter 2, has been implemented in UK or USMARC.

Nor have standards for the creation of bibliographic data remained static. Existing standards have been refined and new standards developed to meet the needs of new materials and bibliographic conditions. A review of ISBD, described as a 'harmonization process', was announced by IFLA in the same year as the publication of *MFBD* and *UKMARC manual*, second edition.[79] Both were committed to ISBD principles and therefore vulnerable to change.[79]

*AACR*2, second edition, 1988 revision[80] contains a number of rule changes, the most substantial the extensive rewriting of Chapter 9 'Computer files'. Other revisions include the reorganization of uniform titles for music and changes in entry for some personal and corporate names. Changes in ISBD and national codes such as *AACR*2 in most cases necessitate alterations to formats which use them as input standards for descriptive and/or author-title cataloguing.

MARC formats for bibliographic data (MFBD) gathered together, in one large loose-leaf version, all previously existing formats: books, films and visual materials, manuscripts, maps, music and serials. *MFBD* was not a single, unitary format, but was presented as an integrated composite, the result of a joint project carried out by LC and RLIN to build a database of MARC content designators which could be used both for maintenance of the formats and, ultimately, as the basis for an integrated USMARC format.[81] It was arranged in order of field tags in columnar fashion, with each column indicating the validity of fields/subfields for one material-specific implementation. All formats adhered to ANSI Z39.2 – 1979 structure, although there were many variations in content designation. Crawford notes that the collocation of the formats made obvious the many ambiguities and inconsistencies that had developed over the years, leading to some questioning about the nature and role of what were now styled the USMARC formats.[82] Inconsistencies among formats posed no problem for agencies which were restricted to one kind of material, or which kept non-book items in separate collections for which there were also separate files of machine-readable records; but as the idea of integration became more popular, assisted by wider movements towards standardization, format inconsistencies became noticeable and inconvenient.[83] The most significant outcome of the MARC format review project conducted for LC by Weisbrod in 1980–1 was the identification of format integration as a top priority. This in turn necessitated formal agreement on fundamental principles for content designation in the USMARC formats. John Attig, a member of MARBI, undertook the task and in October 1982, after much consultation and discussion, *The USMARC formats: underlying principles* was approved by MARBI.[84] It received wide publication and was subsequently included as a preliminary statement in *MFBD*. The *Underlying principles* reflected what was inherent in current USMARC formats and provided a basis for future development. They restated or made explicit certain well-established features, such as the commitment in structure to ANSI Z39.2–1979/ISO 2709–1981; the design of the formats primarily for communication, as distinct from storage or display; a recognition that USMARC formats had been adapted for use in a variety of exchange and processing environments; the distinction between two types of record, bibliographic and authority, which served different purposes; an attempt to preserve compatibility with other national manifestations of MARC, despite the absence of agreement on cataloguing rules and practices; and the relative freedom of the formats from specified standards for data content. A new principle (Section 2.6) introduced the Responsible Parties Rule, which Crawford sees as the most significant of the *Underlying principles*, completing the shift from LC to USMARC.[85] Apart from certain data elements which could be assigned only by particular agencies (e.g. ISBN, ISSN, LC card number) responsibility for all other data would rest with the institution creating the record (identified by subfield codes in the 040 field). This rule, according to Crawford, widened the MARC formats and facilitated the sharing of cataloguing data.[86] Henceforth, format integration was an intrinsic part of USMARC development. In 1984 the USMARC Advisory Group/MARBI agreed that the USMARC bibliographic formats were to be considered a 'single integrated format' with content designation valid, where appropriate, for all kinds of materials.[87] Soundings taken by LC between 1984 and 1986 indicated that format integration was believed necessary, despite the cost.[88] A paper on format integration considerations (Discussion paper no.16) was presented at a MARBI meeting in June 1987[89] and identified several objectives: the accommodation of non-textual serial items and multimedia/multiformat items (e.g. a serial on audio cassette, a tape/slide guide); simplification and coordination of content designation; and the rationalization of data elements to prevent the same data element being coded in different ways. Towards the end of 1987, the LC Cataloging Distribution Service distributed *USMARC formats: proposed changes*, based on comments received and discussed at the June 1987 MARBI meeting. These proposals were subsequently considered at MARBI meetings in January and July 1988, and, in the main, approved.[90]

New and revised USMARC formats, 1980–7

Format revision continued after the publication of *MFBD*, with attention given to improving treatment of non-book materials, mainly stimulated by the appearance of *AACR2*. The name of the films format was in 1985 changed to *Visual materials*, with appropriate alteration in content designation.[91] The new title more accurately reflected the scope of the format, which from the outset had included graphics, sculpture and art objects. Content designators have been continuously revised, with additions of fields to accommodate two- and three-dimensional materials, archival moving images and compact audio discs. The 1973 manuscripts format was revised and renamed *Archival and manuscripts control* (AMC) format. Published in 1983, the revision differed from other formats in its emphasis on archival control and collective, as opposed to separate item, description.[92] Fields completely new to USMARC were added, indicating provenance, action taken, and copy and version identification. A format for machine-readable data files was completed in 1981, although not included in *MFBD* until 1984 (Update 9).[93] A revision of *AACR2* Chapter 9 'Computer data files', led to further revision.[94] The requirements of technical reports were dealt with not in a separate format but in an extension to the books format, entitled *Summary of MARC format specifications for technical reports*.[95] This allowed users to input bibliographic data for reports together with those for general monograph literature. Techniques for handling analytical records had been under discussion since the 1970s, as USMARC, unlike its British counterpart, did not support the making of 'in' analytic records or multi-level description. Several suggestions, including the extension of the directory and the definition of a control field as subrecord directory map, similar to the device used in UKMARC, were put forward and rejected, mainly on grounds of complexity and cost. It was not until 1981 that proposals for record-linking techniques prepared by Sally McCallum of the LC's Network Development and MARC Standards Office, proved to be acceptable.[96] Analytical records in current USMARC are dealt with chiefly by means of linking entry fields which hold data concerning related items and the nature of the relationship present. The techniques are discussed in a separate section of this chapter.

Between 1986 and 1988 LC's Network Development and MARC Standards Office reviewed, redesigned and restructured the existing USMARC documentation, issuing a series of publications which collectively represent a 'full USMARC documentation product line'.[97] MFBD was superseded by USMARC format for bibliographic data, which sets out the content designation identifying all data elements in USMARC bibliographic records and incorporates requirements for national-level bibliographic records.[98] USMARC format for bibliographic data is one of three USMARC communications formats, the other two being USMARC format for authority data[99] and USMARC format for holdings and locations.[100] The structure of the USMARC bibliographic record is described in a separate document: USMARC specifications for record structure, character sets, tapes[101] intended mainly for those involved in the technical aspects of MARC systems design and maintenance. Three USMARC code lists covering countries, languages, relators, sources and description conventions,[102] USMARC character set for Chinese, Japanese, Korean,[103] and USMARC concise formats,[104] complete the set. USMARC specifications are discussed in an Appendix to this chapter.

The first authorities format was published in 1976,[105] and used to distribute LC name authority records in machine-readable form from 1978 onwards. It was redesigned to facilitate the first implementation of the LSP project and republished in

1981.[106] The format is designed to hold in one record all authority data relating to a particular name or subject heading, including cross-references. ('Name' includes all personal, corporate names, names of jurisdictions and meetings, and uniform titles.) As well as its own records, LC distributes authority records created by other organizations under the NACO scheme. The current specification is *USMARC format for authority data*, published in 1988 as part of the review of the range of USMARC formats. Like the format for bibliographic records, it includes information on national-level authority records, which had previously been issued separately. It is possible that authority data from classification schemes may be incorporated.[107]

The *USMARC format for holdings and locations* had its origins in 1981, when a group of research libraries, members of SEARL (South Eastern Association of Research Libraries) received a grant from the Office of Education to develop a shared database of holdings and bibliographic data for serials.[108] LC joined in the project and a committee was set up, comprising representatives from all participating libraries. The possibility only of adding extra fields to the bibliographic formats to accommodate holdings data was rejected in favour of a dual approach: the creation of separate records which could either be linked to or embedded in bibliographic records.[109] The authority format is compatible with ANSI Z39.44–1986, *Serial holdings statements*. It was published as a final draft in 1984 and updated in 1987. Both authorities and holdings formats are discussed further in an Appendix to this chapter.

Responsibility for the USMARC formats rests jointly with LC and the USMARC Advisory Group, of which the chief constituent is MARBI, the Committee on Representation in Machine-Readable Form of Bibliographic Information. MARBI is a committee of the American Library Association, drawn from the Resources and Technical Services Division, the Library and Information Technology Association and the Reference and Adult Services Division. It is often cited as ALA RTSD/LITA/RASD MARBI Committee. The USMARC Advisory Group also includes representatives from the National Agricultural Library, the National Library of Medicine, the National Library of Canada and the bibliographic utilities/networks.[110] Proposals for changes in formats and other matters for discussion are submitted to meetings of MARBI. The process of discussion, referral and consultation with all interested parties is time-consuming and, naturally, not all proposals are ratified.

The *UKMARC manual*, second edition, published in 1980, was the result of a rethinking of the format, incorporating changes necessitated by the appearance of AACR2 and the desire to broaden the format to embrace more satisfactorily a wider range of materials. UKMARC was offered as an integrated, unitary format, with some material-specific fields. The first *UKMARC manual* had linked the format with British text AACR,[111] and the second edition is also linked with AACR2.[112] Most of the examples cite AACR2 rule numbers and act as a guide to the cataloguing policy and practice of British Library Bibliographic Services. The separately published *Cataloguing practice notes* gives further information on BLBS interpretations of AACR2/UKMARC.[113] Publication in loose-leaf form facilitated continuous revision and between 1980 and 1987 approximately 60 amendments were issued. The widening of the format to include more non-book materials produced many changes; for example, in the implementation-codes section of the record label, additional codes for special instructional materials and kits were provided in character position 7, type of record. Many new fields and subfields were incorporated, for example fields to cope with cartographic materials and music data. Major differences between the 1975 and 1980 formats can be seen in the physical description field (tag 300), where subfields were defined to cope with the differing physical descriptions required by AACR2 for audiovisual materials such as tapes, films, sound recordings. Here, as in other parts of the format, changes in content designation occurred. Field 248 (Second level and subsequent level title and statement of responsibility information relating to a multi-part item) was introduced to replace subfields $g and $h (volume or part number and title of field 245 (title area) of the first edition. Use of field 248, which can be repeated when necessary, allows the construction of separate MARC records for individual parts of a multi-part item (excluding serials). Multi-level description, in accordance with AACR2 Chapter 13, can be produced at output. Format revisions made in 1986 included a

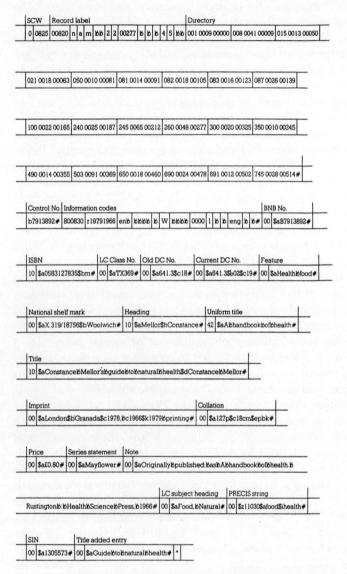

Fig. 3.3 Example from *UKMARC manual*, 2nd edition

(Reproduced from *UKMARC manual*, 2nd ed., with permission of the British Library Board)

change in character positions 21–4 of the record label (the directory map) to align it more closely with ISO 2709 and the flagging of British Library MARC records with a provenance code 'b' in character position 40 of the 008 (Information Codes) field.[114] The latter was introduced in connection with the British Library licensing system, requiring users to retain or create a provenance flag for all records originally created by the Library.

The British Library, through its National Bibliographic Service, is responsible for the maintenance and development of the UKMARC format. As Long has observed, procedures for format revision are simpler and less formal than in the United States.[115] Proposed changes are published, normally in *BLAISE newsletter* and/or *British Library Bibliographic Services newsletter*, and interested bodies, such as the MARC Users Group, are consulted. The *UKMARC manual* is undergoing a phased revision, due for completion in 1990.[116] The revised manual will contain a statement of underlying principles based on that approved for the USMARC formats and will place greater emphasis on the role of UKMARC as the British national format, with British Library policy and practice (for example in the construction of records for the national bibliography) even more clearly distinguished. There will be more examples of audiovisual materials, and in languages other than English. Many fields developed for use in BLD MARC records, i.e. records in UKMARC format produced by or for departments of the Library for its internal catalogues, may be incorporated in the manual and thus made available for wider use.

To date, authority data are held in UKMARC exchange records in the form of cross-references in the 9-- fields. The British Library has its own internal machine-readable format for authority records, based on a simplified version of the USMARC authorities format, and maintains its own authorities database. The question of whether to publish the format and to make authority records available outside the Library is under review. Holdings data are accommodated in local fields in bibliographic records. The format specifications set out in the *UKMARC manual* second edition are discussed in an Appendix to this chapter. An example of a UKMARC exchange tape record appears in Figure 3.3.

US and UKMARC at the end of the 1980s

From a common origin and purpose, the American and British MARC formats diverged, the UKMARC format remaining unitary, the original LC MARC format used as a model for additional, material-specific formats. At the end of the 1980s, the US (bibliographic) and UKMARC formats have come closer together, for despite continuing differences in content designation and data content, each is a single, integrated format, based on common standards for data input and attempting to meet national and international demands for data interchange.[117] A major distinction, however, is the existence in the United States of separate formats for authority and holdings/locations data.

It is generally agreed that MARC has been not only a widely used and effective format for bibliographic data, but an invaluable vehicle for data exchange and shared cataloguing. It may seem, then, that US and UKMARC occupy an unassailable position in Anglo-American library automation. Appearances may, however, be deceptive, as questioning of the role and nature of MARC formats has recently increased, mainly as a result of the spread of online catalogues, the emergence of CD-ROM as an alternative medium for record storage and dissemination and the economic issues raised by adherence to bibliographic standards for data content. Any review of US and UKMARC would in theory involve consideration of all three format components: physical structure, content designation and content, the last directly linked with standards for record creation. There has been some criticism of the physical structure (i.e. the tape-based ISO 2709 structure) of MARC, with its separation of the record into two sections (record label/directory and variable datafields) and the data redundancy resulting from this; but in many cases this problem can be eliminated or alleviated for local processing and online use. Increased computer storage capacity and faster access mitigate many structural problems, but in turn undercut the need for highly structured records.

The most serious criticisms centre on the detailed content designation and data content typical of US/UKMARC and many other national MARC records. Both US and UKMARC formats continue to expand in response to perceived needs for additional data elements and, although conducted in a controlled manner, the add-on approach leads to even more detailed and lengthy records, requiring yet more storage space. An important question is whether a highly formalized, bibliographically detailed record, with structured access points and precise division into fields and subfields, is appropriate or necessary for the practical applications of the majority of MARC records, especially in online catalogues.

Ashford, writing in 1984, gives full credit to the achievement of MARC in demonstrating the feasibility of a structured record for bibliographic data; further, he believes that most deficiencies reported about MARC can be dealt with by any competent database designer and that its defects are far outweighed by its success as an international exchange standard which has radically changed the economics of cataloguing.[118] This is undoubtedly true, but the economics of cataloguing may in the future change the MARC formats, and while it is possible for MARC records to be restructured for local use, some MARC producers and users are now asking whether even at national level highly complex and detailed records are needed and whether such detail is incorporated at the expense of coverage and currency. As much of this discussion occurs within national and local contexts, the issues are dealt with in Chapters 6 and 7.

Other national MARC formats

National formats may be true exchange formats, used for the transfer of records between systems. As with all formats, they may be used as the basis of internal formats in the design of software systems which may not necessarily be intended to communicate with each other but which would usually be able to communicate if required.

After the joint work by the Library of Congress and the British National Bibliography on the MARC format, other countries were quick to join in the activity and develop their own formats. Obviously, the development of a new format or agreement on the adoption of an existing format comes first, but many countries were much slower to make any actual use of a format even when effort had been put into its development. Moreover, some national formats were developed taking, say, LC MARC as a model but without access to hardware or software of the kind that had been used at the Library of Congress, so that the format could not be used until the hardware was obtained and the software developed. Computer science has advanced relentlessly since 1967 when LC MARC began, and now a national bibliography and MARC records could be produced on a microcomputer, but until 1982 or there-abouts a mainframe or a large minicomputer would have been necessary.

Canada

In Canada, a MARC Task Group was set up which developed a recommended Canadian MARC Format for Monographs and a Canadian MARC Format for Serials. The Group looked at Canada's special needs for a machine-readable bibliographic record and studied the MARC formats of the US, UK, France, Italy and Germany. They spoke to a number of people involved in MARC including staff from the US Library of Congress MARC Development Office, British National Bibliography, University Library of Grenoble, France, which used the MONOCLE format, and the Birmingham Libraries Cooper-ative Mechanisation Project (BLCMP). They adopted the LC MARC II format chiefly but took additional fields from the BNB MARC format and MONOCLE. They made sure not to include any fields with tags which would conflict with any of the other national MARC formats. They took the basic subfield identifiers from LC MARC but added extra ones from BNB 'in order to improve the MARC II format'.[119] They retained the LC indicators but added additional ones from BNB and MONOCLE. Since Canada has a bilingual English/French policy, they expanded the 900 series of tags which were used for references to provide the option of selecting data in certain fields in either French or English. They also added a code in the label to indicate the degree of completion of the machine-readable record which included an indication of whether it was fully bilingual or not. The report includes a composite table of MARC formats comparing the monographs format subfield by subfield with Canadian, LC, UK, MONOCLE and the Italian format. The serials format is compared with LC and MASS, the BLCMP serials format. A minority of the members of the Task Group felt it would be better to accept LC MARC in its entirety, but the main reason for adopting their own format was said to be the need to cater for bilingual records.

The format specified in the report was superseded by the national Canadian *MARC format* (CANMARC), which was published in 1974 and revised in 1979.[120]

Australia

The National Library of Australia published its MARC format in 1973 with a second edition in 1975. Its third edition published in 1979 was necessitated by the publication of the second edition of AACR in 1978, which had been reflected in the second edition of UKMARC. These changes had been discussed and agreed in March 1978 at the second meeting of ABACUS (the Association of Bibliographic Agencies of Britain, Australia, Canada, and the US).[121]

The Australian format is very close to that of UKMARC even to the extent of using the 002 subrecord directory for analytics and the level-digit method for data entry which is described in Chapter 2 of this book. However, in 1988, they began to exchange authority records, using the AUSMARC authorities format (published in early 1988 after preliminary drafts in 1983 and 1986). This is based closely on the USMARC authorities format.[122]

Other early developments

Other countries adopted national formats. The Federal Republic of Germany had been following MARC developments and in 1973 published its own format, *Maschinelles Austausch-format für Bibiotheken* (*MAB*1).[123] A main feature of this format is its facility for record-linking between records representing different bibliographic levels, for example analyticals in mono-graphs or volumes in multi-volume monographs, and many of the ideas in that area have influenced other formats, such as UNIMARC. Also in Germany, a national format was developed in 1977 for secondary services, MADOK.[124] This included in the format document comparisons between MAB1, BNB MARC and INTERMARC.

Italy had already developed a format which the Canadian Task Force had studied; this was known as ANNAMARC,[125] and was used as the format for the magnetic-tape service of the

Istituto Centrale per il Catalogo Unico in Rome until 1985. The Danish format DANMARC was first published in 1975 with a second edition in 1979.[126] The Spanish Ministry of Education and Science published IBERMARC in 1976 in the form of a provisional edition.[127] It was then published in another version in 1981.[128] The Swedish format SWEMARC came out in 1980.[129] Norway and Finland followed, basing their formats very closely on UKMARC and following similar principles. Some of these formats were used as the basis of networks, others only as the format of the national institution. Many of these countries were interested in being able to take records from the Library of Congress and the British Library. Since the British Library converted data from the Library of Congress tapes to the UKMARC format, it was advantageous to adopt the UKMARC format to make it possible to take tapes from the British Library which included both LC and BNB records.

Formats influenced by UNIMARC

The next phase of development of national MARC formats was in countries outside Europe and North America. By 1975, the first draft of SUPERMARC, also known as the MARC International Format and later to be called UNIMARC, had been circulated and Japan,[130] South Africa[131] and Taiwan[132] developed formats based on this. This new format was of particular interest to Japan and Taiwan because it was designed to be a more generalized format than LC MARC had been; Japan and Taiwan did not use AACR and also needed a mechanism to deal with non-Roman character sets. Additionally, a different method of treatment was required to deal with non-alphabetic access points.

South Africa published its SAMARC format in 1977, basing it on UNIMARC for 15 stated reasons. The most important reasons were that UNIMARC had been designed cooperatively by acknowledged experts with collective experience of many national formats; it was a multimedia format; it would be easier to exchange data with other countries if an international format were used – it was then expected that international exchange would be effected via UNIMARC from 1980 onwards; it enabled multilingual records; and it allowed linking records and analytical descriptions. A number of fields were added in the

110

900 series to provide for publishing statistics.

In 1986, the National Library in Portugal introduced UNIMARC as a national format and published an operations manual to clarify its use.[133] The National and University Library of Croatia in Zagreb also adopted a format very close to UNIMARC.[134] 'National libraries' in Yugoslavia are organized on a state basis and the National Library in Slovenia based at Ljubljana and the University of Maribor Library in the north-east of the state are cooperating in an automation project which is using UNIMARC as its format mainly to ensure compatibility with the Croatians, though one of the staff at the National and University Library in Ljubljana, Joze Kokole, was in fact the representative of the Union of Library Associations of Yugoslavia on the IFLA working group that developed UNIMARC. This format has now been accepted as the standard format for use in all libraries in Yugoslavia.

Nationalism in format development

In Spain, too, nationalism resulted in the development of a distinct format for the production of the *Bibliografia Nacional de Catalunya*.[135]

When work began to automate the production of this bibliography in 1982, IBERMARC, the Spanish format published in 1976 (to an outsider the obvious choice), was rejected because it had not yet been revised in line with AACR2.

Though an edition of IBERMARC for monographs taking into account AACR2 was produced in 1985, the direction that was being taken in Madrid was to take some aspects from UNIMARC (for sound discs and books) but for cartographic materials to base the format on USMARC. In Barcelona, they therefore decided to develop their own format based on UKMARC which was published in 1987 and called CAT-MARC.[136] This was used for exchange between five different organizations, one of which, the Public and University Library of Barcelona, also takes records from OCLC. Because of the resemblance of CATMARC and UKMARC, they are able to use the standard conversion that OCLC has available from its own format (USMARC) to UKMARC.[137]

This example shows to what extent bibliographic formats have gained a 'political' aspect.

INTERMARC

The mid-1970s had seen a spate of international activities in connection with formats. The British Library Bibliographic Services Division, along with other members of IFLA, was involved with UNIMARC, subject of Chapter 4. At the same time a group of representatives of Western European national libraries sat round a table to develop another international format, which was called INTERMARC and was published in 1975.[138] This was intended to be a regional format; no one from North America was involved. This eventually became the official format of the national libraries of France and Belgium. However, the Bibliothèque Nationale in Paris did not have an automated system at that time and did not actually make use of INTERMARC, though by 1984 it was offering exchange tapes in UNIMARC. The Belgian National Library has continued to use it internally. The format is very much like UKMARC save that it has six indicator positions instead of two. The first two correspond to the two indicators of UKMARC; the third and fourth are used to denote occurrence of repeated field (from 0 to 99) and the last two are used in a similar way to the level indicator in the data-entry format in the British Library's Library Software Package (LSP), which uses a format related to UKMARC and which groups together fields into subrecords when recording analytical entries.

The INTERMARC Group which developed the format was subsequently transformed into a group studying the general problems of library automation, and renamed the INTER-MARC Software Sub-Group, though it consisted of the same core of people. It has changed its name yet again to the European Library Automation Group (ELAG).

INTERMARC was never very much used in France. Even before the Bibliothèque Nationale in Paris obtained the GEAC software package and adopted the UNIMARC format, the Ministère de la Culture, Division du Livre et de la Lecture, which has responsibility for the public-library services in certain localities, had already adopted UNIMARC as the internal format on a software system being developed on Honeywell-Bull computers.

It could be said that INTERMARC never achieved the international status expected of it although it is very often referred to by writers on the subject as being a format of comparative importance. This could well be because of its name, which is presumably an abbreviation for 'international MARC'.

European Documentation and Information System for Education (EUDISED)

The British Library had also become involved in a further project, to develop a format for educational material. The Working Party on EUDISED Formats and Standards met for the first time in July 1972 under the chairmanship of Richard Coward, then of the British National Bibliography Ltd, and completed the first stage of its work the following year with the publication of its report.[139] This contained the EUDISED format on which Michael Gorman and John Linford had started work for a project, funded by the Council of Europe, before their employer, the British National Bibliography, was absorbed into the British Library. This format used as its basis the concept of bibliographic level since it was intended for the recording of educational materials like kits which consist of sub-parts which are sometimes in complex relationships with each other. The draft format defined seven bibliographic levels, Collection, Sub-Collection, Document, Volume, Analytical, Sub-volume and Volume Analytical. The document called for the extension of ISO 2709 to provide a new mechanism to avoid the subrecord directory technique using field 002 which was already used by AGRIS, INIS and UKMARC. Linford gives an interesting history of the format in which he indicates that the format was used operationally in the publication of the *EUDISED R&D bulletin, EUDISED AV bulletin* and *EUDISED EP bulletin*.[140]

The format document was extensively consulted in the design of MERMARC, the format of the MERLIN system, a relational database library-software package that was begun by the British National Bibliography and taken over by British Library Bibliographic Services Division, only to be dropped after six years of development.

113

MEKOF

Developments in Eastern Europe had paralleled those in the West. Eastern European countries tend to adopt international standards wherever possible; since the record structure of the LC MARC format had been adopted as US ANSI Standard Z39.2–1971 and then as International Standard ISO 2709–1973, it was natural for the countries of Eastern Europe to adopt it as the record structure of their international format. ICSTI, the International Centre for Scientific and Technical Information in Moscow, is the centre of an information network in the COMECON countries. They use a format called MEKOF of which there are two versions, MEKOF-1 and MEKOF-2, which differ mainly in their record structure.[141] MEKOF-2 was the first and is the most developed of the two. It uses the standard record of the Normative Technical Prescription (NTP) of ICSTI, no.2[142] which has a more complex record structure than ISO 2709. MEKOF-1 uses the NTP of ICSTI no.1,[143] which is very close to ISO 2709. MEKOF-2, being further removed from ISO 2709, has some interesting features. Its tag consists of four digits to accommodate a level indicator. A multi-level record is treated similarly to the Reference Manual's treatment, except in a more analytical way. Any field within the format can be allocated to any bibliographic level, whereas in the Reference Manual only selected fields are repeated at different bibliographic levels. In MEKOF-2, a review is treated as a separate bibliographic level so that details of a review can be entered in the same record as the item reviewed, to create a link between the two. As in the West, there have been no major developments for many years and the standards are accepted as good, workable standards.

Developments in Latin America

In Latin America, national exchange formats developed in a different way. The MARCAL (MARC Americana Latina) format was published by the Organization of American States in 1981; it was virtually a translation of the Library of Congress MARC Manual but was not extensively used.[144]

Brazil

In Brazil, the national format began as a Master's thesis presented in 1971 which was later published.[145] It was based on the Library of Congress MARC format as it was at the time. It was developed by a member of staff of IBBD (the Brazilian Institute of Bibliography and Documentation), one of the predecessors of IBICT (the Brazilian Institute of Information in Science and Technology) but it was not used as it was felt to be too 'academic', no doubt since it had been developed as a thesis. The CALCO format as used at the Getúlio Vargas Foundation, where the data processing for the National Library automated catalogue takes place, was based on the work done in the thesis and was in use from about 1981.[146]

IBICT set up an office in 1982 called Escritorio CALCO which was intended to promote the CALCO format as a national format to enable exchange of data, but this format was not compatible with the format used by the Getúlio Vargas Foundation, which had made changes to the original format on the lines of changes that the Library of Congress had made to its MARC format. In order to avoid this problem of incompatibility, certain changes were then made to the IBICT format to make it more accommodating as an exchange format and some of these were based on UNIMARC practice and others on the CCF. At first, to help in the acceptance of the new exchange format, it was called the CALCO exchange format, but just before publication it was decided to call it the IBICT format (standing for *I*ntercâmbio *Bi*bliografico e *Ca*talográfico).[147]

Mexico

In Mexico there have for a long time been attempts to develop a national format to enable data to be taken from Library of Congress tapes and used in automated systems in Mexico. However, the national library based at the University in Mexico City only obtained an automated system in the mid-1980s, and so work on developing a national format was completed only in 1987. The format has been closely based on USMARC. A working group was formed in 1985 which took into account earlier work such as an attempt in 1979 to establish the BIBA system (Banco de Información Bibliográfica Automatizada) which had already established objectives for the automation of the national bibliography.

The agreed objectives of the system were the creation of a

115

bibliographic database containing records of Mexican material with the possibility of querying it online. Duplication of data was to be avoided in order to streamline the database. It also had to enable the exchange of information, either via MARC tapes or telecommunications networks and it had to enable the creation of by-products like specialized bibliographies and the cumulative monthly issues of the *Mexican bibliography*.

A number of working groups were set up to assist in the design of the system. The MINISIS software was selected, probably because not only is it a system designed specifically for bibliographic information retrieval; it is also available free of charge for non-profit-making organizations in developing countries. Furthermore, MINISIS had just had developed an interface making it especially suitable for supporting MARC data.[148]

One of the working groups had the task of designing the format. In the design of the total system, this was seen as one of the more important elements. An unpublished paper describes the methodical way in which the format was developed.[149] The MARC format (presumably the USMARC format) was studied with a view to defining the data elements that would be incorporated in the database. From this was constructed a data-element dictionary. Each data element was described in the dictionary according to its attributes as follows: name of data element; maximum length of field; whether numeric or alphabetic; repeatable or not repeatable; whether it had subfields; whether it had any possible validation such as a defined set of values (like coded data fields) or a defined pattern (like an ISBN). Next came a description of the use of each field, examples, observations and points of clarification. Finally, the description of each data element contained an indication of whether it was used in MARC, the CCF and other Mexican systems, those of IIMAS (the Instituto de Investigaciones en Matemáticas Aplicadas y Sistemas) and of the UNAM (National University of Mexico) Library. The data-element dictionary was put into a MINISIS database and the parts of the format manual dealing with data-element definitions were produced from it.[150]

It is interesting that there was very little questioning of the decision to adopt the MARC of the Library of Congress, but at the same time there was an attempt to take into account other formats such as the CCF.

India and South-East Asia
In this area, there has been a resurgence of interest in bibliographic exchange formats with the widespread introduction of microcomputers, though larger computers have been in use for bibliographic processing for many years. The centralized Singapore Integrated Library Automation Service (SILAS) has used LC/USMARC since its establishment in 1986, but other countries have seen fit to develop their own national formats.

India
India has long had databases set up by specialist libraries and documentation centres rather than by national, public or academic libraries. The Bureau of Indian Standards published Indian MARC, which was based very closely on UKMARC, in 1985.[151] It had taken eight years to formulate and it was stated soon after that it needed immediate revision. An exercise was then begun under the auspices of the National Information System for Science and Technology to develop INDIMARC on a framework prescribed by the CCF.[152]

Thailand
In 1976, Stephen Massil, who had just completed two years as Associate Director of the library of the Asian Institute of Technology (AIT) in Bangkok, Thailand, was commissioned by Unesco to develop a format for the National Library of Thailand. THAIMARC was based on UKMARC with a number of adaptations found in the variant of the UKMARC format used by BLCMP and further adaptations pertaining to special characteristics of material in the Thai language, such as books published in commemoration of the deceased on their cremation, names of dignitaries, ecclesiastical names. As a result of this the National Library began to develop computerized systems to process records using this format. Other libraries were interested in mechanization, but in contrast to the situation elsewhere, the National Library was reluctant to allow other organizations to use its format. In consequence, the university libraries formed a sub-committee of the University

117

Bureau to develop a format which was called UNIVMARC and which was really very similar. Later Mahidol University Library and Chulalongkorn University's Academic Resource Centre developed MAHIDOLMARC and CUMARC respectively. The Ministry of Science Technology and Energy's MOSTEMARC was developed in 1989. These last three have been developed by organizations that wish to take data from external sources such as OCLC, either by tapes or from CD-ROM, and they have introduced variants to bring their formats into line with the formats used by the records they are adding to their own databases. At a seminar on Standards for Bibliographic Control held in 1989, it was recommended that the National Library should take steps to improve THAIMARC and allow it to fulfil the needs of libraries on a national basis.[153]

Malaysia

Malaysia also has its own format, MALMARC, based almost entirely on UKMARC and, as in the case of THAIMARC, developed with the assistance of Stephen Massil. While still Associate Director of the AIT Library, he had circulated a paper outlining plans by AIT to take records from the National Library of Australia and to coordinate requests from other libraries in Thailand and the region. Nothing came of this proposal, but subsequently representatives of the National Library of Malaysia and five academic libraries met with the result that Massil returned to South-East Asia to conduct a feasibility study on the use of MARC in Malaysia.[154] A format based very closely on UKMARC was developed as it was decided to use the British Library's LSP package to process records from the British Library and Library of Congress in UK format on the computer of the Universiti Sains Malaysia in Penang.[155] The Universiti Sains became the coordinating centre for this and remained so until 1990 when the MALMARC project as such was disbanded, though the libraries involved continued exchanging data using the MALMARC format.

Indonesia

The National Library of Indonesia also developed a format to promote exchange of data between other organizations and the building up of a national union catalogue, based on state libraries. Originally, INDOMARC was based on SEAMARC, the MARC format for South-East Asia developed for the SEAPRINT (South-East Asian Imprints) project, but when that project terminated through lack of funds, it was decided to base the national format, published in 1989, on USMARC.[156]

International coordination of national developments
In 1984, IFLA's International MARC Programme published the *International guide to MARC databases and services: national magnetic tape services*, with a revised edition in 1986.[157] This listed all the tape services being provided by national libraries and those proposed in the two subsequent years. It also listed a number of national libraries which had no plans to offer a magnetic-tape service for bibliographic records. This does not mean that a national library had not automated or did not have a format. Brazil, for example, was included in the first edition as having no plans to automate. This was surprising as the National Library had had an automated catalogue produced by the Getúlio Vargas Foundation since 1981. This statement was corrected in the second edition and presumably the error had occurred because data processing was done outside the institution. Surveys based on questionnaires enquiring about future activities have to be looked at very carefully, and should certainly not be taken as evidence of activities having taken place.

As regards the future, it is not certain whether countries will continue to develop their own MARC formats or adopt UNIMARC or an existing national format such as US or UKMARC. If the library cooperatives gain customers in developing countries, we may see an increase in the use of their formats, since it is the developing countries alone that have yet to develop national formats.

Notes and references

1 'MARC nomenclature', *British Library Bibliographic Services newsletter*, **44**, October 1987, 3–4.
2 *UNIMARC/A: UNIMARC format for authorities*, London, IFLA UBCIM Programme, 1990.

3 This section draws on several invaluable sources, especially Avram, H., *MARC, its history and implications*, Washington, Library of Congress, 1975; Long, A., 'UKMARC and US/MARC: a brief history and comparison', *Journal of documentation*, **40**, 1984, 1–12; Crawford, W., *MARC for library use: understanding the USMARC formats*, White Plains, NY, Knowledge Industry, 1984.

4 King, G. W. and others, *Automation and the Library of Congress: a survey sponsored by the Council on Library Resources, Inc.*, Washington DC, LC, 1963.

5 Buckland, L. F., *The recording of Library of Congress bibliographical data in machine form: a report prepared for the Council on Library Resources, Inc.*, Washington, CLR, 1965.

6 Avram, H., *op. cit.*, 3.

7 Library of Congress, Information Systems Office, *Project MARC: an experiment in automating Library of Congress catalog data*, Washington DC, LC, 1967.

8 *Ibid.*, 2–3.

9 *Ibid.*, 4–5.

10 *MARC record service proposals: details of the proposals for current British publications on magnetic tape...*, London, Council of the British National Bibliography, 1968 (BNB MARC Documentation Service publications no.1), 1.1.

11 *UKMARC Project: proceedings of the seminar on the UKMARC Project*, ed. by A. E. Jeffreys and T. D. Wilson, Oriel Press, 1970, 2.

12 Avram, H., Knapp, J. F. and Rather, L. J., *The MARC II format: a communications format for bibliographic data*, Washington DC, LC, 1968.

13 *MARC record service proposals* (see note 10).

14 *MARC II specifications (March 1969)*, London, Council of the British National Bibliography, 1969 (BNB MARC Documentation Service publications no.2).

15 *Ibid.*, 1.

16 International Organization for Standardization, *Documentation: format for bibliographic information interchange on magnetic tape*, 2nd ed., Geneva, ISO, 1981 (ISO 2709–1981).

17 *MARC record service proposals*, 2.1.

18 Avram, H., Knapp, J. F. and Rather, L. J., *op. cit.*, 10.

19 *Ibid.*, 23–6.

20 *MARC record service proposals*, 3.1.

21 Crawford, W., *op. cit.*, 119.

22 Council of the British National Bibliography, *BNB/MARC Project: report on the period September 1970 – March 1973*, Council of the BNB, 1974, 2.4.1.

23 Originally entitled *Subscriber's guide to the MARC Distribution Service*, this reached its fifth and final edition: Library of Congress, MARC Development Office, *Books: a MARC format*, 5th ed., Washington DC, LC, 1972.

24 Library of Congress, MARC Development Office, *Serials: a MARC format*, 2nd ed., Washington DC, LC, 1974 (preliminary ed., 1970); Library of Congress, Information Systems Office, *Maps: a MARC format*, Washington DC, LC, 1970; Library of Congress, MARC Development Office, *Films: a MARC format*, Washington DC, LC, 1970; Library of Congress, MARC Development Office, *Manuscripts: a MARC format*, Washington DC, LC, 1973; Library of Congress, MARC Development Office, *Music: a MARC format*, draft, Washington DC, LC, 1973 (includes musical and non-musical sound recordings).

25 Library of Congress, MARC Development Office, *Authorities: a MARC format*, preliminary ed., Washington DC, LC, 1976.

26 Long, A., *op. cit.*, 6.

27 Rohrbach, P. T., *FIND: automation at the Library of Congress, the first twenty-five years and beyond*, Washington DC, LC, 1985, 21.

28 Avram, H., *RECON Pilot Project: final report ...*, Washington DC, LC, 1972. See also Avram H., *MARC: its history and implications*, 13–16.

29 Bourne, R., 'Building a serials file', *Program*, **12**, 1978, 78–85; *American libraries*, **8**, (1), Jan. 1977 (special issue); *The CONSER Project: recommendations for the future: report of a study conducted for the Library of Congress*, Washington DC, LC, 1986 (Network Planning Paper no.14).

30 *Library of Congress information bulletin (LCIB)*, **36**, (10), 11 March, 1977, 165–6.

31 *LCIB*, **37**, (14), 7 April 1978, 228.

32 *LCIB*, **47**, (4), 25 January 1988.

33 'REMARC users', *Program*, **19**, 1985, 195; Martin, S. K., *Library networks, 1986–87: libraries in partnership*, White Plains, NY, Knowledge Industry, 1986, 145; Avram, H., 'Towards a nationwide library network', *Journal of library administration*, **8**, 1987, 101.

34 Library of Congress, MARC Development Office, *Composite MARC format: a tabular listing of content designators used in the MARC formats*, Washington DC, LC, 1976.

35 Library of Congress, Processing Services, *National level bibliographic record: books*, revised draft, prepared by H. F. Schmierer ..., Washington DC, LC, 1978.

36 *LCIB*, **38**, (7), 16 February 1979, 55.

37 *LCIB*, **38**, (45), 9 November 1979; *LCIB*, **38**, (46), 16 November 1979.
38 *LCIB*, **38**, (47), 23 November 1979.
39 *LCIB*, **38**, (45), 9 November 1979, 462–4.
40 Work carried out under the aegis of BLCMP is particularly relevant. See, for example, *BLCMP final report to the British Library Research and Development Department*, Project number SI/G/027, Birmingham, BLCMP, 1976; and the series of *MASS (MARC-based Serials System) working papers* issued by the cooperative.
41 Gorman, M., *Description of the BNB/MARC record: a manual of practice*, London, Council of the British National Bibliography, 1971 (BNB/MARC Documentation Service publications no.5).
42 *UKMARC manual*, 1st standard ed., London, British Library Bibliographic Services Division, 1975.
43 Pringle, R. and Stevenson, S., 'LCMARC off the peg? Automatic upgrading of LCMARC records', *Vine*, **29**, 1979, 19–24; the steps involved in an early conversion program are listed in Council of the British National Bibliography, *BNB/MARC project*, 43–5.
44 Long, A., *op. cit.*
45 Avram, H., 'International standards for the interchange of bibliographic records in machine-readable form', *Library resources and technical services*, **20**, 1976, 25–35.
46 'BLAISE goes live!', *British Library news*, **16**, April 1977.
47 'BLAISE use of MARC fields', *MARC news*, **1**, August 1977, 7–9; 'BLAISE: extension of use to character position 24 in field 008', *ibid.*, 10–12.
48 'Serials on BLAISE', *MARC news*, **2**, November 1977, 2–4.
49 'Format used for Learning Materials Recording Study', *MARC news*, 3, February 1978, 1–3.
50 'Extensions to the UKMARC format', *MARC news*, **4**, January 1979, 7.
51 *Ibid.*, 8.
52 *British Standard Specification for format for bibliographic information interchange on magnetic tape*, BS 4748:1982, London, British Standards Institution, 1982.
53 Gapen, D. K., 'MARC format simplification', *Journal of library automation*, **14**, 1981, 286–92.
54 Gredley, E. J., 'Standardizing bibliographical data: *AACR*2 and international exchange', *Journal of librarianship*, **12**, 1980, 84–101.
55 International Federation of Library Associations and Institutions, Working Group on the General International Standard Bibliographic Description, *ISBD(G): general international standard*

bibliographic description ..., London IFLA International Office for UBC, 1977.

56 Wells, A. J., *The International MARC network: a study for an international bibliographic data network*, London, IFLA International Office for UBC, 1977 (Occasional paper no.3), iii.

57 See, e.g., Rather, L. J. and De La Garza, P. J., 'Getting it all together: international cataloging cooperation and networks', *Journal of library automation*, **10**, 1977, 163–9; Avram, H., 'International standards'.

58 Avram, H., 'Toward a nationwide library network', *Journal of library administration*, **8**, 1987, 95–116.

59 See, e.g., McCarthy, P., 'CD-ROM – an alternative information distribution medium', in *9th International Online Information Meeting, London, 1985*, Learned Information, 1985, 163–9; Akeroyd, J., Brimage, D. and Royce, C., *Using CD-ROM as a public-access catalogue*, British Library, 1988 (British Library research paper 41).

60 *LCIB*, **47**, (36), 5 September 1988.

61 'Compact discs for national bibliography: Britain and France join forces', *British Library Bibliographic Services newsletter*, **46**, June 1988, 1–3.

62 Information obtained from *Access '89: catalogs and technical publications*, Library of Congress Cataloging Distribution Service; *BLAISE newsletter*, **98**, May/June 1989.

63 Buckland, M. K. and Lynch, C. A., 'The Linked Systems Protocol and the future of bibliographic networks and systems', *Information technology and libraries*, **6**, (1), March 1987, 83–8; McCallum, S., 'Linked Systems Project, Part 1: authorities implementation', *Library hi-tech*, **10**, 1985, 61–8; McCallum, S., 'USA – the Linked Systems Project', in *Open systems interconnection: the communications technology of the 1990s: papers from the Pre-Conference Seminar held in London, 12–14 August 1987*, ed. by Christine Smith, Munich, K. G. Saur, 1988 (IFLA Publications 44), 108–18; Denenberg, R., 'The Linked Systems Project, Part 2: standard network interconnection', *Library hi-tech*, **10**, 1985, 69–79.

64 'Proposals for a UK library database system', *British Library Bibliographic Services Division newsletter*, **27**, November 1982, 2–5.

65 *British Library Bibliographic Services Division newsletter*, **34**, October 1984, 2.

66 *Machine-readable cataloging: 1985 MARC services*, Washington DC, Library of Congress Cataloging Distribution Service, 1985.

67 *Ibid.*, 1987.

68 *LCIB*, **47**, (46), 14 November 1987; *LCIB*, **48**, (17), 24 April 1989.

69 Information obtained from British Library Bibliographic Services information leaflets and from issues of *BLAISE newsletter*.

70 'BLAISE records: a new MARC record service', *British Library Bibliographic Services newsletter*, **43**, June 1987, 7.

71 *British Library Bibliographic Services Division newsletter*, **38**, October 1985, 1–2.

72 *Ibid.*, 3–4.

73 'National MARC records and international exchange', *British Library Bibliographic Services newsletter*, **42**, February 1987, 4–5.

74 *UNIMARC: Universal MARC format*, 2nd ed. rev., recommended by the IFLA Working Group on Content Designators, London, IFLA International Office for UBC, 1980.

75 *MARC formats for bibliographic data*, prepared by the Network Development and MARC Standards Office, Washington DC, Processing Services, Library of Congress, 1980.

76 *UKMARC manual*, 2nd ed., London, British Library Bibliographic Services Division, 1980.

77 *CCF: the Common Communication Format*, Paris, Unesco, 1984.

78 *Documentation: format for bibliographic information interchange on magnetic tape*, ISO 2709–1981, Geneva, International Organization for Standardization, 1981.

79 Bourne, R., 'Harmonization of the ISBDs', *International cataloguing*, **15**, (4), 1986, 39–40.

80 *Anglo-American cataloguing rules*, 2nd ed., 1988 revision, prepared under the direction of the Joint Steering Committee for Revision of AACR, ed. by M. Gorman and P. W. Winkler, Ottawa, Canadian Library Association, London, Library Association Publishing, 1988.

81 *LCIB*, **38**, (7), 16 February 1979, 55.

82 Crawford, W., *op. cit.*, 121.

83 Attig, J., 'The concept of a MARC format', *Information technology and libraries*, **2**, 1983, 7–17.

84 'The USMARC formats: underlying principles', *LCIB*, **42**, (19), 9 May 1982, 148–52. See also Attig, J., 'The US/MARC formats: underlying principles', *Information technology and libraries*, **1**, 1982, 169–75. The principles are reproduced in Crawford, W., *op. cit.*, Appendix A.

85 Crawford, W., *op. cit.*, 186.

86 *Ibid.*

87 *Format integration and its effect on the USMARC bibliographic format*, prepared by Network Development and MARC Standards Office, Washington DC, Cataloging Distribution Service, Library of Congress, 1988, 5.

88 *LCIB*, **46**, (41), 12 October 1987.
89 *LCIB*, **46**, (23), 8 June 1987.
90 *LCIB*, **47**, (39), 26 September 1988.
91 *LCIB*, **44**, (18), 6 May 1985.
92 Crawford, W., *op. cit.*, 73–4.
93 *Ibid.*, 63.
94 *LCIB*, **46**, (23), 8 June 1987.
95 *LCIB*, **40**, (17), 24 April 1981, 141.
96 McCallum, S., 'MARC record-linking technique', *Information technology and libraries*, **1**, 1982, 281–91.
97 *LCIB*, **47**, (17), 25 April 1988, 175–6.
98 *USMARC format for bibliographic data, including guidelines for content designation*, prepared by Network Development and MARC Standards Office, Washington, Cataloging Distribution Service, Library of Congress, 1988, 2 vols. Update no. 1 was announced in *LCIB*, **48**, (12) 20 March 1989, and came into force in July 1989.
99 *USMARC format for authority data, including guidelines for content designation*, prepared by Network Development and MARC Standards Office, Washington DC, Cataloging Distribution Service, Library of Congress, 1987. Two updates appeared in 1988 and 1989.
100 *USMARC format for holdings and locations*, Washington DC, Network Development and MARC Standards Office, Library of Congress, 1984; *USMARC format for holdings and locations, final draft, update no. 1*, 1987. Superseded by *USMARC format for holdings data, including guidelines for content designation*, 1989.
101 *USMARC specifications for record structure, character sets, tapes*, prepared by Network Development and MARC Standards Office, Washington DC, Cataloging Distribution Service, 1987.
102 Full citations for *USMARC code lists* appear in the notes and references section of the Appendix to this chapter.
103 *USMARC character set: Chinese, Japanese, Korean*, prepared by Network Development and MARC Standards Office, Washington DC, Cataloging Distribution Service, Library of Congress, 1987.
104 *USMARC concise formats for bibliographic, authority and holdings data*, Washington DC, Cataloging Distribution Service, Library of Congress, 1988.
105 *Authorities: a MARC format*, prelim. ed., Washington DC, Library of Congress, 1976.
106 *Authorities: a MARC format*, Washington DC, Library of Congress, 1981.

107 *LCIB*, **48**, (9), 27 February 1989, 84.
108 Pope, N. F., 'Developing a format for holdings and location data', in *The USMARC format for holdings and locations: development, implementation and use*, ed. by B. B. Baker, New York, Haworth Press, 1988, 3–37.
109 *Ibid.*, 9–10.
110 Crawford, W., *op. cit.*, 201.
111 *UKMARC manual*, 1st standard ed., London, British Library Bibliographic Services Division, 1975, 19.
112 *UKMARC manual*, 2nd ed., London, British Library Bibliographic Services Division, 1980–7, 5/1.
113 *Cataloguing practice notes for UKMARC records*, London, BLAISE, 1981–3.
114 *BLAISE newsletters*, **79**, March/April 1986, 9; **80**, May/June 1986, 2–3.
115 Long, A., *op. cit.*, 7.
116 Verbal communication, British Library Bibliographic Services. Part 1 of the 3rd ed. was formally issued in December 1989.
117 Long, A., *op. cit.*, 8.
118 Ashford, J. H., 'Storage and retrieval of bibliographic records: a comparison of database-management-system (DBMS) and free-text approaches', *Program*, **18**, 1984, 16–45.
119 *Canadian MARC: a report of the activities of the MARC Task Group resulting in a recommended 'Canadian MARC format for monographs' and a 'Canadian MARC format for serials'*, Ottawa, National Library of Canada, 1972.
120 *Canadian MARC communication format: monographs*, 3rd ed., Ottawa, National Library of Canada, 1979– (looseleaf); also *Canadian MARC communication format: monographs*, 2nd ed., Ottawa, National Library of Canada, 1974– (looseleaf).
121 National Library of Australia, *Australian MARC specification: books*, 3rd ed., Canberra, National Library of Australia, 1979.
122 National Library of Australia, *Australian MARC specification: authorities*, Canberra, National Library of Australia, 1988.
123 *Maschinelles Austauschformat für Bibliotheken (MAB1)*, Deutsche Forschungsgemeinschaft, Berlin, Arbeitsstelle für Bibliothekstechnik, 1973.
124 *MADOK: Magnetband Austauschformat für Dokumentationszwecke*, herausgegeben von der Zentralstelle für maschinelle Dokumentation (ZMD), Frankfurt, Verlag Dokumentation, 1977.
125 *ANNAMARC: specifiche relative ai nastri magnetici contenenti i record della Bibliografia Nazionale Italiana nel formato ANNAMARC*, Florence, Bibliografia Nazionale Italiana, 1977.

126 *DANMARC: 1. udgave omfattende monografier*, Ballerup, Biblioteks-centralen, 1979.
127 *Formato IBERMARC para monografías: manual*, Madrid, Ministerio de Educación y Ciencia, Comisaría Nacional de Bibliotecas, Centro de Proceso de Datos, 1976.
128 *IBERMARC(M): esquema del formata IBERMARC para publicaciones monográficas: puesta al día de 1985*, Madrid, [s.n.], 1985.
129 *SWEMARC: format specification*, compiled on behalf of the Bibliographical Institute by Marie-Louise Bacjman and Sten Hedberg, Stockholm, Royal Library, 1980.
130 *Japan/MARC manual*, 3rd ed., National Diet Library, 1988 (includes convention for the recording of Kanji). First edition, 1981.
131 *SAMARC: South African national format for the exchange of machine-readable bibliographic descriptions*, Working Group for Bibliographic Standards, Committee for the Computerized Cataloguing Network, National Library Advisory Council, Pretoria, The Council, 1982.
132 Chinese MARC Working Group, Library Automation Planning Committee, *Chinese MARC format*, Taipei, National Central Library, 1982.
133 *Base Nacional de Dados Bibliográficos: manual de operações*, Lisbon, Biblioteca Nacional, 1986. Cover title: *UNIMARC: manual de operações*.
134 Willer, M., ed., Priručnik za UNIMARC, Zagreb, National and University Library, 1989.
135 Anglada i de Ferrer, Lluís M., *El Format MARC i l'intercanvi d'informació bibliogràfica a Catalunya*, Barcelona, Diputació de Barcelona, 1988, 5.
136 *Manual del CATMARC*, Barcelona, Institut Catalá de Bibliografia, 1987.
137 Anglada i de Ferrer, Lluís M., *op. cit., passim.*
138 *INTERMARC(M): format bibliographique d'échange pour les monographies: manuel*, Paris, Bibliothèque Nationale, 1975.
139 Council of Europe, *EUDISED: standards, format, character representation*, Strasbourg, Documentation Centre for Education in Europe, 1973, containing Linford, J. E., 'Draft EUDISED format'.
140 Linford, J. E., 'The EUDISED format: a structure which will contain any type of formalized document record', in International Symposium on Bibliographic Exchange Formats, *Towards a common bibliographic exchange format?* Proceedings, Budapest, OMKDK, 1978, 116–18.
141 *Meždunarodnyj kommunikativnyj format – MEKOF 2. Soderzanie i*

127

sposob predstavlenija dannyh v zapisi dlja obmena informaciej na magnitnoj lente (NTP-MCNTI 19 – 77) Specifikacija elementov dannyh, Moscow, ICSTI, 1977. [International communication format – MEKOF 2: content and method of presentation of data in the record for exchange of information on magnetic tape: specification of data elements.]

142 *Format dija obmena bibliograficeskoj informaciej na magnitnoj lente*, Moscow, ICSTI, 1974 (NTP ICSTI 1 – 74) [Magnetic tape for bibliographic information interchange].

143 *Kommunikativnyi format zapisi dannyh na magnitnoj lente*, Moscow, ICSTI, 1974 (NTP ICSTI 2 – 74) [Communication format for data records on magnetic tape].

144 Faunce, S. S. A., *MARCAL, manual para la automatización de las reglas catalográficas para América Latina*, Río Piedras, Puerto Rico, Universidad de Puerto Rico, Escuela Graduada de Bibliotecología, 1977 (Manuales de bibliotecario no.9). Based on Library of Congress, *Books: a MARC format* and Library of Congress, *Serials: a MARC format.*

145 Barbosa, Alice Príncipe, *Projecto CALCO, catalogacao cooperativa automatizada*, Rio de Janeiro, Instituto Brasileiro de Bibliografia e Documentacao, 1973.

146 Fundação Getúlio Vargas, *CALCO-BIBLIODATA: manuel*, Rio de Janeiro, The Foundation, 1981.

147 IBICT, *Formato IBICT: formato de intercâmbio bibliográfico e catalográfico*, Brasilia, IBICT, 1987.

148 Woods, E. W., *The MINISIS/UNIMARC project final report*, London, IFLA UBCIM Programme, 1988.

149 Quiroga, Luz Marina and others, Una nueva etapa en la historia de la Bibliografía Mexicana: su automatización, 1987 (unpublished).

150 *Guía para la definición de bases de datos compatibles con el formato MARC*, Mexico City, UNAM, Instituto de Investigaciones Bibliográficas and Biblioteca Nacional, 1987.

151 *Guidelines for data elements and record format for computer-based bibliographical databases for bibliographic description of different kinds of documents*, New Delhi, Bureau of Indian Standards, 1985 (IS 11370 – 1985).

152 Lahiri, A. and Sunder Singh, B. G., 'Bibliographic databases and networks: the Indian scenario', *Astinfo newsletter*, **4**, (3), 1989, 6 – 7.

153 Maenmas Chevalit. Final report: the National Seminar on Standards for Bibliographic Control, Bangkok, 1989, unpublished.

154 Lim Huck-Tee, 'The Malaysian MARC (MALMARC) project', *Program*, **14**, (3), 101–20.

155 Massil, S. W., *Study of the feasibility of using MARC tapes for cooperative processing*, Paris, Unesco, 1977.

156 *Format MARC Indonesia (INDOMARC) untuk buku*, Jakarta, Perpustakaan Nasional R.I., 1989.

157 *International guide to MARC databases and services: national magnetic tape and online services*, 2nd rev. ed., Frankfurt, Deutsche Bibliothek, The International MARC Project, 1986.

Appendix to Chapter 3:
Current UK and USMARC:
Comparative summaries

These summaries are based on current MARC documentation.[1] Although both US and UKMARC are implementations
of ISO 2709, there are minor structural differences between the
two, and more significant divergences in content designation
and content, which mean that conversion programs must be
applied by the Library of Congress and the British Library to
enable exchange records to be distributed and used with
national records. Where terminology differs, the terms used in
the relevant documentation are preferred. It must be noted that
the American documentation is far more extensive than the
British – there are three USMARC communications formats
– and the *USMARC format for bibliographic data* contains many
more fields than its British counterpart. As mentioned earlier,
UKMARC is undergoing a phased revision, the second phase
due for completion in 1990. *BLAISE newsletter* is the main
vehicle for advance notification of format changes.[2] USMARC
formats are also subject to continuous revision; amendments
and changes are regularly reported in *Library of Congress
information bulletins*, and in *USMARC format: proposed changes*,
available on subscription from the Library of Congress.[3]

Magnetic exchange-tape format and labelling specifications
are excluded from these summaries. They may be found in
Section 2 of the *UKMARC manual* and in *USMARC specifications
for record structure, character sets, tapes*, pp.26–37.[4]

UKMARC
UKMARC format specifications are set out in *UKMARC
manual*, second edition, 1980–7. The format described is the
British national MARC format, although heavily influenced by

the needs of the printed *British national bibliography*, which is produced from UKMARC records created by British Library Bibliographic Services. UKMARC is a single, unitary format designed to accommodate all types of material, with some material-specific fields. UKMARC exchange tapes at present contain records only for monographs and first issues of periodicals published in the United Kingdom.

Structure

The physical structure of UKMARC is based on ISO 2709 and BS 4748 (Figure 3.4).

Record label	Directory	Control fields	Variable data fields

Fig. 3.4   UKMARC record structure

(a) *Record label*

The record label (called 'leader' in USMARC) is a fixed field of 24 characters containing coded information about the record which assists processing.

Character position	*Information given*
1 – 5	record length, i.e. total number of characters, including all data and content designation.
6	record status (new, changed, deleted, confirmed CIP, revised CIP). A proposal has been made to change the last code definition to 'increase in encoding level', for records reviewed and augmented by BL as a result of shared cataloguing.[5]
7 – 10	implementation codes, used to indicate type of material and class of record (in other formats styled 'bibliographic level'); although 14 types of record are possible, records on UKMARC exchange tapes currently only have codes 'a' for printed language material, or 'e' for printed cartographic material. Class of record allows for four codes, of which only two, 'm' for monographs and 's' for serials, appear on current exchange tapes.

131

11	indicator count, always '2' in UKMARC, as two indicators are used for each data field.
12	subfield mark count, showing the number of symbols used to identify subfields, always '2' in UKMARC.
13–17	base address of data, giving the total number of characters of the record label and the directory, including the end-of-directory field terminator (to provide the computer with the exact location of the first data field in the record).
18	encoding level, indicates the degree of completeness of the record. Codes currently defined are 'ƀ' for full level, '8' for CIP records. Two further codes are proposed: '5' for partial (preliminary) level records created under the Copyright Libraries Shared Cataloguing Programme; and '7', for minimal level records converted from USMARC.[6]
19–20	unused, contain blanks (spaces).
21–24	directory map, showing the lengths of certain parts of the directory. Character positions 21 and 22 indicate length of 'length of data field' part of each directory entry (value 4 in UKMARC exchange records) and length of 'starting character position' part of each directory entry (value 5 in UKMARC exchange records). Character position 23 holds the 'length of the implementation-defined part' of each directory entry, in conformity with ISO 2709. This is always 0 (zero), as UKMARC does not make use of the implementation-defined part. Character position 24 is unused.

It should be noted that ISO 2709 and BS 4748 use another method of counting character positions in fixed fields, based on the notion of character displacement. As the first character in a string 'displaces' no other characters, it is counted as 0 (zero). USMARC also uses this method. UKMARC uses character positioning, so that the first character in a string is counted as 1 (one). ISO character positions 17–19 in the record label are left for definition by user systems. These correspond to character positions 18–20 in UKMARC, of which only 18 is used, the others being left blank.

(b) *The directory*

The directory begins in character position 25 of UKMARC. It contains a series of 12-character entries, each referring to a data field in the record (Figure 3.5). Repeated fields are represented by separate directory entries.

TAG (3 characters)	LENGTH OF DATA FIELD (4 characters)	STARTING CHARACTER POSITION (5 characters)

Fig. 3.5   Structure of a UKMARC directory entry

The tag, a three-digit label which identifies an associated data field in the record, is held only in the directory, and not with the data in the appropriate field. The length of data field contains four characters, implying that fields may contain a maximum of 9999 characters although in practice only 999 are permitted in UKMARC. All content designation is included. Starting character position is calculated by displacement, and shows the starting character position of the data field to which the entry refers.

082	0011	00092

Fig. 3.6   Example of an entry in the directory, UKMARC

From the example (Figure 3.6) it can be seen that the record to which this directory entry refers contains a field tagged 082 (current Dewey classification number); that the field contains 11 characters, including all content designators; and that 92 characters precede this field in the data portion of the record. Directory entries appear in ascending tag order, with entries for control fields preceding those for variable data fields. Where subrecords are present (i.e. records containing analytical entries, perhaps for individual items within a collection), subrecord directory entries must be added, following the entries for the record as a whole (Figures 3.7 and 3.8).

1. 100.10 $aAdams$hFrancis#
    245.10 $aHistory of the elementary school contest in England$eFrancis Adams$jTogether
    with The struggle for national education$eJohn Morley$eedited, with an introduction, by
    Asa Briggs#
    700.11 $aBriggs$hAsa$r1921-#
    100.10:1 $aMorley$hJohn$c1838-1923#
    245.14:1 $aThe struggle for national education#

2. 100.10 $aUpex$hR. V.#
    245.10 $aEmployment protection legislation$dR.V. Upex#
    505.00 $aIncludes the text of the Employment Protection (Consolidation) Act 1978#
    790.00 $al. Ti 2. Great Britain 3. Employment Protection (Consolidation) Act 1978#
    110.10:1 $aGreat Britain#
    240.40:1 $aEmployment Protection (Consolidation) Act 1978#
    245.00:1 $aEmployment Protection (Consolidation) Act 1978$bElizabeth II. 1978. Chapter
    44#

3. 100.10 $aSimenon$hGeorges$r1903-#
    245.10 $aAfrican trio$dGeorges Simenon#
    505.00 $aContents: Talatala / translated by Stuart Gilbert. Translation of: Le blanc à
    lunettes – Tropic moon / translated by Stuart Gilbert. This translation originally published:
    New York : Harcourt, Brace, 1943. Translation of: La coup de lune – Aboard the Aquitaine /
    translated by Paul Auster and Lydia Davis. Translation of: 45° à l'ombre#
    790.00 $al. Ti 2. Contents(6)#
    100.10:1 $aSimenon$hGeorges$r1903-#
    240.23:1 $aLe blanc à lunettes$rEnglish#
    245.10:1 $aTalatala#
    100.10:2 $aSimenon$hGeorges$r1903-#
    240.23:2 $aLa coup de lune$rEnglish#
    245.10:2 $aTropic moon#
    100.10:3 $aSimenon$hGeorges$r1903-#
    240.20:3 $a45° à l'ombre$rEnglish#
    245.10:3 $aAboard the Aquitaine#

Fig. 3.7 Examples of records containing analytical levels as coded for MARC input

(Reproduced from *UKMARC manual*, 2nd ed., with permission of the British Library Board)

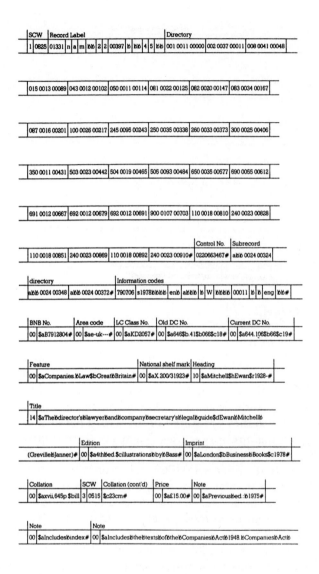

Fig. 3.8 **A record containing subrecords, and spanning two
blocks, as held on the UKMARC exchange tape**

(Reproduced from *UKMARC manual*, 2nd ed., with permission of the
British Library Board)

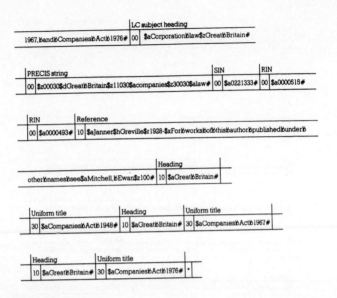

		LC subject heading
1967,bandbCompaniesbActb1976#	00	$aCorporationblaw$zGreatbBritain#

PRECIS string		SIN		RIN	
00	$z00030$dGreatbBritain$z11030$acompanies$z30030$alaw#	00	$a0221333#	00	$a0000515#

RIN		Reference	
00	$a0000493#	10	$aJanner$hGreville$r1928-$xForbworksbofbthisbauthorbpublishedbunderb

		Heading	
otherbnamesbsee$aMitchell,bEwan$z100#	10	$aGreatbBritain#	

Uniform title		Heading		Uniform title	
30	$aCompaniesbActb1948#	10	$aGreatbBritain#	30	$aCompaniesbActb1967#

Heading		Uniform title		
10	$aGreatbBritain#	30	$aCompaniesbActb1976#	*

Fig. 3.8 (cont.)

(c) *Control fields*

Control fields supply information needed for the processing of the record. ISO reserves tags 002–009 for reserved fields required by the implementing agency. Control fields have no indicators or subfield marks. They follow the directory and the order in which they are stored in the record parallels that of the corresponding directory entries. There are three control fields in UKMARC: 001, record control number (corresponds to ISO 2709 record identifier field), 002, subrecord directory data field, and 008, information codes field. For records produced for the *British national bibliography* and associated databases and services, the record control number is at present the ISBN; for items without ISBN, the BNB number is used. The subrecord directory data field (002) occurs only when subrecords are present. A record containing analytical records will therefore contain an 002 field among its control fields. The 002 field, which is automatically generated, holds data on the length and position of each subrecord directory, in sequences of 12-character data elements. The information codes field (008) is a fixed field of 40 characters, containing a wide range of information in coded form. Its main purpose is to allow machine retrieval (or exclusion) of records sharing certain characteristics, without the need for scanning of data fields, which might be time-consuming and costly.

(d) *Variable data fields*
The variable data fields follow the control fields and contain the bibliographic or cataloguing data. Approximately 125 fields have been defined or reserved for use in UKMARC, allowing individual users of the format ample scope for adding fields for local data (normally in unreserved 9-- fields). The variable data fields are arranged in blocks which reflect the areas of a traditional catalogue entry (Figure 3.9). Their structure is illustrated in Figure 3. 10.

TAG	DEFINITION
Control fields	
001	Record control number
002	Subrecord directory datafield
008	Information codes
Coded data fields	
010	Library of Congress card number
015	British National Bibliography number
016	Authority control information field
017	Correction message
018	Amendment message
021	International Standard Book Number (ISBN)
022	International Standard Serial Number (ISSN)
*024	BLAISE number
026	International Standard Cartographic Number (ISCN) (reserved for future use)
031	Relief, projection and prime meridian coded information field
032	Geodetic, grid and vertical measurement coded information field
034	Scale and co-ordinates coded information field
036	Dates (cartographic materials)
037	Physical description coded information field
038	Aerial photography and remote sensing coded information field
041	Languages
043	Area codes
044	Country of producer
046	Coded data – music
047	Form of composition – music (reserved for future use)
048	Number of instruments or voices – music (reserved for future use)
050	Library of Congress classification number
062	Cartographic classification number
080	Universal Decimal Classification number
081	Dewey Decimal Classification number (old edition)
082	Dewey Decimal Classification number (current edition)
083	Verbal feature
085	British Catalogue of Music classification number
*087	National shelf mark
092	British Library Lending Division shelfmark (reserved for future use)
*093	'Back-up' libraries' serial holdings (reserved for future use)
*095	Science Reference Library classmark

Fig. 3.9 Summary statement of data fields

(Reproduced from *UKMARC manual*, 2nd ed., with permission of the British Library Board)

Main entry heading fields

100	Personal name main entry heading
110	Corporate name main entry heading
111	Conference, congress, meeting, etc. name main entry heading

Title fields

222	Key-title
240	Uniform title – excluding collective title
243	Collective title
245	Title and statement of responsibility area
248	Second level and subsequent level title and statement of responsibility information relating to a multipart item

Edition field

250	Edition area

Material specific fields

254	Musical presentation area
255	Numeric and/or alphabetic, chronological or other designation area (serials)
256	Mathematical data area (cartographic materials)

Imprint field

260	Publication, distribution, etc. area

Physical description field

300	Physical description area

Price field

350	Terms of availability

TAG   **DEFINITION**

Series statement fields (cf 800-840)

440	Series area – title of series in added entry heading form
490	Series area – title of series not in added entry heading form

Notes fields

500	Nature, scope or artistic form note
501	"With" note
502	Dissertation note
503	Edition and history note (monographs), relationships with other serials note (serials)
504	Bibliography and index note
505	Contents note
508	Statements of responsibility note
511	ISBN and ISSN note
513	Summary note
514	Title proper, parallel title and other title information note
515	Numbering and chronological designation note (serials)
516	Mathematical and other cartographic data note (cartographic materials)
518	Change of control number note*
521	Audience note
525	Accompanying materials and supplements note
528	Publication, distribution, etc. note
530	Other versions available note
531	Physical description note
532	Series note
534	Reference to published descriptions note
536	Note relating to original (graphic materials and microforms)
537	Program note (machine-readable data files)
538	Numbers borne by the item note
542	Mode of use note (machine-readable data files)
546	Language of the item and/or translation or adaptation note
554	Frequency note (serials)
555	Indexes note (serials)
556	Item described note (serials)
557	Graphic index and characteristic sheet note (cartographic materials)

Fig. 3.9 (contd.)

138

Fig. 3.9 (contd.)

Naturally, not all variable data fields are present in every record. Some fields, such as National Shelf Mark, are reserved for British Library use. Of the 29 defined notes fields (500–557), perhaps only one or two will need to be used for any given record; many are material-specific. Many fields are repeatable.

INDICATORS (2 digits)	FIRST SUBFIELD MARK	SUBFIELD DATA
SECOND AND SUBSEQUENT SUBFIELD MARK	SUBFIELD DATA	FIELD MARK

Fig. 3.10   Structure of variable data field in UKMARC

Data fields for subrecords appear after the last data field for the record as a whole.

Character set

UKMARC exchange-tape records are encoded in modified ASCII (eight-bit extended version). This includes many diacritical marks, graphic characters and letters from languages other than English, (e.g. Polish Ł and Scandinavian ø) but only three Greek characters (α, β, γ). USMARC records reformatted to UKMARC are in the same character set. The US character set, however, contains more characters, some of which cannot be represented in the UKMARC set; these are converted to the nearest equivalents, as shown in the last page of Appendix K of the *UKMARC manual*.

Content designation

Content designators are defined in UKMARC as 'the means of identifying data elements and/or providing additional information about a data element' (Appendix L: Glossary). UKMARC content designators are (field) tags, indicators and subfield marks. Similar functions are served by:

*level numbers; *repeat numbers; information codes; field marks; record marks (* = not held in the machine record; used as input conventions).

(a) *Field tags*

Field tags consist of three digits. ISO 2709 permits any combination of numeric and alphabetic characters, but in UKMARC tags are numeric (001/999). Field tags identify whole fields, defining a particular function or bibliographic condition. They are used at input, but held only once, in the directory, in the machine record.

(b) *Indicators*

Indicators are used in variable data fields, not in control fields. They precede the data in the field and supply information about the contents of the field and/or show how the field is to be manipulated for particular functions, e.g. catalogue production. Two-digit indicators are used in UKMARC; each has its own meaning within the context of a given field.

(c) *Level numbers*

Level numbers are single digits. Their purpose is to tell the computer whether the field refers to a main entry for an item (i.e. the record as a whole) or to an analytical entry within the record. Level numbers are not held in the machine record, but are used to set up the appropriate subrecord directory data field (002) and corresponding subrecord directories following the main directory. (Some software packages may hold level numbers in the machine record.) USMARC does not use this technique.

(d) *Repeat numbers*

Repeat numbers are single digits, also not held in the machine record, but useful at input. They signify valid field repeats. The first occurrence of a field is repeat 0 (zero), the second repeat 1, the third repeat 2, and so on. Repetition of fields depends directly on the nature of the bibliographic record; commonly repeated fields are added entries for personal and corporate names. Repeat numbers are used in particular to link fields containing references to the relevant main and added-entry fields, e.g.

900.10$aDuran$hPeter Spyers-$xSee$aSpyers-Duran,
   Peter$z700/1#

The reference here is linked to the second occurrence of a personal-name added-entry field.

The notes accompanying each field indicate whether or not a field is repeatable. Appendix J of the *UKMARC manual*, which lists valid fields, indicators, subfields, levels and repeats, also shows the number of times a field can be repeated at the same level and gives information on the repeatability of subfields (shown by code 'R').

(e) *Subfield marks*

Each variable data field must contain at least one subfield. Subfield marks in UKMARC consist of a special character (ASCII value 31) represented graphically by a dollar sign, followed by a lower-case alphabetic character: $a, $b, etc. They precede and identify data elements within fields and can be repeated where necessary, e.g. to specify two separate places of

141

publication. Like indicators, they have special meanings within fields. Subfield marks may be given punctuational and typographic values. In UKMARC subfield marks are related, where appropriate, to AACR/ISBD punctuation, and no punctuation appears at subfield boundaries. USMARC does not follow this practice. Only a limited amount of punctuation, therefore, need be supplied by those creating UKMARC records, although punctuation within subfields must be supplied. Subfields are normally input in the order in which they are to appear in the final product; this is usually but not invariably alphabetical. UKMARC also contains many 'non-printing' subfields (i.e. for data to be held in the machine record, but not displayed in printed *BNB* and other products).

(f) *Codes*

Coded data appear in several parts of the UKMARC record (e.g. the record label, the 032, 034, 036 and 037 fields), though most significantly in the 008 field. The coded data recorded here represent information about the record as a whole (its nature, content) and/or about specific characteristics of the record which may be useful for processing and retrieval, e.g. date of publication, presence and nature of illustrative matter, general class of material, form of publication. In UKMARC the codes are mainly lower-case letters, although there are some numeric codes used, and upper-case letters are used for material designation codes. The *UKMARC manual* provides, for the convenience of cataloguers, input subfield marks which can be programmed to cause the codes to be placed in the correct fixed positions. This depends on the software used for data entry and does not form part of the UKMARC format.

Here is an example of an information codes (008) field in UKMARC:

1					6	7	8		
8	9	0	6	0	6	s	1	9	8

					16			19	
8					e	n		b	

			24					29	30
			W					0	0

31	32	33		36					40
0	1	1			e	n	g		b

Explanation:

Character positions	Information
1–6	Date entered on file, i.e. 6 June 1989
7	s = single date of publication, i.e. 1988
8–15	date(s) of publication (date 1 only used)
16–18	en = published in England
19	b = contains maps
24	W = text (corresponds to General Material Designation in *AACR2*)
29	0 = not a government publication
30	0 = not a conference
31	0 = not a Festschrift
32	1 = has an index
33	1 = heading repeated in title area
36–38	eng = main language of text is English
40	b = provenance code for British Library record

Using the input subfield marks provided in the UKMARC manual, this could be coded as:

008 890606 $as1988 $ben $ob $pW $e0 $f0 $g0 $h1 $i1 $leng $nb

(g) *Field marks*
Field marks (ASCII value 30), called 'field separators' in ISO 2709 and 'field terminators' in USMARC, show the end of fields. UKMARC external (graphic) representation is the hash sign (#).

Given that the start of each field is recorded in the directory and signalled in the record by the appearance of the indicators, the field mark is perhaps redundant, but it is considered desirable as a double-checking device and has value for some processing applications.

(h) *Record marks*
Record marks (ASCII value 29), called 'record separators' in ISO 2709 and 'record terminators' in USMARC, follow the field mark of the last data field in each record. UKMARC external (graphic) representation is the asterisk (*).

(i) *Input convention*

The input convention in UKMARC is as follows:

TAG . INDICATORS : LEVEL / REPEAT   FIRST
SUBFIELD MARK   DATA ELEMENT   SECOND AND
SUBSEQUENT SUBFIELD MARK   DATA ELEMENT ...
END OF FIELD MARK

e.g. 300.00 : 0/0 $a350p.$bill.$c28cm#

    245.14 : 0/0 $aThe aims of history$bvalues of the
    historical attitude$dDavid Thomson#

NB: level and repeat numbers are normally omitted when the setting is 0 (zero).

Content

The content of a UKMARC record is the data recorded in the fields. This is determined by external input standards and by the nature of the item being recorded. The UKMARC format is closely linked with AACR2 and the analysis of fields and subfields is based on that present in AACR2. This certainly promotes standardization and encourages the sharing of bibliographic data, but means that the national format does not easily support non-AACR2 catalogue data. A full UKMARC record is a substantial data package, including comprehensive bibliographic description, constructed according to AACR2/ISBD principles, and structured access points for names of persons, bodies and uniform titles, formulated according to AACR2. Fields are defined in UKMARC for several class numbers: Dewey, Library of Congress, UDC, British Catalogue of Music class number and cartographic class number. (MARC users may add extra fields to carry other class numbers.) The verbal subject data fields include Library of Congress topical and geographic subject headings and PRECIS strings. If these are not required, local fields may be added, for example to carry locally generated subject headings or descriptors. Although access points and bibliographic description are for the most part held in different fields – an obvious exception being the 245 (title and statement of responsibility area) field – this distinction breaks down when MARC records are made available online. It must be said that UKMARC is more flexible in its approach to subject data than to bibliographic description, or choice of author/title access points for records.

144

Appendix N: *Recommended standard for bibliographic records exchanged in the UK national network*, was incorporated in the *UKMARC manual* in 1986. Prepared originally by the Cooperative Automation Group as a common input standard for the proposed national library database systems (UKLDS), the provisions have been widened to cover a range of materials (printed monographs, serials, audiovisual and cartographic materials, music) and to facilitate exchange of records between libraries by setting out a recommended level of cataloguing. AACR2 is the required cataloguing standard. Three categories of data elements are indicated:

M = mandatory if applicable
R = recommended if applicable
O = optional

Relationships in UKMARC

UKMARC does not at present support record-to-record links, or explicit links between records and authority files. Some intra-record links, however, are provided. The 9-- fields carry references needed for the generation of printed *BNB*, but are useful also for catalogues and printed bibliographies of other kinds. Each reference field contains an identification of the field to which the reference is made:

900.10 $aLewis$hCecil Day-$xSee$aDay-Lewis, Cecil$z100#

In this example the reference is made to the 100 or personal-name main-entry heading field. The link is one-directional, with nothing in the 100 field to indicate that a reference has been made. USMARC does not use fields with 9-- tags for references of this nature – a separate authority format is used.

UKMARC can carry subrecords, i.e. groups of fields within a record that can be treated as an entity. This enables the display of hierarchical relationships and the making of analytical entries for parts of items, for example individual contributions within a collection. Techniques for handling analytical records have already been described.

UKMARC also supports multilevel description for monographic items. For each separately catalogued part of a multipart item, a separate MARC record is made, containing the entire hierarchy of bibliographic levels. The title of the work

as a whole appears in field 245 (title and statement of responsibility) and special indicator settings in other appropriate fields,
e.g. 250 (edition), 260 (publication area), are used to link data
in these fields either with the part or with the whole work. Only
one extra field is needed to support this technique: the 248
(second and subsequent level title and statement of
responsibility field) carries the title and related data for the
individual part.

USMARC

There are three USMARC communications formats: *USMARC
format for bibliographic data, USMARC format for authority data* and
USMARC format for holdings and locations. All are implementations
of ANSI Z39.2, *American National Standard for bibliographic
information interchange on magnetic tape*,[7] which conforms with ISO
2709. For convenience and brevity, USMARC formats are
referred to as *UFBD, UFAD* and *UFHL*. It must be emphasized
that these abbreviations have no official status.

Structure

The physical structure for all USMARC formats (Figure 3.11)
is described in *USMARC specifications for record structure, character
sets, tapes*. It is similar to the structure of the UKMARC record,
although there are some differences in terminology and in
definition of fields.

LEADER	DIRECTORY	VARIABLE FIELDS
		CONTROL DATA

Fig. 3.11   USMARC record structure

(a) *Leader*
The leader is a fixed field of 24 characters, with positions
counted from 0–23. Character positions 0–4 are occupied by
logical record length (record length in UKMARC and ISO
2709) and character position 5 by record status. Character
position 6 shows type of record: different values can appear
here, depending on whether the record is for a bibliographic
item, authority data, or holdings/locations. Character position
7 is for bibliographic level, defined only for bibliographic and

holdings/locations records. Codes are included for monograph and serial component parts, collections, subunits (i.e. parts of collections), monographs and serials. Codes in character positions 6 and 7 determine the definition of the 008, fixed-length data elements, field. Character positions 8–9 are reserved for future use and left blank in current records. Indicator count and subfield codes count (character position 10–11) are both, as in UKMARC, always '2'. Base address of data holds a five-character numeric string which is the total of the lengths of leader and directory, including the field terminator at the end of the directory. Character positions 17–19 (ISO 'implementation-defined' positions) are used in different ways, according to the type of record (bibliographic, authority, holdings/locations). The entry map (character position 20–3) shows the structure of the entries in the directory; as USMARC does not make use of the 'implementation-defined' fourth part of the directory allowed in ISO 2709, character position 22 is always 0 (zero). Character position 23 is undefined, and also set at zero.

(b) *The directory*
The directory begins in character position 24. Its nature and function are identical to those described for UKMARC, with the following exceptions: (i) USMARC records have less restriction on length of fields, with maximum 9999 characters; (ii) USMARC contains no subrecord directory entries, as analytical records are not handled via the directory; (iii) character positions are counted from zero.

(c) *Variable fields*
Following the directory are the variable fields, comprising control fields and data fields. The control fields precede data fields, as in UKMARC, and have neither indicators nor sub-field codes. Control fields defined or reserved in USMARC are

001 control number, assignable by the agency which creates, uses or distributes the record. Records distributed by LC contain LC control numbers.

002	subrecord map of directory	reserved but never
003	subrecord relationship	defined and deleted
004	related record directory	in 1988

005	date and time of latest transaction (based on ANSI X3.30 and X3.43)[8]
006	fixed-length data elements – additional material characteristics
007	physical description fixed field
008	fixed-length data elements: coded information useful for retrieval and manipulation of data.

Fields 006 and 007 are } not defined in authority records

Definition and content of fields 006–008 depend on the nature of the record.

009	Physical description fixed field for archival collections was made obsolete in 1986. The field is at present reserved for local use.

Data fields in USMARC follow the variable control fields. Their definition depends on the format: bibliographic, authority or holdings/locations. In structure (Figure 3.14), they closely resemble those in UKMARC.

INDICATORS (TWO DIGITS)	FIRST SUBFIELD CODE	SUBFIELD DATA

SECOND AND SUBSEQUENT SUBFIELD CODE	SUBFIELD DATA	FIELD TERMINATOR

Fig. 3.14   Structure of data field in USMARC

Character set

USMARC records are encoded in ASCII (eight-bit) code for information interchange (ANSI X3.4) and ANSEL, the *Extended Latin alphabet coded character set for bibliographic use* (ANSI Z39.47). Three separate character sets containing 14 superscript, 14 subscript and three Greek characters (α, β, γ) may be added. *USMARC specifications for record structure, character sets, tapes*, gives full details of the USMARC character sets, including explanations of techniques used to access alternative graphic character sets. Field 066 (Character sets present) is used in the bibliographic data format to show the presence in the record of alternative character sets, normally in conjunction with data field 880 (Alternate graphic representations). *USMARC character set: Chinese, Japanese, Korean*, lists codes developed by RLIN for the representation and storage of Chinese, Japanese and Korean characters and now used in USMARC records.[9]

Content designation

USMARC uses several kinds of content designators, defined separately for each format: field tags; indicators; subfield codes; coded values; field terminators; record terminators.

USMARC has three-digit field tags, which, as in UKMARC, are stored not with the data for the fields, but in the directory. Some tags (in general those containing the digit '9') are reserved for local implementation: in particular the 9-- fields in each of the formats can be used for local data.

Indicators are two characters, which may be numeric or alphabetic, although only numeric digits are at present used. Undefined indicator positions contain spaces/blanks (ƀ) (ASCII value 32). Their use is as in UKMARC, though UKMARC prefers 'zero' to 'space'.

Subfield codes (known as 'subfield marks' in UKMARC) consist of a delimiter (ASCII value 31, graphic representation ǂ) followed by a data-element identifier, which may be a lower-case letter or a digit. The number 9 and certain other graphic characters are reserved for local use. Subfield codes are for purposes of identification only and do not carry punctuation values, although these can be assigned by program for local use.

Codes are used in the leader, in control fields and in some data fields. Codes common to all formats include:

n   not applicable
u   unknown
ƀ   undefined
| fill character, ASCII value 124 (record creator has not attempted to supply a code, although one is expected).

Codes used in USMARC bibliographic, authority and holdings/locations formats can be found in the *USMARC code lists*, which contain codes for countries, geographic areas, languages, relators (terms indicating relationship between name and work, e.g. 'adapter'), sources (e.g. of subject category codes and terms) and description conventions (e.g. AACR2 or non-AACR2 compatible).[10]

Field terminators ('field marks' in UKMARC) mark the ends of fields. In USMARC ASCII value 30 is used; it has no graphic representation.

Record terminators ('record marks' in UKMARC, and 'group separators' in ASCII) are the last characters in records. ASCII value is 29; there is no graphic representation.

Content

The content of a USMARC record is determined by several factors: the record format (bibliographic, authority, holdings/locations), external input standards and, in the case of bibliographic and holdings records, the nature of the item for which the record is made. Each format incorporates national-level record requirements, i.e. stipulations on content for full-level records intended for contribution to a national database. Four codes are used:

M = Mandatory
O = Optional
A = Mandatory if applicable
U = Unused (undefined, or not relevant for a particular item)

The content of USMARC records is discussed under the separate headings for each format.

Full Level Record Examples

The examples in this appendix reflect the application of USMARC content designators in a full level record context. Although the data is taken from actual bibliographic records, these records are included for illustrative purposes only and are not usable for bibliographic purposes.

Note that the creator of the bibliographic data is not specified: field 008/39 contains code d (Other sources), and field 040, subfields ‡a and ‡c contain the dummy phrase <NUC symbol>. In addition, field 001 contains the dummy phrase <control number>, indicating that the record is an example only. The system-generated portions of the Leader (LDR) are represented by asterisks (*). The records also lack a system-generated Directory. Field 008 character positions have been segmented to improve readability. The exact segmentation varies, however the first two segments are always 0-5 and 6-14, and the last segment is always 35-39.

FULL LEVEL RECORD - BOOK

This example can be identified as a record for language material by code a in Leader/06, and further as a monograph· by code m in Leader/07. The record contains the basic bibliographic information fields (fields 100, 245, 260, and 300), as well as additional fields, e.g., fields 020 (International Standard Book Number), 050 (Library of Congress Call Number), 082 (Dewey Decimal Call Number), 500 (General Note), and 650 (Subject Added Entry - Topical Term).

```
LDR    *****camⱨⱨ22*****ⱨaⱨ4500
001    <control number>
005    19870504050512.0
008    | 820305 | s1982ⱨⱨⱨⱨ | nyuaⱨⱨⱨ | ⱨⱨⱨⱨⱨⱨ | ⱨ00110ⱨ | engⱨd |


020    ⱨⱨ‡a0442281536 :‡c‡15.95
040    ⱨⱨ‡a<NUC symbol>‡c<NUC symbol>
050    14‡aTX745‡b.S49 1982
082    04‡a641.8/6‡219

100    10‡aShakespeare, Margaret N.
245    14‡aThe meringue cookbook /‡cMargaret N. Shakespeare.
260    0ⱨ‡aNew York :‡bVan Nostrand Reinhold,‡c1982.
300    ⱨⱨ‡a240 p. :‡bill. ;‡c25 cm.
500    ⱨⱨ‡aIncludes index.
650    ⱨ0‡aCookery (Meringue).
```

Fig. 3.12   USMARC full-level record – book

(Reprinted from *USMARC format for bibliographic data, including guidelines for content designation,* prepared by Network Development and MARC Standards Office, Washington DC, Cataloging Distribution Service, Library of Congress, 1988–, 2 vols.)

This example can be identified as a record for language material by code a in Leader/06, and further as a serial by code s in Leader/07. This record illustrates the use of several fields related to serial material: field 022 (International Standard Serial Number), field 042 (Authentication Code), field 210 (Abbreviated Title), field 222 (Key Title), field 246 (Varying Form of Title), field 310 (Current Frequency), field 362 (Dates of Publication and/or Volume Designation), and field 780 (Preceding Entry).

```
LDR    *****cas½½22*****½a½4500
001    <control number>
005    19860716101553.0
008    | 791031 | c19789999 | dcuar | 1½½½½½½½ | ½0uuua0 | eng½d |


010    ½½‡a½½½85649389½‡zsc½80000109½
022    0½‡a0273-1967
035    ½½‡a(OCoLC)5629434
040    ½½‡aCtY‡cCtY‡dDLC‡dNSDP‡dDLC‡dNST
042    ½½‡alc‡ansdp
043    ½½‡an-us---
050    00‡aSK361‡b.U63a
082    00‡a639.9/2/0973‡219

210    0½‡aAnnu. wildl. fish. rep.
222    00‡aAnnual wildlife and fisheries report
245    00‡aAnnual wildlife and fisheries report /‡cUnited States Department of Agriculture,
       Forest Service, Wildlife and Fisheries].

246    14‡aWildlife and fish habitat management in the Forest Service
260    00‡a[Washington, D.C.] :‡bWildlife and Fisheries,
300    00‡av. :‡bill. ;‡c28 cm.
310    ½½‡aAnnual
362    1½‡aBegan with vol. for 1978.
500    ½½‡aDescription based on: 1983.

650    ½0‡aWildlife management‡zUnited States‡xStatistics‡xPeriodicals.
650    ½0‡aWildlife management‡zUnited States‡xPeriodicals.
650    ½0‡aWildlife habitat improvement‡zUnited States‡xStatistics‡xPeriodicals.
650    ½0‡aWildlife habitat improvement‡zUnited States‡xPeriodicals.

710    10‡aUnited States.‡bForest Service.‡bWildlife and Fisheries Staff..
780    00‡aUnited States. Forest Service. Division of Wildlife Management.‡tAnnual wildlife
       report‡x0099-068X‡w(OCoLC)2242070‡w(DLC)½½½75644790
850    ½½‡aDLC‡alCarbS‡aOrCS‡aWaU
```

Fig. 3.13   USMARC full-level record – serial

(Reprinted from *USMARC format for bibliographic data, including guidelines for content designation*, prepared by Network Development and MARC Standards Office, Washington DC, Cataloging Distribution Service, Library of Congress, 1988–, 2 vols.)

USMARC format for bibliographic data (UFBD)

USMARC format for bibliographic data (UFBD) is designed to hold bibliographic records for books, serials, archival and manuscript materials, computer files, maps, music, visual materials (including artefacts, kits and audiovisual items). Each type of material is identified in the specifications by a two-letter code (BK, SE, AM, CF, MP, MU, VM). *UFBD* is an integrated format, in the sense that it offers a single set of content designators valid, where appropriate, for all materials. There are in fact many material-specific fields.

Prior to format integration, seven separate formats existed for different materials, each with separately defined leader codes and 008 fields. Format integration posed some problems in specifying characteristics of different materials; these have been resolved by the introduction of a new control field, 006, fixed-length data elements – additional material characteristics, previously a linking field for serials.[11] Briefly, *UFBD* copes with the problems of characteristics of different materials in the following manner:

leader character position 6 denotes type of record within the above seven broad groups (14 types are specifiable: language material, monographic or serial, plus 12 other categories);

leader character position 7 gives bibliographic level (monograph component part, serial component part, collection, subunit, monograph, serial);

008, fixed-length data elements, is a 40-character coded-data field, depending for its definition and content on the leader positions 6 and 7. It is not repeatable. 008 character positions 0–17 and 35–9 have the same definition regardless of form of material; character positions 18–34 may be different, according to the requirements of different kinds of material. In general, where the same data element is common to more than one form of material, it appears in the same position;

007, physical-description fixed field, can be used to hold data for eight kinds of material: maps, globes, projected graphics, micro-forms, nonprojected graphics, motion pictures, sound-recordings and video-recordings. The 007 field is defined differently for each form. It is described in the specifications as possessing a 'generic tree structure', with the value in its first character position determining the nature and content of the field. 007 copes with materials requiring special treatment in physical description; not all records, therefore, will include an 007 field. It may be repeated, for example to specify the different physical forms of a work.

006, fixed-length data elements – additional material character-istics, can be used to hold extra information about items for which the 008 field is inadequate, e.g. non-textual serials and multi-media items. 006 can be defined in seven different ways, the first character position determining the definition.

The above appears complex in comparison with UKMARC, but means that many more physical characteristics can be accommodated in coded-data fixed fields.

Data fields are assigned tags 01- / 89- and are grouped into functional blocks. There are many more fields than in UKMARC, e.g.

024	Standard recording number
027	Standard technical report number
037	Source of acquisition
045	Time period of content
130	Main-entry uniform title
306	Playing time
654	Subject added entry – faceted topical heading
656	Index term – occupation
657	Index term – function

Prior to format integration, there were 15 fields in *UFBD* with tags 3--, compared with 2 in UKMARC and 50 kinds of notes with tags 5--, compared with 29 in UKMARC. (Five 3-- and six 5-- fields have since been made obsolete.) Fields 76- / 79- are not present in UKMARC. Fields with tags 9-- are in USMARC reserved for local use; in UKMARC these may also be used for local purposes, with the exception of those 9-- fields reserved for references. Comparisons of this nature are, of course, liable to become outdated when the revision of UKMARC is completed, as more fields are likely to be added. Field 040, Cataloguing source, which identifies the origin and the contributor of a record, has also been proposed for inclusion in UKMARC, in connection with the Copyright Libraries Shared Cataloguing Programme. In *UFBD* this field contains the National Union Catalog symbol or the name of the organization that created and/or modified the record. Character position 39 in the 008 field also carries a code for the appropriate agency (cf. provenance code in character position 40 of UKMARC 008 field).

Many fields in *UFBD* are repeatable where appropriate; this is shown in the specifications by 'R' or 'NR'. There are no repeat digits used at input as in UKMARC.

There are numerous examples of coincidence in content designation between US and UKMARC, reflecting their common origin and history. Compatibility of content designation with other national formats is of course a stated aim of the USMARC formats. Major fields, such as main-entry headings for persons and corporate bodies, title, physical description and subject added entries, carry the same field tags. There are, however, some differences in other aspects of content designation, e.g. in definition of subfields:

| UKMARC | 100 10 $aSmith$hJohn# |
| USMARC | 100 10 ‡aSmith, John. |

| UKMARC | 245 14 $aThe home garden$dSusan Beresford$e illustrated by Leonard James# |
| USMARC | 245 14 ‡aThe home garden /‡cSusan Beresford; illustrated by Leonard James. |

As the above examples illustrate, end of subfield punctuation continues to be supplied in USMARC, one reason why there are fewer subfields than in UKMARC.

Indicators perform the same function as in UKMARC, supplying additional information about the field and facilitating manipulation of data.

Content

The content of a USMARC bibliographic record depends on the standards used for data input and the type of item recorded. USMARC, as UKMARC, specifies certain data content in its fixed fields (leader, 006, 007, 008). Standards for input to data fields which are specifically mentioned in *UFBD* include AACR2, ISBD, LCSH, DC, LC. Other standards, however, are permitted. Field 100, Main entry – personal name, states only that the content of the field is determined by 'various cataloguing rules'; 245, Title statement, explicitly allows for both ISBD and non-ISBD formulations; field 300, Physical description, mentions also 'various cataloguing rules'; non-ISBD statements are acceptable and can be accommodated. Leader position 18 shows whether records have been catalogued according to ISBD and AACR2. There are fields in *UFBD* for all types of subject headings, including those drawn from recognized thesauri and lists of subject headings (e.g. LCSH, MESH) and fields for uncontrolled subject-index terms.

If used in full, *UFBD* would produce a highly detailed bibliographic record, suitable for a variety of applications. Fullness of bibliographic information and/or content designation is shown in leader position 17: code 'b' indicates a complete USMARC record, code '7' indicates that the record is minimal level, meeting the national-level bibliographic record minimal-level requirements. (Five other codes are possible, describing various degrees of fullness.) Requirements for national-level bibliographic records and minimal-level records are shown with each field description and are summarized and illustrated in Appendix A.

Relationships in USMARC
UFBD provides for several kinds of inter- and intra-record links. These are supported primarily by a block of linking-entry fields: 76- /79- . Originally defined to link related serials, they were developed to handle a wider range of relationships between different bibliographic items, including those which are physically separate and those contained within a parent or host item. Major kinds of relationships recognized are chronological, horizontal and vertical, the last including the hierarchical or whole/part relationships. A distinction is made between the 'target item' (the principal item around which the bibliographic record is constructed) and 'related items' (items having some relationship to the target item; details of these may or may not be needed to obtain the target item). Data for related items appear in the linking-entry fields.

Inter-record (record-to-record links)
This kind of link is achieved mainly by three mechanisms:

(1) an alphabetic code in position 19 of the leader, showing whether a record for a related item is needed for full processing.

(2) use of a linking-entry field (76- /789); content designators in each of these fields show the type of relationship between items and whether notes for display purposes are to be generated from data within the linking-entry field or from elsewhere in the record; the data in the linking-entry field may be actual bibliographic data (e.g. the author and title of an item), or coded data (e.g. a record number, control number, standard number).

(3) use of a linking-entry complexity note (580) which shows relationships between items that are too complex to be expressed by reference only to the data in a linking-entry field; if 580 is used, it is provided in addition to an appropriate linking-entry field and holds the full note which is to be displayed to the user.

A major use of this technique is the construction of analytical records, i.e. records for component parts of items. The bibliographic record is constructed for the component part and the appropriate linking-entry field (773, Host item entry) contains details of the containing item. Field 773 carries the display constant 'in', which is automatically generated for visual presentation. For this application, character position 7 (bibliographic level) of the leader holds a suitable code: 'a' for monograph component part, or 'b' for serial component part. This technique will not support multilevel description, described in Chapter 1 and discussed earlier in relation to UKMARC. This kind of technique has been proposed for UKMARC and is in use in some sections of the BL; for many years, a similar technique was used in processing *British education index*, although it was not formally labelled a linking technique.

Other inter-record links
Linking-entry fields can be used to make other types of record-to-record links, for example between a special issue of a serial and the record for the serial as a whole; between a work and its translations; between a serial and one which supersedes or precedes it; between a series and its subseries.

Intra-record links
Field-to-field linkage is used in *UFBD* for alternative graphic

representations of data. The linking mechanism is the subfield code $\ddagger$6, which connects pairs of associated fields, e.g. a main-entry heading in English and a corresponding main-entry heading in Chinese. Introduced to cope with the problem of including data in non-Roman scripts, especially Chinese, Japanese and Korean, the method relies on the presence in the record of one or more 800 (Alternate graphic representation) fields to carry the non-Roman data. Field 066 (Character sets present) signals the presence in the record of character sets other than the normal USMARC sets and is an indication that special processing techniques may be needed. $\ddagger$6 is always the first subfield code and the subfield contains the tag number of the associated field, together with other data necessary for matching and identification. Field 880 can be repeated, so that main entry, added entry and descriptive data may be carried both in Roman and vernacular scripts within the same record. Data within linked fields must exactly correspond in terms of subfield definition.

The above is a highly selective account of *UFBD* linking devices; the reader is advised to consult the specifications and appropriate items in the bibliography.[12]

USMARC format for authority data (UFAD)

Authority records hold data on standard forms of names and subjects which provide access points for bibliographic records, and data needed for the construction of *see* and *see also* references between headings. 'Names' covers personal, corporate and meeting names, names of jurisdictions, name/title combinations and uniform titles. 'Subjects' includes topical and geographic headings and terms used as subdivisions under names and subjects. USMARC authority records carry the code 'z' in Leader position 6 (Type of record). The two major kinds of authority records are for established and unestablished headings: the precise type is shown by one of seven possible codes in the 008 field, character position 9. Code 'n' in position 17 of the leader shows that the record meets the national-level record requirements for content and content designation.

Data in authority records are grouped in blocks, currently:

0-- *Control information, identification and classification numbers*. Certain fields in this group can be used to make links with bibliographic records: 014 (Link to bibliographic record for serial or multipart item) contains the control number copied from field 001 of a USMARC bibliographic record for a serial or multipart item catalogued as a set. The field can be repeated to hold control numbers of all records associated with a series heading. 020 (ISBN) and 022 (ISSN) also provide a similar machine link between the authority record for a series and the bibliographic record(s) in which the series heading occurs.

1-- *Headings (established and unestablished)*. Established headings are authoritative forms of names and subjects that may be used in the main and added-entry fields of bibliographic records. Unestablished headings are not used in bibliographic records. They are described in *UFAD* as headings 'used within an authority file to organize or to refer'. The most common type of unestablished heading is the variant form of name/subject, from which a *see* reference would be made.

2-- *Complex 'see' references*.

3-- *Complex 'see also' references*. Data in these fields are used to generate references between headings which are too complex to be derived from data in the 4-- and 5-- fields, e.g. references containing explanatory text.

4-- *'See from' tracings*.

5-- *'See also from' tracings*. These are used to generate simple *see* and *see also* references to data in 1-- fields. Cross-references can lead from an unestablished heading to an established heading (*see* reference) or from one established heading to another (*see also* reference).

6-- *Series treatment decisions, notes, etc*. These include decisions on the treatment of series headings named in 1-- fields, and additional fields for complex references relating to names.

9-- *Reserved for local implementation*.

In order to facilitate machine linking possibilities between bibliographic and authority records, consistent content designation has been maintained across certain fields in both types of record. In bibliographic records, the fields are those with tags 1--, 4--, 6--, 7--, 8--, i.e. all those fields that might be subject to authority control. In authority records the relevant fields are: 1--, 4--, 5--; e.g.

159

UFBD	UFAD
100 Main entry – personal name	100 Heading – personal name
110 Main entry – corporate name	110 Heading – corporate name
111 Main entry – meeting name	111 Heading – meeting name

In these fields, indicators and subfield codes are also consistently defined. The policy of parallel content designation between bibliographic and authority record fields is made explicit in *The USMARC formats: underlying principles*, Section 6.5.

Linking between authority and bibliographic records, for example by recording authority control numbers in bibliographic records, has been more fully developed in UNIMARC.

The content of USMARC authority records is determined by external standards, such as AACR2 and Library of Congress Subject Headings (LCSH). Other standards are permitted. 008 (Fixed-length data elements) field uses character position 10 to identify the descriptive cataloguing rules used to formulate the headings or reference data: six codes are possible, including 'c' for AACR2, 'd' for AACR-compatible and 'z' for other rules. Character position 11 identifies the subject-heading system or thesaurus used to establish the subject name or terms: 'a' is for LCSH, 'c' represents Medical Subject Headings (MESH). Seven other codes are possible, including 'z' for other schemes.

It has been suggested that *USMARC format for authority data* be extended to cover authoritative data from classification schemes such as Dewey and Library of Congress.[13]

USMARC format for holdings and locations (UFHL)
This is the most recent of the USMARC communications formats, originating in a format for serials holdings statements although now applicable where appropriate to monographic items. It accommodates all types of data required to furnish local holdings information: copy-specific, organization-specific, and that needed for internal processing. The format is designed to be used independently; in certain cases, however, holdings and locations data may instead be embedded in bibliographic records.

Leader position 6 indicates the type of record: 'x' for single-part item and 'y' for multipart/serial item. Leader position 17 (Encoding level/level of specificity), shows whether the record meets ANSI Z39.44 – 1986, *Standard for serial holdings statements at the summary level*. At present only three blocks of data are defined:

0--   *Control numbers and codes.* These include the record control number (001), the control number for the parent bibliographic record (004) and a copy-specific physical-description fixed field (007). The physical form of an item must be shown in the 007 holdings field.

         Holdings data of course have no significance unless attached in some way to bibliographic records. Certain fields, e.g. Library of Congress Control Number (010), ISBN (020) and ISSN (022) provide links with data in associated bibliographic records.

         Linking fields in *UFHL* have content designation consistent with that in bibliographic records. Linkage number (014) can be used to record the system control number of the holdings record and the system control number of an associated bibliographic record within bibliographic utilities or cooperatives such as RLIN and OCLC.

         System control number (035) can be used locally to record system control numbers of holdings and bibliographic records.

         Multiple holdings records can be linked to a single bibliographic record, for example in the case of a serial held in both printed text and microform.

8--   *Holdings and locations data.*

         843-845 contain notes on reproductions and terms governing use.

         852 contains location/call number.

         853 –868 are for holdings data. The arrangement here is complex, resulting from a tripartite division into nature of publication, enumeration and chronology or publication pattern, and actual holdings. Three types of publication are identified: 1) basic bibliographic units; 2) supplements and accompanying materials; 3) indexes. Each is allocated a pair of fields, the first of which is devoted to definition of enumeration and chronology or publication pattern, the second to the holdings proper. Separation of fields in this way allows for separate usage, e.g. for serials checking, where only the first field need be used. For display purposes, data from both fields would be combined.

853/863 are the fields for definition of enumeration and chronology/publication pattern for basic bibliographic units.

854/864 duplicate the function for supplements and accompanying materials.

855/865 duplicate the function for indexes.

Alternatively, fields 866/867/868 may be used to combine all holdings statements for each of the three types of publications. Field 853 (Action note) from the bibliographic format can be used also in the holdings format, for example to record preservation actions and other copy-specific information.

9-- *Reserved for local implementation.*

This is a much simplified account of the holdings and locations format. More adventurous readers will need to consult the specifications, for example to investigate the detailed subfield listings in fields 853–68, and the role of the indicators in these fields in data compression and expansion for the display of holdings statements. The *UFHL* supports considerable manipulation of data for management as well as display purposes.[14]

Format conversion between UK and USMARC

UKMARC and USMARC bibliographic records cannot be used in their original state in the same database. Conversion between formats is necessary. LC/USMARC records, reformatted to BNB/UKMARC, have been available in the United Kingdom for almost 20 years (Figure 3.15), although the LC began to offer reformatted UKMARC records only in the mid-1980s. The BL's specification for conversion of LC MARC to UKMARC records was issued as a separate document in 1981.[15] The chief purpose was to achieve 'basic record compatibility' so that reformatted LC records where possible had the same content designation and coded values as UKMARC. Steps in the conversion process are too numerous to be listed here, but the major types of conversion are content designator to content designator, and content designator to punctuation. Examples include:

● deletion of punctuation marks occurring immediately before subfield marks, field marks and record marks

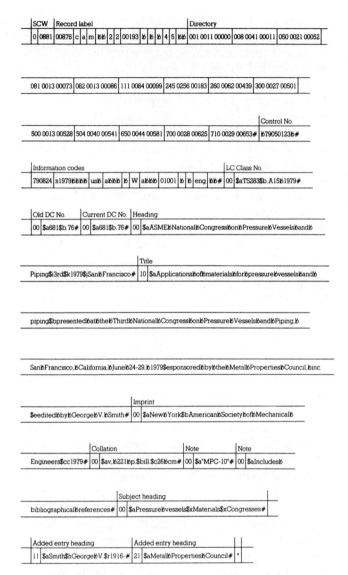

Fig. 3.15 A Library of Congress record reformatted to UKMARC

(Reproduced from the *UKMARC manual*, 2nd ed., with permission of the British Library Board)

- conversion of other punctuation to UKMARC subfield marks, e.g. to create subfield $h, inverted element of name, in 100 (personal-name main-entry heading) field
- conversion to zeros of spaces (blanks) in indicator positions in data fields
- conversion of field 007 to UKMARC 037
- conversion of some codes in the 008 field to UKMARC equivalents
- if no 1-- fields are present, conversion of first indicator 0 (zero) or 1 in field 245 to 3
- conversion of certain LC subfield codes in 7-- fields to punctuation marks in cases where UKMARC lacks corresponding subfields
- conversion of 730 (added entry – uniform title) to UK-MARC 740 (uniform-title added-entry heading)

Fields for which there are no UKMARC equivalents are left unconverted. For many years, the conversion programs were designed also to delete LC MARC records for British imprints (identified by the presence of the code GB*** or a BNB serial number in field 015, national bibliography number). From January 1988, however, the British Library discontinued supplying Library of Congress subject data in official UKMARC records and as a measure of support for customers requiring such data, the practice of excluding LC MARC records for British imprints has been halted.[16] The *UKMARC manual*, Appendix H, gives details of differences between reformatted LC/USMARC records, although these are based, as are the 1981 conversion specifications, on the 1980 *MFBD* and some changes have since taken place.

In 1986 LC issued notes arising from queries concerning conversion of UKMARC records to USMARC.[17] A major point of interest is the PRECIS string, for which there is no USMARC field. PRECIS data is converted into the 653 field (Subject access – uncontrolled) and additionally into the 886 field (Foreign MARC information field), along with other UKMARC fields not recognized in the reformatting programs. UKMARC 9-- fields (references) are the major examples here. Second indicators in UKMARC LC class number and DC class number fields (050, 082) are changed to '4', showing that the class numbers have not been assigned by the LC. Similar treatment is given to fields containing subject data (6--), since names, titles and geographic subject headings are not based on the LC authority files.

UKMARC records contain LC card numbers in field 010. These are copied from the work in hand, and do not always represent valid, current LC control numbers. They are, however, retained in field 010.

Notes and references

1 Specifications consulted: *UKMARC manual*, 2nd ed., London, British Library Bibliographic Services Division, 1980–7; *USMARC format for bibliographic data, including guidelines for content designation*, prepared by Network Development and MARC Standards Office, Washington DC, Cataloging Distribution Service, Library of Congress, 1988 – , 2 vols. (update no.1 forthcoming); *USMARC format for authority data, including guidelines for content designation*, prepared by Network Development and MARC Standards Office, Washington DC, Cataloging Distribution Service, Library of Congress, 1987 – ; *USMARC format for holdings and locations*, Washington DC, Network Development and MARC Standards Office, Library of Congress, 1984; *USMARC format for holdings and locations*, final draft, update no.1, 1987. Part 1 of the 3rd edition was formally issued in December 1989.
2 *BLAISE newsletter* is published by British Library Bibliographic Services and issued as part of their subscription to clients of BLAISE Online Services and BLAISE Records. Contact: British Library Bibliographic Services, 2 Sheraton Street, London W1V 4BH.
3 *Library of Congress information bulletins (LCIB)* are issued weekly by the Information Office of the Library of Congress. Contact: Information Office, Library of Congress, Washington DC, 20541. *USMARC format: proposed changes* available on subscription from Cataloging Distribution Service, Library of Congress, Washington DC, 20541.
4 *USMARC specifications for record structure, character sets, tapes*, prepared by Network Development and MARC Standards Office, Washington DC, Cataloging Distribution Service, 1987.
5 *BLAISE newsletter*, **98**, May/June 1989, 7–9.
6 *Ibid.*

7 *American National Standard for bibliographic information interchange on magnetic tape, ANSI Z39.2–1979*, New York, American National Standards Institute, 1979.

8 *Representation for calendar date and ordinal date for information interchange* (ANSI X3.30); *Representations of local time of the day for information interchange* (ANSI X3.43).

9 *USMARC character set: Chinese, Japanese, Korean*, Cataloging Distribution Service, Library of Congress, 1987.

10 *USMARC code list for countries*, prepared by Network Development and MARC Standards Office, Washington DC, Cataloging Distribution Service, Library of Congress, 1988; *USMARC code list for languages*, prepared by ND and MARC Standards Office, Washington DC, CDS, 1987; *USMARC code list for relators, sources, description conventions*, prepared by ND and MARC Standards Office, Washington DC, CDS, 1988; *USMARC code list for geographic areas*, prepared by ND and MARC Standards Office, Washington DC, CDS, 1988.

11 *Format integration and its effect on the USMARC bibliographic format*, prepared by Network Development and MARC Standards Office, Washington DC, Cataloging Distribution Service, Library of Congress, 1988.

12 See especially McCallum, Sally H., 'MARC record linking technique', *Information technology and libraries*, **1**, 1982, 281–91; Crawford, W., *MARC for library use: understanding the USMARC formats*, White Plains, NY, Knowledge Industry, 1984, Chapter 8: 'Links within and among USMARC records'.

13 *LCIB*, **48**, (9), 27 February 1989, 84.

14 *The USMARC format for holdings and locations: development, implementation and use*, ed. by Barry B. Baker, New York, Haworth Press, 1988, offers a good introduction to the format itself and its use in practice.

15 British Library Bibliographic Services Division, *Specifications for conversion of LCMARC records to UKMARC*, London, BLAISE, 1981.

16 *British Library Bibliographic Services newsletter*, **46**, June 1988, 7.

17 *LCIB*, **45**, (33), 18 August 1986, 294–6.

4
International MARC activities and UNIMARC

International MARC Network

The International MARC Network is defined in Wells's report on the International MARC Network[1] as '[a network of] the group of countries, including organizations within those countries, participating in the exchange of bibliographic data by machine. These are the countries mentioned in the terms of reference, namely: Australia, Belgium, Canada, Denmark, Federal Republic of Germany, France, Italy, Netherlands, South Africa, Spain, Sweden, United Kingdom, United States.'

From the time of the creation of LC MARC and the MARC II project, the number of national MARC formats being developed had steadily increased. The early cooperation between the Library of Congress and the British National Bibliography and subsequent collaborative arrangements set up between the Library of Congress, the British Library, the National Library of Canada and the National Library of Australia were seen as models for the establishment on a global basis of an international network of bibliographic records.

The differences between national formats and the problems they posed for exchange of bibliographic data were a matter of concern at the start of the 1970s. Among the resolutions passed at The International Seminar on the MARC Format and the Exchange of Bibliographic Data in Machine-readable Form in 1971 was a recommendation that efforts be made to define and overcome effects of variations which already existed in different MARC formats. The most frequently occurring themes in the literature of the period were the need for agreement on content designators for a common format and for greater uniformity in cataloguing practices.

This kind of activity has to be seen in the overall climate of cooperation of the time. The Conference of Directors of National Libraries was set up in 1974 and met during the IFLA General Conference to discuss matters of concern for their cooperation. Unesco and ICSU/AB (International Council of Scientific Unions – Abstracting Board) were jointly planning a World Information System for the Sciences which was being implemented by Unesco's UNISIST programme. The Unesco Department of Documentation, Libraries and Archives set up the NATIS (National Information Systems) Programme on the recommendations of the Intergovernmental Conference on the Planning of National Documentation, Library and Archives Infrastructures.

In 1975, when the Directors of National Libraries met for the second time, they had before them two papers which were concerned with the exchange of machine-readable data by national libraries as part of a world information system. These papers were 'Proposals for a focus for the international exchange of bibliographic data in machine-readable form' by Stephen Green of the British Library[2] and 'The role of national libraries in national and international information systems' by R. M. Duchesne, formerly of the British National Bibliography but then of the National Library of Canada.[3] Duchesne, incidentally, had already put forward at the International Seminar on the MARC Format and the Exchange of Bibliographic Data in 1971 the idea of SUPERMARC, a 'genuinely international communications format which is in essence a superset of national implementations'. This was probably the first suggestion of a universal format, and it was proposed after the author had made a comparison of the UK and US formats and found that they diverged in a number of not insignificant places. 'SUPERMARC' would therefore drastically reduce the number of translation programs as each national agency would require only two programs, from national format to SUPERMARC and from SUPERMARC to national format.[4]

As a result of these presentations in early 1975, a meeting was held in October 1975 to consider the development of an International MARC Network. This meeting decided that in view of the complex bibliographic and communication problems involved it would commission a group of short studies which could form the basis for decisions that had to be taken to set up the network.

The background papers commissioned by the study, which were coordinated by the IFLA UBC Office (constituting its first incursion into the world of automation), were completed in September 1976. A general report was approved in draft by the International MARC Network Steering Committee in March 1977, submitted to the meeting of the Conference of Directors of National Libraries and published as the *International MARC Network: a study for an international bibliographic data network*.[5]

The International MARC Network study

The report assumed the desirability of establishing international systems for the exchange of bibliographic data. It discussed the 'state of the art' in the international exchange of data. The national formats reflected the fact that there were different national cataloguing rules. Many of these differences were historic but reflected cultural and linguistic differences. More standards were needed. The International Standard Bibliographic Descriptions (ISBD) were a good starting point as far as bibliographic standards were concerned, but dealt only with the descriptive area of the record. As far as name access points were concerned, Henriette Avram had stated that 'standardization of choice and form of heading is a major problem for which there is no near-term solution'.[6] In the field of subject indexing, whether by means of subject headings, descriptors or classification, there was still less possibility of universal agreement. Work was needed on multilingual indexing systems. More encouraging was the fact that national agencies had the will to tackle the problem of universal bibliographic control even if they had not yet solved all the problems. National agencies were producing records for most printed monographs and had access to serials records. ISBN and ISSN systems had been established in many countries and the standard numbers were being printed extensively on the documents they identified. Even the problem of the delay between publication of a book and its record appearing in a national bibliography or a database was being tackled by the introduction of CIP (Cataloguing in Publication) programmes which involved the national agency producing a catalogue record from the proofs of a book which could then be incorporated when the book was sent to press.

The report dealt with the necessity to share the burden of hosting bibliographic databases. The network would consist of a number of linked databases. Each country would be responsible for the creation of records relating to the publications of that country and different countries would be given responsibility for the areas outside the network members' areas. It was felt preferable to concentrate on cataloguing current material rather than attempting retrospective coverage, since earlier material would have been catalogued already in manual form. Indeed, it would be better to concentrate limited resources on current non-book materials.

Other practical problems of an International MARC Network, merely noted with the recommendation that they must be tackled, were the problems of overlap of coverage, the identification of items which were of national interest only, the development of standard agreed statuses for records and the lack of a standard procedure for the upgrading of records. The need for duplicate checking in large databases with records coming from different sources is still recognized. Less obvious is the need to mark records of items of national interest only. Any item could surely be of interest to anyone. However, the need for status codes and a procedure for upgrading of records in networks have both been discussed ever since and still await a solution.

Having discussed the problems, Wells makes recommendations for standardization separating the problem into five categories, which are summarized below.

Normalization of descriptive data

The first category related to problems concerning descriptive data which Wells in turn divided into a further four subcategories. ISBD had been established here, so the mandatory set of data elements for the bibliographic record should be the full ISBD data elements. Subsets of this could be established for CIP or restrospective conversion records. Each record should contain a code indicating its level of completeness. Another problem mentioned under the head of descriptive data concerned record linking, how to relate records of analytical entries to the records of the works containing them or records of monographs in a series to the record of the series. The report states that an emerging consensus favours the adoption of a system which established a series of linked records.

The second subcategory related to the structure of access points: Michael Gorman, the joint editor of the first and second editions of AACR (at the time he was working on the second edition) worked in the British Library MARC Office and was the ideal person to make a study of the problem of name access points in different languages.[7] Wells interpreted the conclusion of this paper as indicating that the differences between access points in different languages were 'relevant only at output and not inherent in the description and identification of parts of the bibliographic record'. Gorman had suggested that access points in a record could be coded in a way that would identify the smallest element of every access point, such as the name of a person. This would enable an agency receiving the record to reconstruct it according to its own rules. Thus, if one set of rules needed Surname, Forename, Title and another needed Surname, Title, Forename, each could derive its preferred form by algorithm. In fact this particular example is a difficult one, since US practice has followed the first method while UK practice follows either depending on the actual title.

$aHookway$eSir$hHarry   generating   Hookway, *Sir* Harry

$aFisher$eJohn$dSaint   generating   Fisher, John, *Saint*

UKMARC therefore has alternative subfields for title depending on the position of the title. LC MARC only needs one subfield here, though on conversion to UKMARC, the appropriate alternative subfield is generated. It is doubtful whether Wells's suggestion that 'A solution appears to lie in the coding of elements and the units of an element found in access points descriptively rather than coding the elements in terms of how they are presented in this or that cataloguing code' would work in every case. For even to describe a data element descriptively requires a cataloguing code to help one make decisions.

The third type of problem related to linguistic problems in access points. Users of an English database would prefer (for instance, for the names of countries) an English form of a name rather than the vernacular. Any additions to names in access points would also be made in the language of cataloguing. The recommended solution for this was the establishment of an international authority file which would be circulated to all participants in the network.

The fourth area concerned character sets, a problem in databases with records in many different languages. The best solution seemed to be to provide for all the different characters required and to avoid transliteration. This was not practically possible as not all systems would have the hardware to output all the different characters. The second best, but more practical, solution was to draw up a set of characters which everyone could process and a set of so-called 'semi-legitimate' characters which could be stored by all systems against the time when they could be output. Until then, agencies needing to use these in their records would have to provide transliterated alternative data using only the standard set. Eventually there should be developed a character set which would include Roman, Cyrillic, Hebrew, Greek, Arabic numerals, mathematical symbols, punctuation marks and control characters.

Normalization of subject data

The second main category dealt with was normalization of subject data. All MARC records appeared to include subject data in the form of subject headings and classification numbers. The report came down on the side of subject headings as being preferable given the then 'state of the art'. The recommendation was that the International MARC Network should consider undertaking at a very early stage a thorough investigation of the precise information-retrieval requirements of the Network and formulate a policy in the light of existing subject data in the MARC record, investigating the possibility of the extended use of existing internationally used classification systems and taking into account current research and development programmes in the field of translingual indexing and classification systems.

Communications network

The third category concerned the mechanism of communication. At the time of the study, international networks were in the future. The only major international online systems related to banking and airline booking. In North America and Canada, national MARC databases could be accessed via TYMNET. In Europe, however, EURONET was only in the future as a proposed data network run by the European Community which, as things turned out, became little more than a concept when the packet-switching networks grew up as the responsibility of the separate telecommunications authorities. A straw poll conducted by the chairman of the International MARC Network established the number of transactions that would be likely to occur in an international network and the resulting estimate of one million records annually was said by a consultant to be very low if a dedicated network were projected. Indeed the consultant stated that 'The projected network would be more remarkable by its round-the-world coverage than by the volume of its traffic'.[8] With the benefit of hindsight, we know that telecommunications have advanced technologically and because of the way they have been structured, the costs of using public telecommunications networks are such that no one would consider an international dedicated network for bibliographic data.

It was clear that the network should support a limited number of access keys based on standard elements such as record control number, international standard number, or, where this was not available, national bibliography number, names and titles and codes constructed from them, subject keywords and subject-classification numbers.

National agencies should set up databases drawing records from within their country. These could be distributed, both within the country and internationally, on tape to reduce the requirement for online access to the national databases; in short, real-time online use would supplement not supplant batch processing. This would result in the International MARC Network consisting of several large or very large MARC databases containing unique national files but with a certain amount of duplication of other material. The first recommendation for study in this area was that an investigation should be made of the use of access keys and command languages via interface computers in online MARC database systems with a view towards achieving systems compatibility. Command languages are the codes used to make a search in a computer. They include terms for expressing a search and printing the results out to the screen or a printer. Standardizing command languages necessitates agreement on data elements since they have to include codes to indicate to the computer the name of the data element on which the search is being made.

The second recommendation for study was to determine the nature and number of searches likely to be made on MARC databases throughout the international communications network.

Bibliographic data exchange policies

It was becoming clear from the experience of record-sharing cooperatives such as OCLC in the US and BLCMP in the UK, both of which derived many of their records from their respective national bibliographic agency, that record ownership was going to become a problem, the fourth category of problem. Who would own a record and be entitled to the royalties from its transfer to another system if that record had begun life in one national database and then been substantially modified by another? This could be further complicated if a national agency did not create all the national records itself, as would be the case with non-book materials which were often not the responsibility of the national bibliographic agencies.

The report recommended a special study of the conditions under which national MARC agencies supplied records to other national agencies and to individual institutions, together with an analysis of the effect of royalty and non-royalty options in an international online bibliographic-data network. The matters for particular study were to include: the problems arising from a mixture of copyright and non-copyright databases; the problems arising from differential charging for different classes of user; the problems arising from differential charging for access to the same records duplicated in a distributed network; the definition of 'modification'; the relation of copyright to retrospective files, that is files of records converted into machine-readable form from hard-copy catalogues; techniques for exercising control over copyright records and the design of a standard international contract.

Cooperative planning and development

The fifth category of problem concerned what can be called the organizational network. Given the experience of international cooperation up to that date, groups of MARC users with some characteristic in common had got together to engage in co-operative activities. The Library of Congress and the British National Bibliography had begun this followed by the creation of the INTERMARC Group which achieved the first international format. ABACUS, the meeting of representatives of the British Library, Library of Congress, and the National Libraries of Australia and Canada, had met to increase coordination in the forward planning of their MARC services. Yet another group was formed of representatives from different countries that had been involved in the early work in the IFLA Working Group on Content Designators which was working on what was later to become UNIMARC.

Moreover, the standards to be used by the network had to be maintained. The report recommended the establishment of a specialist committee to advise the heads of the national libraries on priorities for the development of the network and for ensuring that necessary technical developments were carried out. This committee would need a secretariat which could be accommodated at one of the national agencies or at a suitable international office.

Since groups of users had been established on an *ad hoc* basis, it was necessary to impose some system on these groups. It was recommended that MARC Network Groups should be set up on a regional basis to include all national agencies that were producers of MARC records. Each Group should have a Centre with objectives such as promoting the most efficient use of machine-readable bibliographic data in the Group; providing information and training for members of the Group converting to MARC systems; coordinating studies on bibliographic and technical matters of concern to the Group; and providing a channel of communication between members of the Group and the International MARC Network Advisory Committee, IFLA, ISO, Unesco, ISDS and any other related organization on matters of standardization concerning network development.

175

Outcome of recommendations

Some of these recommendations have been abandoned, others have been followed through. The International MARC Network Study Steering Committee, as it was called for a time, published in 1980 *International access to MARC records*[9] which looked at the ownership aspects and included a recommended text for bilateral agreements for record exchange. These issues are discussed further in Chapter 6.

The ISBDs have become accepted even outside networks, but we are no nearer universal conventions for name access points. No international authority file has been established, though a UNIMARC Authorities Format has been developed. UNIMARC has adopted a limited group of standard character sets, including only those that have been formally approved as international standards, and not those validated by the European Computer Manufacturers' Association (ECMA) on behalf of ISO. Escape sequences developed by ISO have been adopted to indicate the transfer from one set to another instead of establishing one large set.

Dewey and the Library of Congress Subject Headings (LCSH) have continued to be used as subject data and the latter have been translated into many languages.

Networking has advanced, exemplified by the Linked Systems Project in North America and efforts made in Canada and elsewhere to set up national networks. These ventures have been carried out by individual countries, but within the framework inspired by the International MARC Network Study. The organizational network has become the responsibility of the Conference of Directors of National Libraries and, so far, no regional centres have been set up formally within the International MARC Network. The IFLA UBCIM Programme Office acts as an international centre, but in practice is primarily a publisher, though acting as an information point for the expertise which is distributed throughout the network of national libraries interested in UNIMARC.

UNIMARC: the standard International MARC Network exchange format

In view of the UNIMARC programme, no special study was

made or recommended on the requirements for an international bibliographic exchange format and the report did not question this. This was how UNIMARC achieved a high profile and became a point of discussion at the top level of national library cooperative efforts.

UNIMARC itself had already been conceived and thus became a useful tool for the International MARC Network. Although the record structure which became ISO 2709 was accepted early on, during the very first cooperative project between the Library of Congress and BNB, there had been disagreement on content designators. In August 1971, a recommendation was made to IFLA that they assume the responsibility for establishing an international standard for content designators. In August 1972, at the IFLA General Conference in Budapest, the IFLA Committee on Cataloguing and the IFLA Committee on Mechanization jointly sponsored the IFLA Working Group on Content Designators. This Working Group had the task of exploring the reasons for the differences between the different MARC formats and arriving at a standard for the international exchange of data in machine-readable form. It limited its investigations to the requirements of the library community, i.e. libraries and national bibliographies. However, to ensure coordination of efforts as widely as possible, all working papers were submitted to the ISO TC46/SC4 Working Group on Content Designators as well as to the UNISIST Working Group on Bibliographic Descriptions which were both involved with formats for the secondary services. During deliberations, it was realized that each country needed to retain or establish its own format because of differences between national requirements, relating partly to the fact that national bibliographic agencies differed from each other in their roles and partly because of the language barriers that exist between nations. Each national agency would also arrange for the development of conversion programs to convert the data in its own national format into that of the international format. One feature that was agreed on was that the International Standard Bibliographic Descriptions should be the basis of the data elements relating to the descriptive area of the catalogue record. This was a wise move; not only were the ISBDs becoming the basis of national cataloguing codes; their adoption in UNIMARC gave the new format an international flavour and a reference point which librarians not yet familiar with automation could understand. Another feature that was agreed upon was that it should eventually be hospitable to all materials. This was a departure from the Library of Congress practice of having a format for each different type of material and one that gave UNIMARC an advantage over other formats when a country newly developing a national format sought models on which to base it. UNIMARC was published in 1977 at a crucial point in the history of the International MARC Network, between the completion of the International MARC Network Study document and its approval for publication.

The second edition of UNIMARC was published in 1980. This new edition was spurred on by the completion of ISBDs for cartographic materials and non-book materials, and by the revision of the ISBDs for monographs and serials. In the second edition of UNIMARC it is stated that:

> A number of national libraries including those of Australia, Canada, Japan, Hungary, South Africa, the United Kingdom and the United States have already agreed to use UNIMARC as their exchange format with implementation to take place early in the 1980s. To facilitate this the International MARC Network Study, which has already authorized and published several studies relating to the developing network of automated national libraries, is giving priority to further studies required to assist the conversion of national MARC formatted data to UNIMARC format.[10]

As a token contribution to compatibility at a wider level, Dorothy Anderson, as Director of the IFLA International Office for UBC and publisher of UNIMARC responsible for editorial work on the document, persuaded the Working Group to allow her to indicate with an asterisk the data elements regarded as mandatory for the identification and description of a bibliographic item by the Ad Hoc Group on the Establishment of the Common Communication Format.

The International MARC Network Study was in the meantime placed under the umbrella of a subgroup of the Conference of Directors of National Libraries called the International MARC Network Study Steering Committee or alternatively the International MARC Network Advisory Committee. The IFLA UBC Office continued to publish papers relating to the study which henceforward were under the authorship of this subgroup. UNIMARC remained an important preoccupation of the group and the format became less the intellectual property of the IFLA Committees on Cataloguing and Mechanization though members of those Committees continued to be involved as members of staff of national libraries interested in UNIMARC.

UNIMARC test

In 1981, the Conference of Directors of National Libraries agreed that a test should take place to attempt to ascertain the potential effectiveness of UNIMARC. This was one of the 'further studies' mentioned in the second edition of UNIMARC as cited above. A number of national bibliographic agencies took part in the test. Each agency was sent a number of photo-copies of title pages to catalogue and to code according to the UNIMARC format. The returned worksheets were collated by the IFLA UBC Office with help from the British Library Bibliographic Services Division and circulated to all who had taken part in the test. They were studied by various experts and it was clear to all concerned that the UNIMARC standard itself needed expanding or interpreting in order to enable compilation of records to compatible standards. The International MARC Network Study Steering Committee agreed that the work should be undertaken as soon as possible. Speed was essential to avoid UNIMARC itself becoming fragmented in its usage. The obvious location for the undertaking of the work was the Deutsche Bibliothek which was on the point of setting up an International MARC Programme which had been proposed a number of years earlier; this was intended to complement the IFLA UBC Office hosted by the British Library. But staff at the Library of Congress were particularly keen to start the UNIMARC project and did not want to wait for the establish-ment of the new office at Frankfurt; and the British fell into line with them. The Library of Congress was exchanging its tapes with other countries but was unable to use foreign tapes since, in order to do so, computer programs would have to be written to convert data from each foreign format to its own. The Library of Congress therefore wished to arrive at a workable international format as soon as possible. Then they would need only one conversion program, into and out of their USMARC format, as everyone else would supply their own data in the international format.

For technical reasons it was preferable to have the British as a partner as their format was very close to that of the US; the German format, MAB1, was different and had much more complex record linking.

UNIMARC handbook

So it was that in November 1982 the British Library transferred a member of staff who had previously worked on another international exchange format, the UNISIST Reference Manual, in the UNISIST International Centre for Bibliographic Descriptions to work on the *UNIMARC interpretive handbook*. Library of Congress staff felt that only by using someone who had experience of developing a bibliographic exchange format could the work be completed quickly. This member of staff worked closely with colleagues from the Bibliographic Standards Office in the British Library and the MARC Office of the Library of Congress.

The work was begun in November 1982 and, after circulation to the organizations that had taken part in the test, was completed in May of the following year, extremely quickly for an international quasi-standard document. It was published towards the end of 1983 as the *UNIMARC handbook*,[11] the word 'Interpretive' having been dropped from the title. In order to achieve that speed, the staff involved were not permitted to change anything in the second edition of UNIMARC, merely to interpret what was there; at times this was difficult, as the test had uncovered a few problems in the format definition. Field 203, General material designation, exemplifies the problem. Although this data element would seem to be sufficiently distinct to warrant a field of its own according to data-processing theory, it is located, according to ISBD rules, embedded in another field, the title field, only rarely appearing at the end of it. It therefore needs to be treated from the processing point of view as a subfield of the title field though, if one followed the principle that fields correspond to ISBD areas, it should be a field. Data which appear in the descriptive area of the record are, according to ISBD, ordered as on the document from which they are taken, and so cannot be arranged by logic. The General material designation, though not reproduced from the document, nevertheless must, according to ISBD rules, always occur after the main part of the title, the title proper, and so comes in the middle of the title field, before any subtitle or other title information. This kind of problem meant that a further revision had to be made to the *UNIMARC handbook*.

Developments in national formats elsewhere

In the meantime, many national libraries were able to forge ahead with their projects for national formats and international exchange based on the *UNIMARC handbook*. In Croatia, one of the states of Yugoslavia, an adaptation in Croatian[12] was made of the *UNIMARC handbook* in order to suit the requirements of the national cataloguing rules. In 1988, this was adopted as the standard for the whole of Yugoslavia. In Portugal, a similar exercise was undertaken with UNIMARC. In Spring 1984, Deutsche Bibliothek began to convert data in their MAB1 format to UNIMARC beginning with single-volume monographs without links.[13]

UNIMARC manual

When the British Library was satisfied with the commitment of other national libraries to UNIMARC, work recommenced on the *UNIMARC handbook* revision. This time there was no need for such great haste and more time was allowed for consultation. As a result, it was possible to make some fundamental changes to the format, most noticeably the inclusion of extra fields for new materials. The majority of the smaller changes related to anomalies which had been discovered during the work on the *UNIMARC handbook* and the subsequent practical use made of it.

Also during the 1980s, a review had taken place of the ISBDs for cartographic material, monographic material, non-book materials and serials. Described as a 'harmonization process', the review was designed to ensure consistency, to provide further and more varied examples, to consider the particular problems of non-Roman scripts and to modify ISBD(NBM) to make it hospitable to many kinds of material without its assuming the function of a cataloguing code.[14] It was completed in 1986 and though the four ISBDs were not published until 1987 and 1988, they were in a definite enough state to be considered in the revision of the *UNIMARC handbook*.

The revised handbook was published in 1987 under the title of *UNIMARC manual*,[15] incorporating changes to the basic format document and so becoming the third edition of UNIMARC. Thus, UNIMARC ceased to be contained in a basic standard-like document, but was embedded in an interpretive document. It was expected that this edition would herald a period of relative stability for UNIMARC.

International MARC Network Committee: further activities
In 1983, a further project of the International MARC Programme had been set up at the Deutsche Bibliothek at Frankfurt. It produced a newsletter and then published a report of a survey of national bibliographic systems entitled *International guide to MARC databases and services*. During IFLA's General Conference in Tokyo in 1986 it was agreed to merge the International MARC Programme with the other IFLA core programme, that for Universal Bibliographic Control, when Deutsche Bibliothek ceased its involvement at the end of that year. The combined programmes became known as the Universal Bibliographic Control and International MARC Programme (UBCIM). Although it did not have as much administrative independence in the British Library as it had had in the IFLA UBC Office, its intellectual independence and that of its policy were guaranteed by the British Library.

CD-ROM
A word on the international MARC community's efforts on standardizing for CD-ROM is appropriate here. In 1986 the Conference of Directors of National Libraries set up discussions under the umbrella of the International MARC Network Committee with a view to achieving a common applications-software standard for the publication of databases of national bibliographies on CD-ROM. The ultimate aim of the standard was to allow the easy interchange of CD-ROM products from different agencies. The discs would be accessed, searched and downloaded using the local search language and it would be possible to switch between discs without changing language. At

a meeting in London in December 1987 attended by representatives from the national libraries of France, the Federal Republic of Germany, Portugal, Spain, Norway, the Netherlands and the United Kingdom, and at which input was received from the US Library of Congress and the National Library of Canada, it was decided that the British Library and the Bibliothèque Nationale of France should go ahead with a joint CD-ROM production.[16] This consisted of about 30,000 records in UKMARC from the BNB MARC database and the same number of records in UNIMARC from the French database. The BNB records were of books on the history of Europe and included records from the whole range of BNB production, starting in 1950 and going up to 1988, with their varying standards and quality. One aim of the project was to see whether records produced according to different cataloguing rules could happily be placed in one CD-ROM. The disc has since been evaluated within the national libraries of the European Community with help from the Commission[17] which gave funding within the context of the promotion of better and easier access to European national bibliographies and the quest for economies in library cataloguing through an increase in the exchange of bibliographic data. The records may be viewed in UKMARC or in UNIMARC, depending on the source, both in a diagnostic-type format where tags and indicators precede the data, and in full ISBD display. An ISO 2709 interface was added as a result of enquiries for it. At a seminar entitled 'Innovations and initiatives' organized by the UK Library Association Cataloguing and Indexing Group in 1989, Robert Smith of the British Library reported on the future directions of the cooperative CD-ROM research. It was hoped to develop the retrieval interface, though it would not be capable of complete standardization. MARC conversion was to be a priority to bridge the different formats in use. At that time there was not an effective microcomputer conversion program available, but Smith said it would soon be feasible. Character sets were going to be high on the agenda, and the multilingual interface would have to be extended as the Commission wanted all Community official languages to be included. Ultimately, what was needed was a common shell for all the different national bibliographies. While searching in one bibliography, it would be possible to pull down a 'window' and look into another bibliography. This was then feasible as compared with two years earlier, since the development of Microsoft Windows, a software package available on the latest IBM personal computers, enabling a number of programs to be run at once.

This project, though not uniquely under the aegis of the International MARC Network, was very much continuing the spirit of the original study.

UNIMARC – technical details

Features stated in the UNIMARC documentation

UNIMARC was designed on the basis of a set of nine principles which were published in the first and second editions as 'Guidelines for Format Design'. These were based on experience which had been gained in the various national MARC formats and are summarized below.

The main feature of UNIMARC was that it should have one set of tags or subfield identifiers covering all materials; there would be one format rather than a separate format for each kind of bibliographic material. Indicators and subfield identifiers should be used as consistently as possible across different fields. There would be no specified order for subfields in UNIMARC, so that they could be placed in the order required by the cataloguing codes and the formats from which the data were converted. One interesting guideline states that descriptive information carried in notes is not intended for use as access points; in UNIMARC data required to generate access points are to be added to the record, even if they are present in a note. This guideline illustrates that UNIMARC records had to be capable of providing catalogue entries and added entries as required in a card catalogue. Cross-reference data was to be kept out of 'the generalized format for the exchange of bibliographic data'. The way in which UKMARC, for example, included references to headings in the bibliographic record containing them was not to be followed. Instead, links to authority files were proposed which resulted, later, in the development of the UNIMARC authorities format.

Additional features relating to UNIMARC as an exchange format

The principles outlined above were required by virtue of the fact that UNIMARC was developed as an exchange format and data would be converted into that format from other formats. Other principles and practices were added later. For example, a 'fill character' was established for use in coded data fields in the record label, and coded subfields where the source format provides no indication of what the UNIMARC value should be.

Another important principle was that ISBD punctuation should not appear at the subfield boundaries in the descriptive area. Some MARC formats do this; others do not as it can be generated automatically. UNIMARC requires that this punctuation is stripped out on conversion. However, UNIMARC makes no such provision for punctuation in other data such as access points, since cataloguing codes treat them in different ways. An agency may therefore include punctuation in the record at subfield boundaries or remove it on conversion to UNIMARC.

The coded data elements usually follow Library of Congress MARC practice, a practice which has in fact been followed by most national MARC formats. However, many of the Library of Congress codes have been expanded or rationalized to make them more generally applicable. An example of such a code is that indicating that the record relates to a government publication. One-character codes are listed for different tiers of government, such as county/department, state/province, intergovernmental.

The types of record codes include all the different types at present supported by the UNIMARC fields. Four categories of bibliographic level are supported, monographic, serial, analytic and collection; these are defined in the same way as in the majority of MARC formats. There is also an encoding-level field which indicates whether the record was created from inspection of the original document, or whether it was produced without the item being examined or whether it was a pre-publication record. A further code indicates the extent to which the record conforms to ISBD.

An interesting feature of the format is the inclusion of fields in blocks defined by type of data element. Up to the development of UNIMARC, the major national MARC formats had ordered the different fields in a way that reflected the order of the fields on a traditional catalogue card. UNIMARC avoided this bias towards one particular end-product of a machine-readable bibliographic record and put all name access points in one block instead of using different blocks for author as main entry and author as added entry.

All title access points are defined in the 500 block other than title proper in field 200 which begins the descriptive block, as the title is usually required as an access point in the same form as in the descriptive area. The 100 block is for coded data. Field 100 includes codes common to all materials and each type of material has another field for codes specific to that type. The blocks and the fields they contain are reproduced in Figure 4.1.

Linking techniques

The most novel feature of UNIMARC is its treatment of links between one bibliographic item and another. Bibliographic items have relationships with each other. They may have previous editions; they may, as in the case of serials, have related, earlier or later titles. Moreover, they may be in the same journal or series as each other. In special cases, some bibliographic items are translations of others. Another kind of relation is the sharing of common subject or authorship. UNIMARC has a number of different ways of showing these linking relationships.

Relationships between bibliographic items are indicated by means of fields in the linking-entry block, fields 410 to 488. The largest number of these relate to serials, such as 'Continues', 'Continues in part', 'Changed back to', 'Merged with x and y to form'. The names of these linking fields in UNIMARC are in fact the text that would be associated with the name of the serial in a note generated for the link in a traditional catalogue record.

Applicable to monographs and serials alike are the fields 'Series' and 'Subseries'. These can be used in monographs and serials to link to a containing series and subseries. Links can be made to other editions and to translations or from a translation to its original.

```
0— IDENTIFICATION BLOCK
    001  Record Identifier Field
    010  International Standard Book Number (ISBN)
    011  International Standard Serial Number (ISSN)
    020  National Bibliography Number
    021  Legal Deposit Number
    022  Government Publication Number
    040  CODEN

1— CODED INFORMATION BLOCK
    100  General Processing Data
    101  Language of the Work
    102  Country of Publication or Production
    105  Coded Data Field:  Books
    106  Coded Data Field:  Books-Physical Attributes
    110  Coded Data Field:  Serials
    111  Coded Data Field:  Serials-Physical Attributes
    120  Coded Data Field:  Cartographic Materials
    122  Coded Data Field:  Cartographic Materials-Situation Date(s)
    123  Coded Data Field:  Cartographic Materials-Scale and Coordinates

2— DESCRIPTIVE INFORMATION BLOCK
    200  Title and Statement of Responsibility
    204  General Material Designation
    205  Edition Statement
    206  Material Specific Area:  Cartographic Materials—Mathematical Data
    207  Material Specific Area:  Serials-Numbering
    210  Publication, Distribution, Etc.
    215  Physical Description
    225  Series

3— NOTES BLOCK
    300  General Note
    301  Notes Pertaining to Identification Numbers
    302  Notes Pertaining to Coded Information
    303  General Notes Pertaining to Descriptive Information
    304  Notes Pertaining to Title and Statement of Responsibility
    305  Notes Pertaining to Edition and Bibliographic History
    306  Notes Pertaining to Publication, Distribution, etc.
    307  Notes Pertaining to Physical Description
    308  Notes Pertaining to Series
    310  Notes Pertaining to Binding and Availability
    311  Notes Pertaining to Linking Fields
    312  Notes Pertaining to Related Titles
    313  Notes Pertaining to Subject Access
    314  Notes Pertaining to Intellectual Responsibility
    315  Notes Pertaining to Material (or Type of Publication) Specific
         Information
    320  Bibliography Note
    321  Availability of Indexes and Abstracts Note
    324  Facsimile Note
    326  Frequency Statement Note (Serials)
    327  Contents Note
    328  Dissertation (Thesis) Note
    330  Summary or Abstract
```

Fig. 4.1   The UNIMARC blocks and the fields they contain

(Reproduced from *UNIMARC handbook*, with permission of IFLA
UBCIM Programme, London)

4— LINKING ENTRY BLOCK

410	Series	444	Absorbed by
411	Subseries	445	Absorbed in Part by
421	Supplement	446	Split into
422	Parent of Supplement	447	Merged with xxx to form
423	Issued with	448	Changed back to
430	Continues	451	Other Edition in Same Medium
431	Continues in Part	452	Edition in a Different Medium
432	Supersedes	453	Translated as
433	Supersedes in Part	454	Translation of
434	Absorbed	461	Set Level
435	Absorbed in Part	462	Subset Level
436	Formed by Merger of	463	Piece Level
440	Continued by	464	Piece-Analytic Level
441	Continued in Part by	488	Other Related Works
442	Superseded by		
443	Superseded in Part by		

5— RELATED TITLE BLOCK

500 Uniform Title
501 Collective Uniform Title
503 Uniform Conventional Heading
510 Parallel Title Proper
512 Cover Title
513 Added Title-Page Title
514 Caption Title
515 Running Title
516 Spine Title
517 Other Variant Titles
520 Former Title (Serials)
530 Key-Title (Serials)
531 Abbreviated Title (Serials)
532 Expanded Title (Serials)
540 Additional Title Supplied by Cataloguer
541 Translated Title Supplied by Cataloguer

6— SUBJECT ANALYSIS BLOCK

600 Personal Name Used as Subject
601 Corporate Name used as Subject
602 Family Name Used as Subject
605 Title Used as Subject
606 Topical Name Used as Subject
607 Geographical Name Used as Subject
660 Geographic Area Code (GAC)
661 Chronological Coverage Code (CCC)
670 PRECIS
675 Universal Decimal Classification (UDC)
676 Dewey Decimal Classification (DDC)
680 Library of Congress Classification

7— INTELLECTUAL RESPONSIBILITY BLOCK

700 Personal Name - Primary Intellectual Responsibility
701 Personal Name - Alternative Intellectual Responsibility
702 Personal Name - Secondary Intellectual Responsibility
710 Corporate Body Name - Primary Intellectual Responsibility
711 Corporate Body Name - Alternative Intellectual Responsibility
712 Corporate Body Name - Secondary Intellectual Responsibility
720 Family Name - Primary Intellectual Responsibility
721 Family Name - Alternative Intellectual Responsibility
722 Family Name - Secondary Intellectual Responsibility

8— INTERNATIONAL USE BLOCK

801 Originating Source Field

Fig. 4.1 (continued)

188

There is additionally a set of linking fields entitled 'Levels' which enable links to be made between items in a bibliographic hierarchy. These link to Set, Subset, Piece and Piece-analytic. Since processing of records containing hierarchical links is more complex, character position 8 in the record label is reserved to indicate if this technique has been used in a record. Organizations which have not developed conversion programs for records including these links can thus be warned that they will not be able to process them correctly. Also, it shows that data from other records will be required for the complete processing of the record that contains these fields. This code has been adopted from character position 19 of the USMARC leader.

In all these cases, the linking fields can be used in two different ways. A link can be made to another record, or the data relating to the related record can be embedded in the linking field. Since one of the main aims of MARC records is to produce catalogue records in printed form, an indicator, the second indicator, specifies whether the field is to be used to print a note: the first indicator is always blank. Following the indicators, the subfield identifier is $1. There then follows, if a link is being made to a record control number, the record control number preceded, for identification, by 001, the tag for the record control number or identifier.

If the embedded-record technique is used, each field in the embedded record follows the tag which indicates the relation and each field is preceded by $1. These embedded fields are not found in any directory, so processing of these fields in the embedded record is quite different from processing of fields in the main body of the record.

In the record for the serial *Bus & coach* which was preceded by *Motor transport* would appear in field 434 the following:

__1$15300__$aBus & coach [__ represents space]

The first two characters are indicators of field 434; $1 indicates start of the first embedded field 530; 0__ are indicators in the embedded field; $aBus & coach are the data which follow immediately. 434 occurs in the directory with pointers to the data string shown above.

If a link were being made to a record number and the record

189

number of *Bus & coach* was T01564, then the field would appear as follows:

＿1$1001T01564

UNIMARC was the first in the family of MARC formats to include this kind of linking mechanism. Hitherto, formats had indicated relationships in other ways, and these methods are also retained in UNIMARC itself.

In a traditional catalogue, series relationships are indicated by means of added entries. An item in a monographic series will have an added entry under the name of the series and, if applicable, the number within that series. In UNIMARC, the series statement, which is primarily intended as part of the description of the monograph according to traditional cataloguing practice, may be used as an access point if it is the established form. Otherwise, field 410 must be used to contain an embedded record relating to the series. The embedded record may consist of the title of the series; or it may include both author and title if cataloguing rules would require an author/title access point.

If the linking field contained a record control number, then the program could proceed as follows when it produced the record in the catalogue from this record: if the record to which the link were made (that of the series) had a main entry under author, an author-title added entry would be produced for this item in the series. If the record of the series on the other hand was entered under title, then a title added entry for the series would be produced in the record of the monograph as in Figure 4.2.

UNIMARC contains an additional way of treating former titles of serials. This is by means of field 520, Former title (serials). This field holds only the title of the serial and has no special linking mechanism. This method has been included to avoid having to make links between records in those systems that enter serial records under the latest title of the serial. Those systems will not have records for earlier titles, and consequently have to include access to earlier titles in the record by means of this 'Former title' field.

```
Label bibliographical level code: m
001     20055
010     $a92-2-106396-8
100     $a19890208d1988        fOENGy0103a
101 0 $aeng
200 1 $aFrom a developing to a newly industrialised country
        $ethe republic of Korea 1961-82$fTony Michell
210     $aGeneva$cILO$d1988
215     $axii, 180 p
225 2 $aEmployment, adjustment and industrialisation$x0257-3415$v6
461   1$100120054$12001 $v6
700   1$aMichell$bTony
```

Record of series
```
Label bibliographical level code: s
001     20054
011     $a0257-3415
100     $a19890208s19869999        fOENGy0103a
101 0 $aeng
200 1 $aEmployment, adjustment and industrialisation
210     $aGeneva$cILO$d1986
712 02$aILO$31092
```

Output in AACR form

```
Michell, Tony
    From a developing to a newly industrialised
country : the republic of Korea 1961 - 82 / Tony
Michell. -- Geneva : ILO, 1988. -- xii, 180 p. --
(Employment, adjustment and industrialisation,
ISSN 0257-3415 ; 6). -- ISBN 92-2-106396-8
```

ADDED ENTRIES
```
CORPORATE AUTHOR(S): ILO
SERIAL TITLE:          Employment, adjustment and
                       industrialisation
                            Record no: 20055
```

Fig. 4.2 **Record of a monograph containing a link to a monographic series**

The second kind of relationship, common subjects or common authorship, is indicated in a traditional catalogue by the records of the items filing together. There are other possibilities in the machine environment. UNIMARC includes in access-point fields representing subjects or persons or corporate bodies responsible a subfield ($3) for an Authority Record Number. This enables a link to be made to an authority record identified by an Authority Record Number which can contain not only the text of the subject heading or author but also references referring to it. A format has been devised called UNIMARC Authorities to hold these records. The example

191

above shows such a number. The record of the series contains in field 710 the subfield $31092. 1092 is the authority record number relating to the record for ILO which would appear as follows so that references could be generated:

CORPORATE BODY NAME : ILO
  USE FOR: BIT
  USE FOR: Bureau international du travail
  USE FOR: International Labour Office
  USE FOR: International Labour Organizaation
  USE FOR: OIT
  USE FOR: Organización Internacional del Trabajo
   CODE : 1092

At the present time any bibliographic agency using an Authority Record Number will have to allocate its own authority record numbers which would be meaningful only to other agencies which were supplied with the authority records. The above record is taken from a system which, when exporting records in UNIMARC, always converts to the full UNIMARC form as in the example in Figure 4.2 and does not even include the authority number in the records it exports. In consequence, all the corporate body headings are available in full in each record. To allow authority records to be used to the greatest possible extent it would be necessary for an International Standard Authority Number to be allocated to subject headings, persons and corporate bodies. This would be expensive to administer; it would be more difficult to administer than the ISBN or ISSN and it would probably not so easily gain the cooperation of the publishing world as the ISBN and ISSN, since it would be of little advantage to any organization other than those producing high-quality catalogue records.

History of UNIMARC authorities

From the outset, there had been problems in many MARC formats of how to incorporate references. LC/USMARC did not include them. UKMARC included in each record every reference required for all the headings in that record. The logical way forward was for a format which would facilitate the setting up of databases of authority records. As illustrated in the example above, UNIMARC may include in an access-point

192

field a subfield, $3, to allow the entry of a code. The intention was that in the future this would be an international authority number but until these were developed it would be a number allocated to a heading in a particular system.

To facilitate the exchange of authority information, in 1979 the IFLA Sections on Information Technology and Cataloguing jointly set up the IFLA Working Group on an International Authority System. This submitted in 1983 the *Guidelines for authority and reference entries (GARE)*[18] which set out the data elements that should appear in authority and reference entries, using conventions akin to the punctuation in ISBD.

Then followed the development of a companion format, based on the underlying principles of UNIMARC and under the auspices of a Steering Group on a UNIMARC Format for Authorities. An additional principle was added, that subfield codes should be as in the bibliographic format, though the tags would have to differ because of the different functions of the fields in the different formats. The different functions can be seen by comparing the table of functional blocks reproduced from the UNIMARC Authorities (Figure 4.3) with those of the UNIMARC format for bibliographic material in Figure 4.1. For example, the 2-- fields are reserved for the descriptive area in the bibliographic format whereas they contain the heading fields in Authorities. The format document was circulated three times round the Steering Group between May 1984 and March 1987 before being revised and published in draft form for wider circulation in January 1988. It was finally published in 1990.[19]

Critique of UNIMARC

Although UNIMARC has been adopted as a national format in many countries, it is intended as an international exchange format into which national agencies will convert their national records to reduce the bilateral conversion arrangements in which they would otherwise have to engage. As an international exchange format, it has to be able to cater for all the idiosyncrasies of existing national formats.

For this reason, the UNIMARC format contains some redundancy; one reason why the *UNIMARC handbook* was commissioned was to give users of UNIMARC guidance as to which option to take in those circumstances where data could be

The fields of the authority or reference record are divided into functional blocks; the first (left most) digit of the tag indicates the block of the field.

0— Identification Block: contains numbers that identify the record or the authority.

1-- Coded Information Block: contains fixed length data elements (frequently coded) describing various aspects of the record or data.

2— Heading Block: contains the authority, reference, or explanatory heading for which the record has been created.

3-- Information Note Block: contains notes, intended for public display, that explain the relationship between the record heading (2--) and other headings.

4-- See Reference Tracing Block: contains variant headings from which a reference is to be made to see the heading of the record.

5— See Also Reference Tracing Block: contains related uniform headings from which a reference is to be made to see also the heading of the record.

6— Linking Heading Block: contains a form of the record heading (2--) in another language or script and links to another record in which that form is the 2-- heading.

7— Classification Number Block: contains classification numbers that are related to the heading of the record.

8-- Source Information Block: contains the source of the record, rules under which it was created, and cataloguer's notes about the data not intended for public display.

9-- National Use Block: contains data local to the originator of the record. Field tags will not be defined in UNIMARC/Authorities for intersystem exchange.

Fig. 4.3   Functional blocks, in UNIMARC Authorities, draft, 1988

(Reproduced with permission of IFLA UBCIM Programme, London)

transferred from one field in a national format to two in UNIMARC. One can see a certain amount of overlap between Uniform titles, Collective uniform titles, Uniform conventional headings and Topical name used as a subject.

UNIMARC may be required to hold records created by different cataloguing rules. Some codes, and the number is increasing as adaptations are made for automation, do not rely on the concept of main entry. The problem is recognized in UNIMARC, which provides (in its Intellectual Responsibility Block) an alternative method of coding records created by codes embodying the main entry concept. Compatibility of records from different sources is discussed further in the context of a definition of compatibility which is treated in Chapter 7.

Impact of UNIMARC

What has been the impact of UNIMARC? The *International guide to MARC databases and services*[20] gives us some clues. The first edition of the report listed 16 countries offering magnetic-tape services; of these, nine were using AACR2 (or AACR2-based) cataloguing codes. USMARC and UNIMARC were offered by five countries. Some, like Australia, offered records to overseas subscribers either in the national format or in USMARC. Twenty countries were planning a magnetic-tape service; 23 were not offering or planning such a service. By 1986, when the second edition of the guide appeared, considerable progress had been made. Nineteen countries offered national magnetic-tape services; 12 countries provided national online services and 14 were planning neither tape nor online access. Eleven countries were using AACR2 or AACR2-based rules for descriptive cataloguing. Comparatively few exchanges in UNIMARC were taking place, though some national agencies had constructed their formats along UNIMARC lines, and several national libraries had made a commitment in principle to accept UNIMARC as an exchange format. Of the four ABACUS libraries (Britain, Australia, Canada and the US) only the US was offering exchange records in the UNIMARC format. Cathro[21] notes that there was little incentive for the Australian Bibliographic Network to develop a UNIMARC interface as records it wished to obtain were readily available in USMARC format.

Hope Clement, who had chaired the International MARC Network Committee since 1979, also expressed her disappointment at the slow development of UNIMARC conversion programs.[22] She felt this lack of effort was due to four factors: the length of time required to write the complex conversion programs; the fact that many libraries already had conversion programs for the sources they used; the conflicting priorities within national agencies of exchange within their country and international exchange; and the lack of a large body of records in UNIMARC which would make the writing of any conversion program worthwhile. She also made the point that differences in implementations of UNIMARC still complicated the writing of conversion programs and could lead to loss of detail and content of the converted records. These reasons were probably among those why the British Library has not adopted UNIMARC, even though it played such a large part in the development of the *UNIMARC handbook*. However, the British Library's hosting of the IFLA UBCIM Programme ended in 1990 and the work transferred to the Deutsche Bibliothek, the national library of the Federal Republic of Germany which, along with the Library of Congress and Bibliothèque Nationale in Paris, was the main supporter of UNIMARC among the national libraries of the world's major industralized countries.

Why had initial enthusiasm for UNIMARC apparently begun to wane? The answer must surely lie in economics. At the start of this chapter it was noted that early developments of UNIMARC began in the spirit of cooperation of the time. By the end of the 1980s a different spirit held sway. Exchange of bibliographic data was only one of many activities that had to adapt to financial constraints imposed on public sector organizations. National libraries could no longer spend limited resources on developing an exchange format which would not bring an easily-visible benefit. Only extra publicity for UNIMARC and its advantages will enable the International MARC Network to come to fruition. A workshop on UNIMARC was held during the IFLA General Conference in Sydney, Australia in 1988, which may be the start of a series.[23] Additionally, as a result of its implementation by a number of national libraries in Europe, UNIMARC was chosen for use in a project concerned with the use of records from different countries in retrospective conversion, part of a European Community initiative. These activities may help to rekindle the early sparks of enthusiasm.

Notes and references

1 Wells, A. J., *The International MARC Network: a study for an international bibliographic data network*, London, IFLA International Office for UBC, 1977 (Occasional paper no.3).
2 Green, S. P., 'Proposals for a focus for the international exchange of bibliographic data in machine-readable form', unpublished paper.

3 Duchesne, R. M., 'The role of national libraries in national and international information systems', unpublished paper.

4 Duchesne, R. M., 'MARC and SUPERMARC' in *The exchange of bibliographic data and the MARC format: proceedings of the International Seminar on the MARC Format and the Exchange of Bibliographic Data in Machine-readable Form, Berlin, 1971*, 2nd ed., Berlin, Verlag Dokumentation, 1973, 37–57.

5 Wells, A. J., *op. cit.*

6 Avram, H. D., 'International standards for the interchange of bibliographic records in machine-readable form', *Library resources and technical services*, **20**, (1), Winter 1976, 25–35.

7 Gorman, M., 'Proposal on the structure of name access points in exchange records', unpublished paper, 1976.

8 Wells, A. J., *op. cit.*, 14.

9 International MARC Network Study Steering Committee, *International access to MARC records: a summary report with recommended text for a bilateral agreement for the international exchange of MARC records*, London, IFLA International Office for UBC, 1980.

10 *UNIMARC: Universal MARC format*, 2nd rev. ed., London, IFLA International Office for UBC, 1980, 1.

11 Hopkinson, A., *UNIMARC handbook*, London, IFLA International Office for UBC, 1983.

12 Willer, M., *ed.*, *Prirucnik za UNIMARC*, Zagreb, Nacionala i sveucilisna biblioteka, 1989. In 1986 this was available in draft, well before final publication which was delayed to await publication of the *UNIMARC manual*.

13 *IFLA journal*, **13**, 1987, 168.

14 'IFLA activities',. *International cataloguing*, **12**, (1), 1. The documents under review were *ISBD(M)*, *ISBD(NBM)* and *ISBD(S)*. The latest versions which were available in draft when the *UNIMARC manual* was in preparation are *ISBD(CM): cartographic materials*, rev. ed., London, IFLA UBCIM Programme, 1987; *ISBD(M): monographic publications*, rev. ed., London, IFLA UBCIM Programme, 1987; *ISBD(NBM): non-book materials*, rev. ed., London, IFLA UBCIM Programme, 1987; *ISBD(S): serials*, London, IFLA UBCIM Programme, 1988.

15 Holt, B., *UNIMARC manual*, London, IFLA International Programme for UBC, 1987.

16 'Compact disc for national bibliography: Britain and France join forces', *British Library Bibliographic Services newsletter*, **46**, June 1988, 1–3.

17 McSean, Tony, 'Sharing the data: developments in MARC record supply', in Horsnell, V., ed., *Mechanisms for library*

    cooperation: getting our act together: proceedings of the 13th Annual Seminar of the MARC Users' Group, Aldershot, Gower, 1988, 71.

18   *Guidelines for authority and reference entries* / recommended by the Working Group on an International Authority System, London, IFLA International Programme for UBC, 1984.

19   *UNIMARC/A: UNIMARC format for authorities*, London, IFLA UBCIM Programme, 1990.

20   *International guide to MARC databases and services: national magnetic tape services*, 1st ed., Frankfurt, Deutsche Bibliothek for the International MARC Project, 1984; 2nd rev. and enl. ed., 1986.

21   Cathro, W., 'The exchange of cataloguing data in the Australian Bibliographic Network', *International cataloguing and bibliographic control*, **17**, (2), April/June 1988, 19–21.

22   Clement, H., 'The International MARC Network and national libraries', *Alexandria*, **1**, (1), 1989, 23–34.

23   *UNIMARC in theory and practice: papers from the UNIMARC workshop, Sydney, Australia, August 1988*, ed. by S. H. McCallum and W. D. Roberts, London, IFLA UBCIM Programme, 1989.

Additional readings

The history of the International MARC Network and UNIMARC can be traced in more detail in the following journals:

International cataloguing and bibliographic control, London, IFLA UBCIM Programme, 1988– , 17– , which succeeded *International cataloguing*, London, IFLA International Office for UBC, 1972–1987, vols. 1–16.

IFLA journal, Munich, Saur, 1975– , 1– .

5

Other international formats

Non-MARC formats

No book on bibliographic data exchange is complete without mention of those exchange formats that are not strictly speaking members of the MARC family. These are formats not used by library networks, national or international, and so are not regarded as true MARC formats. They are related to those formats by virtue of the fact that they owe their record structure and much of their methodology to the early work done on MARC formats in national libraries. There are many formats developed by systems for their own use, for exchanging data within a network. There are other formats which have been devised purely as a means of outputting data for external users; some established systems have offered their tapes to customers to mount on their own computers. The recipient system devises or purchases programs which will interpret the tapes and integrate the data with its own data. Many of the formats used by these tape services are related to ISO 2709 to enable the recipient who may already have programs that can read ISO 2709 tapes to use the records with the minimum of difficulty.

The INSPEC tape format and Chemical Abstracts (CAS) format are examples of exchange formats. They predate MARC and are not based on ISO 2709. In the case of the CAS format, one of the main areas of incompatibility with ISO 2709 was that it included the facility of indicating data by bits rather than bytes or characters which is the only way permitted by ISO 2709. Tapes using formats like these and, in some cases, software to process them are supplied to subscribers. Other formats have achieved a slightly higher status because they have been developed by international organizations. These tend to use ISO 2709 for the record structure. The AGRIS format

(Agricultural Information System) of the UN Food and Agriculture Organization and the INIS format (International Nuclear Information System) of the UN International Atomic Energy Agency are examples of these formats. Because they were in existence early on, they have influenced systems in their subject area throughout the world since systems have been developed at regional or state level to hold records which are contributed to the international system. Also in the case of these two systems, the responsibility for data entry is distributed to organizations in member states. Originally, worksheets were prepared in the member states and sent to headquarters to be converted into machine-readable form by either manual data entry or optical character recognition (OCR). The only format that the remote institution saw was the worksheet. Now, in many cases, data are sent on tapes and diskettes, produced on systems in the member states.

These systems are not truly library systems. They are often referred to as 'secondary services' or 'abstracting and indexing services'. They are regarded as making up, together with national libraries and their dependent local library services, the 'total information community'. This is a term which has often been used in connection with the next two exchange formats which are discussed in greater detail.

UNISIST reference manual

History and use

All the formats discussed so far were developed for the library sector of the information community. However, computers were already being employed by secondary services before they were introduced into libraries. In the context of the exchange of data the secondary services were to follow the libraries. Since the record structure of the MARC format had been made a national standard in the USA, ANSI Z39.2–1971,[1] it was the obvious standard for the information community as a whole to follow. In the United States, the Chemical Abstracts Service followed the Library of Congress in setting up a similar cooperative project to that which the Library of Congress had set up with the British National Bibliography, this time with UKCIS, the UK Chemical Information Service. They took and adapted Z39.2–

1971 as their exchange record structure. In the UK, the Institution of Electrical Engineers started in 1969 a tape service for bibliographic references, automating their abstracting and indexing service which had begun as *Science abstracts* in 1898. This, too, used a similar record structure. The need for a standard set of data elements for the exchange of bibliographic data was spreading to the secondary services, so they began to look for something akin to the MARC formats. They based their format on the same record structure, though they adopted their own system of tags for the data elements.

Resolutions adopted at the 14th and 15th Sessions of the General Conference of Unesco which took place in 1966 and 1968 authorized the Director-General of Unesco to undertake and complete jointly with the International Council of Scientific Unions (ICSU) a feasibility study on the establishment of a World Science Information System (UNISIST).[2]

The UNISIST-ICSU/AB Working Group on Bibliographic Descriptions, set up in 1967 as part of the UNISIST programme, decided that it was necessary to develop a standard for the recording and exchange of data in machine-readable form. The outcome of this was the UNISIST *Reference manual for machine-readable bibliographic descriptions*[3] and the group that had worked on it included representatives from the British National Bibliography, the Centre National de la Recherche Scientifique, France, the Institution of Electrical Engineers which had set up INSPEC, and Chemical Abstracts.

When the format was being developed, the Working Group had only the early MARC formats as models. The members thought that they should take great care not to cause confusion with the existing MARC formats and decided that tags should begin with an alphabetic character, and subfield identifiers should be numeric. Because the International Serials Data System was engaged in the control of serial titles, it was decided that the Reference Manual should not include the treatment of serials as a whole, so no provision was made for them. However, fields were included for the treatment of contributions in serials. The Manual included matrices or tables giving the fields required for each combination of bibliographic level (e.g. analytic in monograph in series; monograph; monograph in series) and it was made clear that this format should not be used

201

for serials by excluding the category of 'serial only' from the table, and by excluding holdings data. Interestingly enough, the ISDS system, when it got under way, dealt with international registration of serials, but did not deal with an individual library's holdings so the Reference Manual would not have duplicated ISDS had it included facilities for the recording of runs of serials. Many of the organizations using the Reference Manual needed to record the serials of interest to their own databases, and no doubt did so by the inclusion of private fields permitted by the format.

It is interesting to note that the importance attributed to the collection level in the Reference Manual may have been due in part to the fact that the French word for a monographic series is 'collection'. The developers of MARC had used 'collection' to mean something completely different, a collection of documents brought together for the convenience of library housekeeping. Given the fact that ISDS was going to record serials much more exhaustively than monographic series, it must have been clear to the Working Group on Bibliographic Descriptions that monographic series had to be included in the Reference Manual. As in the case of serials, there was no opportunity, as indicated by the matrices, for the collection to be recorded as a complete entity. Fields at the collection level could be included only when fields at the monographic level were present.

After publication, it was felt that the format needed a maintenance agency to look after it. The idea of the establishment of the ISDS Centre to control serial publications had just been proposed and accepted within the UNISIST Programme, and the Government of the Republic of France had agreed to host the centre and find accommodation for it in Paris. There was a feeling in certain circles in the UK that participation in UNISIST at a similar level to that of France was essential, so the UK government agreed to host a UNISIST Centre which was set up to maintain the Reference Manual. The UK focal point for the UNISIST Programme had been the Office for Scientific and Technical Information which later became the British Library Research and Development Department. So the UNISIST International Centre for Bibliographic Descriptions (UNIBID) was placed there and Harold Dierickx who was working on the AGRIS project in FAO was appointed its

Director. Unesco gave it a token grant each year and contributed towards travel and subsistence costs for foreign travel. In consultation with Unesco, the British Library established an Advisory Committee to oversee the work of the Centre.

Take-up of the format seemed rather slow, a result, perhaps, of the diverse nature of the secondary services agencies and the difficulty of achieving consolidation between them. Furthermore, in contrast with the library community, the larger members of the secondary-service community and many of the smaller ones tend to be in the private sector and to be in competition with each other.

There existed a number of organizations coordinating these secondary services, such as the (US) National Federation of Abstracting and Indexing Services (NFAIS), the European Association of Scientific Information Dissemination Centres (EUSIDIC), the Association of Information Disseminating Centers (ASIDIC) and ICSU/AB. The organizations that had helped in the preparation of the Reference Manual were for the most part members of one or more of the coordinating organizations and some of them were invited to join the Advisory Committee set up to monitor the work being done by UNIBID in maintaining the Reference Manual. These organizations generally had their own formats, which is why they had been involved in work on the Reference Manual, and they were being asked to help others as much as to design a format that their own organization would be likely to use. Potential users of the Reference Manual also had ideas for improvement and put pressure on the coordinating organizations for certain changes to be made to it. In 1977, the so-called Four-Ways Committee (because it was composed of representatives of ASIDIC, EUSIDIC, ICSU/AB and NFAIS) with support from the US National Science Foundation, Division of Scientific Information, called a meeting in 1977 to put forward their views to UNIBID.[4] One feature they wanted was a field to contain personal author names in a standard format with the forenames stripped down to initials to facilitate online searching. This was provided as a subfield in the second edition of the Reference Manual. A year or so later, ASIDIC decided no longer to give their support to the format, ostensibly because their members did not feel it a worthwhile exercise to which to devote any time or resources. The 1977 meeting had revealed the difficulties of achieving agreement in this area of standardization among the potential users of the Reference Manual.

Nevertheless, UNIBID continued to maintain the format supported by Unesco. Other features were requested by members of the UNIBID Advisory Committee and other interested parties. The second edition of the manual, which was published in 1981 in loose-leaf form, includes 'guidance for the description of serials as entities in their own right',[5] and a chapter entitled 'A brief guide to database documentation'[6] which is intended to ensure that the features of a secondary service are sufficiently well outlined in manuals and other documentation they produce.

In 1982, the British Library Research and Development Department suffered severe cuts and was unable to continue to host UNIBID. There had been a certain amount of criticism within the British Library that the Library was supporting both UNIMARC and the UNISIST Reference manual which to many seemed to be rival formats serving the same function. Additionally, there was criticism that the publication of the revision of the Reference Manual had taken as long as it had, four years, though there was little understanding that this kind of international work can be protracted because it requires the agreement of so many parties to make any advances.

The functions of UNIBID were therefore transferred to the Unesco Division of the General Information Programme which continued to provide copies of the Manual to enquirers. Eventually, the second edition was superseded in 1985 by a third edition incorporating all the loose-leaf amendments.

The Manual was widely circulated by Unesco and it had great influence on systems that were being developed. It was used as a source of data elements by organizations developing formats. It was used by the International Development Research Centre in Ottawa as a format on which to model the format for DEVSIS, the Development Information System, and was then adopted for the MINISIS software system. This package, developed by IDRC (International Development Research Centre) as a package to be made available to organizations in developing countries for their library databases is prominent among software packages in having four-digit alphanumeric tags (one alphabetic character followed by three numeric, the last of which is a subfield identifier). The package has only recently had additional software written for it to enable it to support ISO 2709-based formats which have the usual three-digit tags. Users of the package were encouraged to use their own fields and field definitions, since it was part of the philosophy of IDRC that nothing should be imposed on users from above, though reference was made in the manuals to documents like the Reference Manual and the use of official international standards has always been encouraged.

A further interesting success story involving the Manual is that of the American Geological Institute's abstracting service GeoRef. This organization was one of the first agencies to adopt the Reference Manual as the basic format of its automated bibliographic information system. They specialize in indexing all English-language material in their subject field. Mulvihill[7] tells how when they decided to extend the coverage to French material by means of a cooperative agreement with the Centre National de la Recherche Scientifique (CNRS) in France, they had no difficulty in merging files with each other; since CNRS had been heavily involved in the design of the Reference Manual, its format was compatible with that of GeoRef.

Another major format was based on the Reference Manual: the CEPAL format of the Comisión Economica para America Latina, a UN agency, has had much influence in Latin America.

Technical features of the format

The major feature of the format is that it gives equal prominence to bibliographic records whether they relate to analytics (meaning journal articles and contributions in journals as well as works found published separately elsewhere but here bound together), monographs or serial titles. The format was designed to do this because it was developed by secondary services which give equal prominence to the different bibliographic levels. It does this in a so-called 'flat' record structure. The record contains no distinctive feature to permit a hierarchy to be indicated; instead, different tags are allocated to fields at a particular level. Thus, a computer program interpreting the record has to hold a table in which each field is separately identified as to its bibliographic level. Additionally, certain

Tag	Name of Field/Data Element	Status Bibliographic Level A/S	A/M	A/M/S	A/M/C	M	M/S	M/C	S	C
A01	ISSN	E		E			E		E	
A02*	CODEN									
A03	Title of Serial	E		E			E		E	
A04*	Serial Designation									
A05	Volume Identification Data (First Order Designation)	E	E²	E	E³		E	E³		
A06	Issue Identification Data (Second Order Designation)	E	E²	E⁴	E³		E⁴			
A08	Title of Analytic	E		E	E					
A09	Title of Monograph		E	E	E	E	E	E		
A10	Title of Collection				E			E		E
A11	Person associated with Analytic	E	E	E	E					
A12	Person associated with Monograph		E	E	E	E	E	E		
A13	Person associated with Collection or Serial									E
A14	Affiliation - Analytic	E	E	E	E					
A15	Affiliation - Monograph						E⁵			
A16*	Affiliation - Collection or Serial									
A17	Corporate Body associated with Analytic	E	E	E	E					
A18	Corporate Body associated with Monograph		E	E	E	E	E	E		
A19	Corporate Body associated with Collection or Serial									E
A20	Collation - Analytic	E	E	E	E					
A21	Date of Publication	E	E	E	E	E	E	E	E	E
A22*	Date other than Date of Publication									
A23	Language of Text	E	E	E	E	E	E	E	E	E
A24*	Language of Summary									
A25	Publisher: Name and Location (Monograph, Collection or Serial)		E	E⁶	E	E	E⁶	E	E	E
A26	ISBN		E	E	E	E	E	E		E
A27	Edition		E	E	E	E	E	E		E

Fig. 5.1 List of fields in Unesco's Reference manual for machine-readable bibliographic descriptions, 3rd ed., 1986.

Tag	Name of Field/Data Element	Status								
		Bibliographic Level								
		A/S	A/M	A/M/S	A/M/C	M	M/S	M/C	S	C
A28	Collation - Collection									E
A29	Collation - Monograph					E	E	E		
A30	Name of Meeting[7]	K	K	K	K	K	K	K	K	K
A31	Location of Meeting[7]	K	K	K	K	K	K	K	K	K
A32	Date of Meeting[7]	K	K	K	K	K	K	K	K	K
A33	Identification of Patent Document	P			·	P				
A34	Person Associated with Patent Document	P				P				
A35	Corporate Body associated with Patent Document	P				P				
A36*	Domestic Filing Data of Patent Document									
A37*	Convention Priority Data of Patent Document									
A38*	Reference to Legally Related Domestic Patent Document									
A39	Report Number		R	R		R	R			
A40*	Name of Performing Organization									
A41	University or Other Educational Institution		T			T	T			
A42*	Type of Degree									
A43	Availability of Document		R	R		RT	RT			
A44*	Abstract									
A45*	Number of References									
A46	"Summary Only" Note[8]									
A47*	Citation Number									
A51	Country of Publication Code		E	E	E	E	E	E	E	E
A52*	Secondary Source Citation									
A69*	Source Data Base									
A70*	Bibliography Note									
A72*	Contract or Grant Number									
A80*	Target Audience Code									
A90*	Related Record									
A99*	Ancillary Data									

Fig. 5.1 (continued)

Tag	Name of Field/Data Element	Status								
		Bibliographic Level								
		A/S	A/M	A/M/S	A/M/C	M	M/S	M/C	S	C
BØ1*	Broad System of Ordering Code									
BØ2*	Dewey Decimal Classification Number									
BØ4*	Universal Decimal Classification Number									
BØ8*	Other Classification Scheme Number									
B21*	Controlled Index Term									
B22*	Uncontrolled Index Term									
B3Ø*	Type of Bibliographic Entity⁹									

NOTES

(1) The symbols heading the columns indicate single bibliographic levels or combinations of bibliographic levels in documents to be described. The meaning of the symbols is as follows:

A = analytic level
M = monographic level
S = serial level
C = collective level.

In the columns of the table, the "mandatory" or "essential" status of a data element in a particular field, at a given bibliographic level or combination of bibliographic levels, is indicated by the symbol "E". In principle a "status E" data element is essential for any type of bibliographic entity described at the indicated bibliographic level or combination of bibliographic levels. When a data element is essential only for either a conference document, patent, report or thesis, this has been indicated by the symbols "K", "P", "R", and "T" respectively.

(2) Essential only in case of a multi-volume monograph of which the individual volumes and/or parts have no individual title but individual page numbering. In this case first and/or second order designation may apply.

(3) Essential only in case of a collection of numbered monographic items. Also, in that case, only a first order designation may be applicable.

(4) Essential when the monographic level describes a serial issue or part treated as a single document (monograph) and when the issue or part carries a volume and issue identification or equivalent.

Fig. 5.1 (continued)

208

(5) Essential only for serial issues or parts treated as a single document (monograph).

(6) Not essential for serial issues or parts treated as a single document (monograph).

(7) The data elements in fields A30, A31 and A32 are essential - regardless of type of bibliographic entity and bibliographic level - if, and only if, the document described is formally designated as being or being part of the published or otherwise disseminated proceedings of a meeting, conference, etc.

(8) This data element is essential whenever the document described is a summary of another work.

(9) Field B30 may be used to record any type of bibliographic entity in addition to that indicated in character position 6 of the record label (see 3.1.2). Any code in character position 6 of the record label may also be repeated as the first entry in B30.

* Tags followed by an asterisk indicate data elements which are never designated as essential.

Fig. 5.1 (continued)

fields such as ISBN and publisher are not identified as belonging to any particular bibliographic level; in most cases the level of these fields is implied, as publisher, for example, relates to the monograph level. As mentioned above, the group developing the format avoided enabling the format to be used for serial titles, and in the matrix in the first edition giving combinations of fields for types of material there is no column for serial title. Tag A08 is the field identifier for title of analytic, A09 title of monograph and A10 title of collection level. A03 is the field for title of serial. In the second edition of the Reference Manual, the scope of fields A13 and A19 (person and corporate body associated with collection) has been extended to include responsibility for serials.

Figure 5.1 gives the list of fields in the Reference Manual and Figure 5.2 is a reproduction of the matrix which indicates the fields required for the description of serials at the serial level (as opposed to analytics in serials) introduced in the second edition.

Unesco Common Communication Format

History
Although Unesco had developed the Reference Manual with the help of ICSU/AB, it had not been accepted unquestioningly by

the audience it was intended to serve. Many organizations continued to approach Unesco for assistance in developing bibliographic information systems; sometimes these organizations were related to national libraries and needed to establish databases that were compatible with MARC. Sometimes they were organizations that straddled the divide conventionally believed to exist between the libraries and secondary services. Some were even situated within national libraries but were secondary services, so it was difficult to see whether they should follow the Reference Manual, developed for the secondary services, or UNIMARC, developed by and for national libraries. In order to solicit wider opinion on the problem and thereby to help in its decision-making, Unesco sponsored the International Symposium on Bibliographic Exchange Formats. This took place in April 1978 and was organized by UNIBID, the office supported by the Unesco General Information Programme and the British Library which was responsible for maintaining the Reference Manual. The symposium also enjoyed the sponsorship of ICSU/AB, IFLA and ISO. Papers were given on a number of issues relating to the then state of the art of exchange formats, and outlines were given of the main features of the major international formats. The proceedings were published in late 1978.[8]

As a result of resolutions passed at the Symposium, Unesco set up the Ad Hoc Group for the Establishment of the Common Communication Format. This Group contained experts from ICSU/AB, ISDS (the International Serials Data System), IFLA, ISO and UNIBID, as well as an expert from the group that had devised MEKOF, the format of the COMECON (Eastern European) countries.[9] The Group worked on the basis that the new format must be compatible with the MEKOF, UNIMARC and UNISIST Reference Manual formats. It also took into account derivatives of these formats, namely the USSR/US Exchange Format (based on UNIMARC) and an ICSU/AB Extension to the Reference Manual developed by the Four-Ways Committee. The Group agreed that the record structure of the format should be that specified in the ISO 2709 standard, which was in any case used by all the formats being taken into account. A consultant prepared a data-element directory which included the majority of the data elements from those formats.[10]

Name of field/data element	Tag	Status*
ISSN	AØ1	E
CODEN	AØ2	O
Title of Serial	AØ3	E
Series Designation	AØ4	O
Person associated with Collection or Serial	A13	O
Affiliation - Collection or Serial	A16	O
Corporate Body associated with Collection or Serial	A19	O
Date of Publication	A21	E
Language of Text	A23	E
Language of Summaries (1)	A24	O
Publisher: Name and Location (Monograph, Collection or Serial)	A25	E
Availability of Document	A43	O
Abstract (2)	A44	O
Citation Number	A47	O
Country of Publication Code	A51	E
Secondary Source Citation	A52	O
Source Data Base	A69	O
Target Audience Code	A8Ø	O
Related Record	A9Ø	O
Ancillary Data	A99	O
Broad System of Ordering Code	BØ1	O
Dewey Decimal Classification Number	BØ2	O
Universal Decimal Classification Number	BØ4	O
Other Classification Scheme Number	BØ8	O
Controlled Index Term	B21	O
Uncontrolled Index Term	B22	O
Type of Bibliographic Entity	B3Ø	O

* E = essential (mandatory)
  O = supplementary (optional)

(1)   This field may be used to indicate the language(s) in which summaries of contributions to the serial are given.

(2)   This field may be used for a statement of the general purpose of the serial, its scientific or other spheres of interest and, in general, any kind of information considered useful and not covered or in insufficient detail in other fields.

June 1981

Fig. 5.2   **Data elements for the description of serials at the serial level from Unesco's Reference manual for machine-readable bibliographic descriptions, 3rd ed., 1986**

(From *Reference manual for machine-readable bibliographic descriptions*, 3rd ed., 1986. © Unesco 1986. Reproduced by permission of Unesco)

211

In the early days of the Group, much of the discussion centred on the adoption of a basic set of mandatory data elements. It was clear that the secondary services were not prepared to adopt the mandatory elements of ISBD. For instance, the statement of responsibility was not provided by many of their databases. The libraries community was persuaded that, though the ISBD elements were, in principle, desirable, records without certain of them from sources without the tradition of fullness of the record that is found in the national libraries would nevertheless be useful to them. The format was aimed at operations which needed to provide records to and receive records from both library and secondary service communities, and as many of these organizations were in developing countries, it was decided to keep the format simple in terms of its data elements and data-element definition. Taking into account the fact that there was not then, and indeed still is not, any international agreement on cataloguing rules, the format was kept free of anything amounting to cataloguing rules. In order to achieve compatibility between the different record structures of the formats and their differently defined bibliographic levels, a record structure was defined for the CCF implementing the latest version of ISO 2709. The structure of the format has at times been criticized as over-complex. It might be true that it is not easy for cataloguers to understand: that is because it requires a different approach from that of traditional cataloguing on which, incidentally, secondary services' practices also are usually based. However, the CCF is, as a standard, required to be implemented only as an exchange format, so the total computerized system should take this into account, and allow records to be created in a way that more closely resembles data-entry practices in other automated systems. This will require a data-entry format which is different from the exchange format. It may be obvious to many users that this can be done to simplify data entry. However, there are other users who are still of the opinion that to follow the CCF it is necessary to use the data elements as described in the manual, and their identifiers, at every possible level in the system. This is possible for the MARC formats as they were developed to automate existing manual systems geared up to the production of catalogue cards. The CCF on the other hand was designed from a data-element directory.

The format was first published in 1984.[11]

Users of the format

Even before the format was formally published, two major organizations were already using it. The Dag Hammarskjöld Library of the UN in New York adopted the CCF but could not implement it fully as it could not be held in the internal format of their existing software system. However, they adopted it to the extent that it would enable the records to be converted to the CCF standard format at some future date, implementing the tagging scheme of the CCF, though not its subfields or segments. A data-entry manual has been published, the *UNBIS reference manual.*[12]

The Office for Official Publications of the European Communities was developing new software and adopted the CCF because of its flexible record structure. They were interested not only in providing a mechanism for linking bibliographic records to each other but also in providing the facility for the linking of the actual text. They publish the *Official journal* of the European Community which consists of small items of information in a daily journal with weekly supplements. These have been put in a large database, each item including its text constituting one record. The main aim is to enable the journal to be printed from tapes in different centres throughout the European Community. The bibliographic levels and segments of the CCF have been used to the full to enable the data from the different sections in the publication to be arranged in their appropriate segments. FORMEX has been published and from the document it can be seen that it adheres very closely to the CCF.[13]

Probably the first network to adopt the CCF was the ICONDA Group developing an international construction database. They had originally planned to use the UNISIST Reference Manual, but, because they were intending to merge databases which had already adopted data-entry rules, they found the CCF easier to implement and have based their manual on it.[14]

Since publication of the CCF, a number of organizations have been helped by Unesco to investigate the advantage of using the format, and, where it has proved advantageous, to adopt it in one way or another.

The situation in Brazil makes an interesting case study.[15] Brazil naturally participates in the many regional subject-based secondary services that have been established in Latin America: Pan-American Health Organization (PAHO) for health information, Documentation System on Population (DOCPAL) for population, etc. Brazil is also a member of international networks such as AGRIS (agriculture) and INIS (nuclear information). The country also has at least one cooperative cataloguing agency, the Getúlio Vargas Foundation, which uses a format derived from LC MARC. It is situated in Rio de Janeiro near the National Library and soon after the software was completed, the National Library became one of the libraries in the cooperative. However, the use of the format was in this case only as a basis for data entry into the system.

Brazil has attempted to develop an information infrastructure following Unesco guidelines and in so doing has tried to coordinate efforts within both the library and the secondary information (predominantly scientific) sectors. Many information systems had been developed using different international formats. There is for example a network based at the Ministry of Agriculture which uses a format close enough to that of the FAO to enable exchange of records with FAO's AGRIS system to be facilitated. BIREME (Biblioteca Regional de Medicina) in São Paulo is the Brazilian node of the Latin American health information system, part of the Pan-American Health Organization which uses the CEPAL (Comisión Economica para America Latina) format. The Instituto Brasileiro d'Informação em Ciência e Tecnologia (IBICT) was charged by the Conselho Nacional de Desenvolvimento Científico e Tecnológico (CNPq) with developing a common format for all sectors in order to prevent the problem which already existed when an organization had to enter data into two systems by manually creating two worksheets for each system.

It was a national policy decision to set up a network for bibliographic information. However, many organizations were already providing data for an international network or an inter-regional network and using a particular format for it. The national network needed a national format. How was the problem of conflicting formats to be resolved? The solution was

214

as follows: many of the secondary services in Latin America were using the CEPAL format which was based very closely on the UNISIST Reference Manual and adapted slightly to suit the capabilities of the software. The national library format was under development but was based on USMARC on which UNIMARC was based. The CCF was compatible not only with these two formats, but also with the formats of AGRIS and INIS which had both been influenced by the MARC formats and the UNISIST Reference Manual. The national format, known as CALCO, was the one based on the USMARC format. However, because it had been developed ten years earlier, and had not been brought up to date, it had deviated slightly from the US format and needed certain revision in any case. The solution to the problem of bibliographic information interchange in Brazil involved bringing the CALCO format into line with CCF and embarking on an exercise to convert the other formats into CCF. As the new CALCO was not accepted readily by cataloguers who felt that data entry would become more difficult into a system where data entry was done via a format which was not made primarily for data entry, it proved essential to develop two national formats: one for the cataloguers so that all cataloguers were inputting records in the same format, and one for the systems themselves which is much closer to the CCF. It is of course the computer which makes the conversion between the two formats, which amount to an input and exchange format. IBICT also developed a 'language' for the specification of format conversions. This was stimulated by the need to be able to convert between the CCF-based national format and the formats used by the existing networks in Brazil including the CALCO data-entry format.

The CCF has also been used in Colombia as the basis for the national format for similar reasons to those that persuaded the Brazilians to make use of it. However, since previous to the exercise to develop a national format they had had no provisional or draft format, they were able to start afresh. Simmons[16] relates how COLCIENCIAS, a semi-autonomous government agency, took on the task of creating and coordinating a cooperative national information system to include the resources of documentation centres, libraries and archives, many of which were microcomputer-based. These organizations were separately funded and chose their own computer hardware and software. A 'switching format' based on the CCF was designed called the Formato Común de Comunicación Bibliográfica para Colombia (FCCC). Each participating agency required a pair of programs to be written, to convert its records to FCCC and back. Programs will also enable the conversion from FCCC to CCF and back.

The FCCC is at first glance far removed from the CCF. The format does not include the ISO 2709 record structure. It has no indicators or segments. It retains compatibility by limiting relationship types in a record and by ensuring that all data required for a full CCF record can be generated automatically or stored in an FCCC field or subfield.

The International Coordinating Committee for Development Associations (ICCDA) has developed an implementation of the CCF on the CDS/ISIS Microcomputer Software Package which is intended for producing databases which can be exchanged between participants. A manual accompanies the software package.[17] The work on the package was coordinated by the OECD Development Centre and supported by IDRC. This package is being used as a model for other similar implementations outside the development community wishing to use the CCF and the CDS/ISIS package.

In China, too, the CCF has been translated and is beginning to be promoted in organizations that need to participate in both the library and secondary services communities.

The second edition of the format was published in May 1988,[18] and in April 1989, the first Users' Meeting took place at the International Bureau of Education in Geneva, sponsored by Unesco, at which progress reports, technical papers and practical demonstrations were given on topics such as implementing the CCF on particular software systems, future extensions to the format for additional kinds of material and conversions between the CCF and other formats.[19]

Technical aspects

As mentioned above, the record structure of the CCF has been criticized as over-complex. In fact, as a machine-readable format it is the opposite, and it can be thought of as complex only when it is regarded as a data-entry format which it was not

216

intended to be. It is complicated for cataloguers to enter data into the format, especially if they try and create manually the links between records or between segments in a record.

There are two main features of the format that distinguish it from other formats. The first feature is its simple set of data elements that can be used at any bibliographic level and are disassociated from cataloguing codes. The second is the logically defined record structure which uses the fourth element of the ISO 2709 directory to denote bibliographic level and field occurrence. The use of both of these features is a product of the circumstances in which the format was devised. Since the format was designed to be compatible with a number of other already existing international formats, it was necessary to include either all data elements from these other formats, or a subset. Including all data elements, in particular those that are seldom used, would have decreased the level of compatibility in the CCF. It is in the lesser-used data elements that formats have gone their own way. Therefore it was decided to include the basic elements in the format for exchange and let the less commonly used data elements be added as private data elements between parties to an exchange agreement. Another reason for there being fewer data elements than there would otherwise be is that data elements relating to different bibliographic levels are not allocated to different fields at each level but appear only once at one designated field. Field 200 is the field for title. If the title is the title of a monograph, it will be designated to a segment containing all the fields relating to the monographic level. If the title is that of an article it will be designated to a segment containing all the fields relating to an article.

The record structure of the CCF was devised to take into account different structures in the format from which records would originate. The Reference Manual and formats related to it have fields designated for different bibliographic levels. UNIMARC has fields designed primarily for the monographic and serial level but can also use those fields embedded in linking fields as fields describing an analytic. The Reference Manual has four bibliographic levels, analytic, monograph, serial and collective, whilst UNIMARC has analytic, monograph, serial and collection. Collective in the Reference Manual corresponds to multi-volume monograph in UNIMARC (only a subset of monograph). In both source formats, the fields relating to appropriate bibliographic levels can easily be identified. However, the relationships could more easily be converted into a third more logical structure than into the structure of the other of the original formats, so the structure of the CCF was designed to be logical. It was designed to make use of a then new feature of ISO 2709, the fourth element of the record directory, so that each field is denoted (in this fourth part of the directory) as belonging to its bibliographic level and each field in the record is uniquely identified there by an occurrence identifier.

It is possible to take a bibliographic item such as a series of annual conference proceedings where each member of the series has its own individual articles and create one record containing all the data relating to what would amount in most bibliographic systems to a number of records (see Figure 5.3).

However, to comply with the CCF, this record will contain a segment for each separately occurring instance of each bibliographic level. One of these segments has to be labelled the primary segment and this will contain certain elements of control information such as record control number. If the format had been designed from first principles it would have probably contained a control segment in each record which would always be present and would contain information as to which segments would make up a complete bibliographic record. As it is, it is the primary segment which contains this control information.

A CCF record relating to an article in a volume of a multi-volume monograph in a series is reproduced in Figure 5.4.

Field-to-field links have also been included in the CCF. The second edition includes codes to denote links between an author name and affiliation (which will usually be entered in its own field and may be formatted like a corporate body if the rules permit) and between publisher and ISBN where a record includes two publishers of a simultaneously published work.

In evaluating the CCF it is necessary to remember three points:

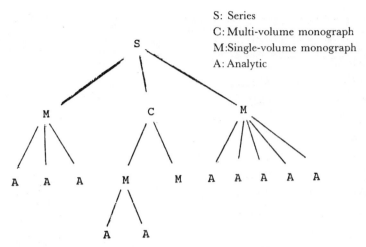

S: Series
C: Multi-volume monograph
M:Single-volume monograph
A: Analytic

Fig. 5.3   Relationships in a complex CCF record

a) *Relationship with existing formats*
The CCF was not designed from first principles but was based on major existing international exchange formats and was intended to be used for the transfer of records between systems which were already capable of providing output into these major exchange formats. It was not expected to have to do anything that could not be done by any existing exchange format.

b) *The CCF is an exchange format*
The CCF is intended as an exchange format and as such has to contain bibliographic data for exchanging between systems. It does not govern what can be done within the systems themselves, so it cannot be looked to as a guide for creators of online public-access catalogues or other systems. Of course, the definition of data elements will affect the internal architecture of systems using these data elements, but there is a large amount of agreement between organizations as to the definition of the key data elements in a record. This can be noted by comparing the data elements in a national bibliography and in a secondary service publication. The data elements author, title, publisher, date, to mention only a few, will be there in every case although they may be presented in different forms, according to different cataloguing codes.

219

Bibliographic level: a (shown in character position 7 in the record label).

Tag	Seg Iden	Occur Iden	Data Fields
001	0	0	25-943
020	0	0	00@BDOCPAL
021	0	0	11@AA
022	0	0	00@A19790615
030	0	0	00@B2
031	0	0	00@Aspa
040	0	0	00@Aspa
050	0	0	00@A010
060	0	0	00@A105
200	0	0	00@AInmigración italiana@Lspa
300	0	0	00@AMellafe@BRolando
490	0	0	00@B246-280
620	0	0	00@AInmigración@AAsimilacion de Migrantes
015	1	0	00@Am
040	1	0	00@Aper
080	1	0	00@A02@B0
080	1	1	00@A01@B2
086	1	0	00@A48010@BOT@C08011
200	1	0	00@ASão José dos Campos. Estudo de caso: dinâmica populacional, transformações socio-econômicas, atuação das instituições
260	1	0	02@A1

Fig. 5.4   Component part in a volume of a multi-volume monograph which is in a series

(From *CCF: the Common Communication Format*, 2nd ed., 1988. © Unesco 1988. Reproduced by permission of Unesco)

220

310	1	0	10@ACentro Brasileiro de Análise e Planejamento@DSão Paulo@EBR@F020
400	1	0	00@ASão Paulo@BCentro Brasileiro de Análise e Planejamento
440	1	0	10@A19780000
460	1	0	00@A305@Btbls
480	1	0	00@ACEBRAP. Estudos de População, 6
490	1	0	00@AVol. 1
015	2	0	00@Ac
080	2	0	00@A02@B1
200	2	0	00@APesquisa Nacional sobre Reprodução Humana
310	2	0	00@ACentro Brasileiro de Análise e Planejamento @DSão Paulo@EBR@F020
440	2	0	10@A19780000-
460	2	0	00@Btbls. grafs
015	3	0	00@As
080	3	0	00@A02@B1
200	3	0	00@ACEBRAP. Estudos de População

Comments. This record describes a Spanish contribution to a Portuguese journal. The record was produced in Spanish by the Latin American Population Documentation System (DOCPAL) in their own format, which is based on the Reference Manual. The agency puts only one component part in each record; it is the target item in the record. The component part is published in a monograph (shown in Segment 1) which is one volume of a multi-volume monograph (shown in Segment 2); that volume has also been given a number in a series (shown in Segment 3). Note that both the records at the multi-volume level (Segment 2) and the serial level (Segment 3) are linked to the record at the monographic level (Segment 1).

In Segment 1 it is necessary to show that 'Vol. 1' in Field 490 refers to the volume in relation to the multi-volume monograph, rather than the serial. Therefore, a reciprocal link is established in Segment 1 (Field 080, occurrence 1) indicating that the segment links to the multi-volume monograph and a link is made between that linking field (Field 086) and Field 480.

The numbering of the monograph within the monographic series is indicated only by means of a series statement (Field 480 in Segment 1).

Fig. 5.4 (continued)

c) *The CCF is intended for exchange of bibliographic data*
Thirdly, when the system was developed it was intended for the exchange of those data elements of the bibliographic record that were needed for the identification of a document in a catalogue or bibliography. It does not contain fields that would be required for library circulation systems or inter-library loan. An individual system using the CCF as an exchange format to facilitate record creation by taking records created externally in the CCF may add any other fields required for its own purposes. Moreover, systems wishing to exchange data elements other than those provided for in the CCF are free to allocate unused tags to those data elements or to allocate alpha-numeric tags (e.g. AAA, BAZ, H97).

ISDS format

History
Another system with its own format is the ISDS (International Serials Data System). This could almost be called a MARC format, since it owes much to the national formats of the countries from which the team involved in its development came. Moreover, many national ISDS Centres are hosted by national libraries.

Like the Reference Manual format mentioned above, this format was developed as part of the UNISIST programme.[20] The UNISIST/ICSU-AB Working Group on Bibliographic Descriptions recommended among other things the establishment of a world list of journal titles, to be assisted by the creation of an International Network for Periodical Titles. INSPEC, the information-system arm of the Institution of Electrical Engineers in London, carried out a feasibility study and recommended the establishment of an International Serials Data System. The French government, along with Unesco, agreed to put up funds for an International Centre for the Registration of Serial Publications (known as CIEPS from its French title) which, in 1974, started work to set up an operation for an automated system for the registration of serials. National centres and in some cases regional centres were set up to record serials and distribute the records to local users.

The International Centre devised cataloguing rules including a methodology for formulating a 'key title' which would be unique for each serial throughout the system. The Centre also became responsible through the national and regional centres for the assignment of International Standard Serial Numbers (ISSN). A format was devised to hold data formulated according to the ISDS cataloguing rules. The tags of the LC-MARC serials format were adopted with additional distinctive fields for relationships with other serials.[21]

Technical details

Figure 5.5 gives a list of these relationship fields as incorporated in the second version of the format described in the *ISDS manual*.[22] Each of these fields has two subfields, &t Key title and &x ISSN (& is the convention used in the *Manual* for the initial character of the subfield identifier).

759 2__ Is other language edition of
760 2__ Is subseries of
762 2__ Has subseries
769 2__ Has other language edition(s)
779 2__ Is inset in or supplement to

780   Former titles:
  __0 Continues
  __1 Continues in part
  __4 Formed by the union of . . . and . . .
  __5 Absorbed
  __6 Absorbed in part

785   Successor titles:
  __0 Continued by
  __1 Continued in part by
  __4 Absorbed by
  __5 Absorbed in part by
  __6 Split into . . . and . . .

787 2__ Related title(s)
789 2__ Has inset or supplement(s)

Fig. 5.5   List of relationship fields in ISDS format

The format has had a great influence on serials formats in automated systems in national libraries throughout the world; not least because many automated serials systems have been set up to provide data for the ISDS.

There was a long controversy over certain incompatibilities between records formulated according to ISDS and those created according to national cataloguing codes based on ISBD. There are good reasons for incompatibility since the records serve different functions. The problematic field has always been the title. The ISDS record includes a fabricated key title as the main title of the record. ISBD requires the title taken from the item with the associated statements of responsibility transcribed from the document. Problems of incompatibility were resolved by removing minor inconsistencies between the data elements, so that it became possible for one record to be produced by an agency which could provide both the input to ISDS and the entry following ISBD for the national bibliography. Thus, by concerted effort between the International Centre and various national agencies, with encouragement from Unesco, the controversy was largely resolved.[23]

Notes and references

1 *American National Standard Format for bibliographic information interchange on magnetic tape*, New York, ANSI, 1971 (ANSI Z39.2–1971); 2nd ed., 1979.
2 *ISDS manual*, Paris, ISDS International Centre, 1983, 1.
3 *Reference manual for machine-readable bibliographic descriptions*, ed. by M. D. Martin, Paris, Unesco, 1974 (SC.74/WS/20).
4 *Report on the 2nd Four-Ways ASIDIC, EUSIDIC, ICSU-AB and NFAIS meeting, June 26–29 1977, Creaton, England*, Washington DC, National Science Foundation, 1977.
5 *Reference manual for machine-readable bibliographic descriptions*, 2nd rev. ed., comp. and ed. by H. Dierickx and A. Hopkinson, UNISIST International Centre for Bibliographic Description (UNIBID), Paris, Unesco, 1981, (PGI/81/WS/22), 0.1. A 3rd ed. was published in 1985.
6 *Ibid.*, Chapter 5.
7 Mulvihill, J. G., 'GeoRef coverage and improvements in the bibliography and index of geology', in Pruett, N. J., ed., *Keeping current with geoscience information*, Washington, DC, Geoscience Information Society, 1981, 55–64.

8   International Symposium on Bibliographic Exchange Formats, *Towards a common bibliographic exchange format?: proceedings*, Budapest, OMKDK, 1978.

9   *International interchange format: MEKOF-2: specification of data elements*, Moscow, ICSTI, 1977 (MEKOF-2/SPEC (Ed.1) 1977).

10   Simmons, P., *Data element directory*, Paris, Unesco, 1979 (PGI/CCF/I/2.1). Distribution limited.

11   *CCF: the Common Communication Format*, Paris, Unesco, 1984 (PGI-84/WS/4).

12   *UNBIS: reference manual for bibliographic description: a manual for the preparation of bibliographic data for input into and retrieval from the United Nations Bibliographic Information System*, New York, UN Dag Hammarskjöld Library, 1985.

13   Guittet, C., ed., *FORMEX: formalized exchange of electronic publications*, Luxembourg, Office for Official Publications of the European Communities, 1985.

14   *ICONDA communication format: format for the exchange of records in the frame of the International Construction Database*, Stuttgart, IRB Verlag, 1985.

15   Hopkinson, A., *Report on a Unesco mission to Brazil*, unpublished.

16   Simmons, P., 'Using CCF: the Common Communication Format', *Information technology and libraries*, **5**, 1986, 285–94.

17   Di Lauro, Anne, *IDIN manual for the creation and management of a bibliographic database using Micro-ISIS*, Paris, OECD, 1988, includes diskette.

18   *CCF: the Common Communication Format*, 2nd ed., Paris, Unesco, 1988 (PGI-88/WS/2).

19   Simmons, P., ed., *Proceedings of the First CCF Users' Meeting*, Paris, Unesco, to be published.

20   *ISDS manual*, 1.

21   Library of Congress, MARC Development Office, *Serials: a MARC format*, Washington DC, Library of Congress, 1970.

22   *ISDS manual*, 137–8.

23   Anderson, Dorothy, 'Compatibility of ISDS and ISBD(S) records in international exchange: the background', *International cataloguing*, **12**, (2), 1983, 14–17.

225

6

MARC and national systems

This chapter deals with MARC in national networks. Networking is a topic which has produced an enormous body of technical and descriptive literature and it has wide ramifications which cannot be explored here. Discussion is therefore limited to aspects relating directly to MARC formats. Although many of the major British and North American library cooperatives or utilities may be termed 'national', since their membership is countrywide, sometimes even international, they are not discussed individually. Our main concern is with those systems, normally coordinated by the national library, which are intended to achieve national coverage and to be accessible to the entire nation. This in no way detracts from the importance of the library cooperatives, whose contribution to MARC record production is considerable, and whose relationship with national libraries has helped to shape national developments.

The situation in the United States and the United Kingdom is outlined, and brief summaries provided for Canada and Australia, which offer interesting and contrasting examples. These four countries form the ABACUS grouping (Association of Bibliographic Agencies of Australia, Britain, Canada and the United States), which has been in the forefront of networking developments. Information on the many other national MARC-based systems may be found in *International guide to MARC databases and services*[1] and in the journal *International cataloguing and bibliographic control*,[2] which regularly includes surveys of national networks.

National MARC networks and bibliographic control
The goal of Universal Bibliographic Control is, as we have seen,

the creation of an international system for the control and exchange of bibliographic information. This can be achieved only by the cooperation of every country in establishing a system for the control of its own publishing output. Complete success also depends ultimately on the acceptance of standards for record construction and the availability of records in machine-readable form. The national MARC network, by which we understand a nationwide system of libraries and other organizations acting cooperatively to create, exchange and share bibliographic records in MARC format, exists not only for the interchange of bibliographic data within nations, but also as a component part of the International MARC Network on which UBC depends. Although the national MARC network can be conceived as an independent entity, availability of MARC records is in practice inextricably linked with the wider national network, the broad aim of which is access, for all users regardless of location, to the bibliographic resources of the whole country: 'the nation's library' as it is described in the *Network planning papers* of the LC's Network Advisory Committee.[3] The end result is, of course, document delivery, the *raison d'être* of all bibliographic records, irrespective of their machine format. UBC and UAP (Universal Availability of Publications), both core programmes of IFLA, must be paralleled at national level.

The chief instrument of bibliographic control is the national bibliography, appearing as printed (catalogue) cards, printed books (in varying combinations of weekly, monthly, quarterly and annual issues) and/or in machine-readable form (tapes, disks). Many national bibliographies are now produced from MARC records generated by the national bibliographic agency. IFLA's *Guidelines for the national bibliographic agency and the national bibliography*,[4] drawn up after the 1977 International Conference on National Bibliographies (ICNB), recommend the establishment of a national bibliographic agency whose responsibility is the preparation of a comprehensive, authoritative bibliographic record, in accordance with accepted standards, for each new publication and its speedy inclusion in a regularly issued national bibliography. There are obvious advantages if the national bibliographic agency is part of, or has close links with, the national library, although differing national literary and publishing histories have brought about differences in the approach to national bibliography.[5] In some countries, it has been undertaken by government institutions; in others, by private organizations, professional associations, publishers and librarians. In the UK, responsibility for the national bibliography passed in 1973 from an autonomous body, the Council of the British National Bibliography, composed jointly of publishers and librarians, to the Bibliographic Services Division of the newly created British Library, the national library of the UK. In the US there is no official national library or national bibliography: the Library of Congress and the *National union catalog: US books* come closest to performing these roles. Bell offers a comprehensive account of current national bibliographies and a succinct survey of developments since the 1977 conference.[6]

It is possible that online databases may in time replace printed national bibliographies, drawing additionally on the resources of libraries outside the national collections. In the 1986 *International guide to MARC databases and services*, 12 countries were listed as offering MARC-based national online services which were available also to users outside the country, and an additional 14 maintained national bibliographic databases for internal use. Peter Lewis, former Director General of British Library Bibliographic Services, believes that bibliographic control can be achieved only by connecting the machine-readable catalogues of the nation's major libraries, thus ensuring the necessary access to documents.[7] This type of linkage would greatly enhance a national MARC network, but it presupposes that all participating libraries use the national MARC format, or that conversion programs are technically possible and economically viable.

CD-ROM is also considered to be a likely medium for the distribution of national bibliographies. Its advantages include high capacity, compactness and portability and it is suitable for use in areas where access to sophisticated database systems and telecommunications is difficult or impossible. The International MARC Network Advisory Committee in 1986 initiated discussions towards the establishment of a standard for applications software for CD-ROM for use in national bibliographies and some experiments attempting to link CD-ROMs into networks have already been carried out. Following the success of the joint British Library/Bibliothèque Nationale CD-ROM project, a European programme for the cooperative development of national bibliography on CD-ROM, involving the British Library and several other European libraries, has been proposed.[8] A significant aspect of such a programme would be the development of MARC format conversion software for use in microcomputer systems.

National MARC networks: nature and operation
The main purpose of the national MARC network is the interchange of bibliographic records in the national MARC format, but records in other national MARC formats may be included. US and UKMARC records, for example, feature in the magnetic-tape and online services of many other nations. Ideally, all types of materials should be covered, although in practice there is considerable variation: books are the major, and in some cases the only, material for which MARC records in the national format are available. The availability of retrospective records also varies: most countries can offer only current MARC records; few have records prior to 1970, the major exceptions being the UK (1950) and the US (1968). Authority records and holdings records, if available, can be included in exchange programmes.

Until recently, the most appropriate focal point of a national MARC network was believed to be an integrated, centralized, national database, controlled by the national library or national bibliographic agency. This view is now changing, influenced by developments in technology apparent in networks operating below the national level, where the heavily centralized systems of the 1970s, relying on large central databases, are giving way to more widely distributed, decentralized structures, using improved technology to link different parts of the network. The change is reflected by a preference, in some quarters, for the expression 'nationwide network' rather than 'national network', which for many has overtones of excessive centralization, loss of autonomy and monolithic structure.[9]

There is no prescribed pattern for a national MARC network, although IFLA's conception of the International MARC Network assumes certain characteristics and functions at national level. The most common arrangement is the national

MARC network operating under the aegis of a national library/national bibliographic agency, which originates and distributes national MARC records and also acts as a channel for the flow of foreign MARC records into the country, their conversion to national format and subsequent distribution. MARC records from other countries are typically used as a source of derived cataloguing, to assist in the processing of publications acquired from the originating country. Subject to agreement, they may also be made available in online databases in the recipient country.[10] Movement of MARC records is mainly from national agency to other organizations, with varying degrees of movement in the reverse direction or between organizations. In the future, multi-directional exchange and a more loosely coordinated structure are likely to become the norm, especially in countries such as the UK and the US, where strong, independent cooperative systems are well established. Clearly, there must be some measure of control and coordination, even in a hybrid system of linked national, regional and local databases, although opinion differs on where this control should be vested and to what extent it should be exercised. Avram has noted the fear in the US of a 'locus of any kind, even for the planning of a nationwide library network, let alone the administration and operation of such a network'.[11] This apprehension is not confined to the United States, as the history of the proposed UK Library Database System has shown. An effective national MARC network must embrace not only the pool of MARC records generated by the national bibliographic agency, but also those of the major cooperatives, the major libraries, the book trade and appropriate specialist collections. Access to records in the network must also be possible for all who need it. Further, successful networking demands at any level a sound financial and organizational basis and agreement among participants on common purposes, guidelines and standards. Are these realistic demands? The potential for conflict between local/regional and national requirements is all too apparent. The following sections turn to a number of other problems which are raised by the development of a national MARC network.

Copyright and ownership of data

Intellectual property rights are legal rights resulting from intellectual activity in the fields of literature, arts, industry, science and technology. Copyright is a form of intellectual property, designed to give copyright owners protection against unfair use of their work. Broadly speaking, it is the ownership of, and the legal right to control, the reproduction of a work. It has both negative and positive aspects: the right of the owner to prevent certain uses is balanced by the right of the public to fair use and reproduction. According to the provisions of the 1988 UK Copyright, Designs and Patents Act, which took into account the technological changes that had occurred since the Copyright Act of 1956, copyright exists in original literary, dramatic, musical and artistic works, in sound recordings and films, in broadcasts (including satellite transmission), in cable transmissions, and in published editions of works. 'Literary works' specifically includes computer programs, tables and compilations, and extends in general to any 'computer-generated' work.[12] A particular problem, important for inter-change of MARC records at all levels, is whether copyright extends to bibliographic records and databases of records. In what sense are these 'original' and therefore subject to copyright? It is not possible here to explore the complexities of intellectual property law and copyright, which have national, European and international ramifications. It is true to say, however, that the legal situation varies from country to country, and that existing legislation is often unclear; moreover, that it is frequently outstripped by rapid changes in technology which have made it difficult, if not impossible, to enforce laws originally designed to cover traditional documents and inadequate to cope with new information carriers such as computer files and machine-readable databases.[13] Ownership of records has become a legal issue, not so much with regard to individual records (which are not normally copyrighted) but to collections held in computers.[14] In the particular case of a database of MARC records, contributed by the members of a library cooperative, who owns the records? The contributing libraries individually? Or the cooperative as a whole? Under US copyright law, databases of bibliographic records are considered 'compilations' (i.e. works arising from the selection, coordi-

231

nation and arrangement of pre-existing materials)[15] but the provisions of the Act are ineffective in dealing with the complex issues presented by databases, compared with literary compilations. Avram, noting the ambivalent attitude taken by American courts in deciding questions of copyright ownership, argues that new legal structures are needed to deal with the problem.[16] The attempt in 1982 by OCLC to seek copyright of its database created considerable disquiet, as the records concerned are either LC MARC records or records created by member libraries, whose freedom to make further use of their own records appeared thereby to be curtailed. Martin notes that the US Copyright Office found itself in an unprecedented situation, but finally in 1984 registered the copyright.[17] The purpose of the application was to prevent appropriation and reproduction of the database, e.g. its reproduction on CD-ROM and sale by an unauthorized party at a reduced cost. This, it was argued, would have resulted in increased charges to members, loss of revenue, decline in quality and the ultimate demise of the database itself. On the other hand, the decision was seen by some as a serious setback to the future of co-operation and free exchange of records. In 1987, however, in a conciliatory move, OCLC issued new guidelines permitting members to transfer records of their own holdings without restriction to other libraries (Figures 6.1 and 6.2).[18] Subject to certain conditions, libraries may also transfer records to commercial firms.

Contracts and exchange agreements

The 1977 Wells report on the International MARC network recommended *inter alia* the design of a standard international contract for MARC record exchanges.[19] A study made by Joseph Rosenthal, commissioned in 1978 by the International MARC Network Study (IMNS) Steering Committee of the Conference of Directors of National Libraries (CDNL), specifically addressed key issues concerning copyright of MARC records and the nature of exchange agreements between national bibliographic agencies for their supply, distribution and use. *International access to MARC records*,[20] published in 1980, was based on Rosenthal's analysis of 25 national agencies, 18 of which had reported actual or potential use of MARC formats.

Guidelines for the Use and Transfer
of OCLC-Derived Records
Revision of November 22, 1988

I. GUIDELINES
(See Definitions in Part II below.)

1. Each member and nonmember library may use records without restriction, and may transfer records of its own holdings without restriction to other libraries.

2. In addition to transfers to libraries, each member and nonmember library may transfer records of its own holdings without restriction, to (a) state and national library agencies and (b) all other noncommercial organizations.

   a. The use and transfer of records in or by library systems or projects operated by or under the aegis of one or more state or national library agencies will be as provided in separate understandings with OCLC. Such understandings may include (i) arrangements to incorporate state or national bibliographic databases into the OCLC system, (ii) paid-up licenses to use records in state or national programs and/or (iii) any other understandings that will facilitate state or national programs as well as the maintenance and enhancement of the OCLC database.

   b. The use and transfer of records by any other noncommercial organizations to which transfers are made under this Guideline 2 will be as provided in separate understandings with OCLC.

3. In addition, each member and nonmember library may transfer records of its own holdings to commercial firms which the library has employed and agreed to pay to process such records, provided that each commercial firm has first signed an individual agreement with the library, or OCLC has advised the library that the commercial firm has signed a general agreement with OCLC, in either case containing measures agreed upon by OCLC and the commercial firm for protection of the records it has been employed to process. In addition, each member and nonmember library may make any other transfers of records to commercial firms, subject to prior written agreements with OCLC. However, there is no requirement for prior written agreements (a) for transfers made under Guideline 1 above to libraries operated by commercial firms or (b) for transfers to commercial firms by former OCLC member libraries of records of their holdings, so long as the libraries maintain no continuing user status with OCLC.

4. When a nonmember organization makes bibliographic information available to OCLC which is subject to usage or transfer restrictions imposed by such nonmember organi-

zation, and OCLC nevertheless elects to accept the information for addition to the OCLC database, OCLC will notify libraries to which it makes the information available, and rights to use and transfer records based on such information will be subject to the same restrictions.

5. When transfers under Guideline 1 above are made to machine-readable union catalogs accessible by nonmember libraries, it is requested that machine-readable copies of the records of such union catalogs be submitted to OCLC. OCLC, at its own expense, will have the right to add such records to its database for all uses consistent with its chartered purposes.

6. The Guidelines above apply to all uses and transfers of records except where a mutually acceptable agreement establishing broader or narrower rights is made with OCLC relating to a specific product or service.

II. DEFINITIONS

1. The term **"member library"** means a general member of OCLC as defined in its Code of Regulations.

2. The term **"nonmember library"** means any library other than a member library.

3. A **"commercial firm"** is any organization permitted, under applicable law, to operate on a for-profit basis.

4. The term **"records"** means bibliographic records and holdings data (including copies thereof) derived from the OCLC database, including derivative works made from such records, and either received in machine-readable form or converted by the transferee into machine-readable form. The term also includes such records when held only in eye-readable form, in the case of proposed transfers to commercial firms. However, records do not include, as to any member or nonmember library (a) bibliographic records designated in the OCLC database as original cataloging by such member or nonmember library and (b) bibliographic records derived by such member or nonmember library from sources other than the OCLC database and to copies of which in the OCLC database its holdings symbol has been attached by tapeloading. Such excluded records are freely transferable and are not dealt with in these Guidelines. OCLC-derived records held only in eye-readable form are freely transferable except to commercial firms.

5. The terms **"transfer"** and **"transfer of records"** refer to all sales, exchanges, gifts, sharing and other transfers, and all online access except online access provided to end-user patrons of a library in authorized possession of the records.

International

7th Floor, Tricorn House   51-53 Hagley Road   Edgbaston
Birmingham, B16 8TP   United Kingdom

Pub. No. 1012
8902/3478 · 2M, OCLC

Fig. 6.1   Guidelines for the use and transfer of OCLC-derived records

(Reproduced with permission of OCLC)

Code of Responsible Use
for
OCLC Participating Libraries

OCLC is a cooperative library service. Participants accept a responsibility to use efficiently the OCLC systems as well as a responsibility to share resources and services. Use of the system should benefit the membership as a whole and support the mission and goals of each institution.

All participants will:

1. Provide basic and continuing training and education for staff to enable them to use the system effectively and responsibly.

2. Avoid creating duplicate records.

3. Improve the quality of the Online Union Catalog by reporting errors promptly.

4. Input current cataloging promptly to promote resource sharing and collection development.

5. Input original cataloging according to current national standards and practices as promulgated in OCLC *Bibliographic Input Standards*.

6. Enter current cataloging into the OCLC Online Union Catalog using the appropriate MARC formats.

7. Limit use of OCLC Online Union Catalog subsystems to OCLC-authorized institutions.

8. Use the information from the Online Union Catalog only for purposes which do not violate cooperative use of the OCLC systems among participants.

OCLC Online Computer Library Center, Inc.
6565 Frantz Road
Dublin, Ohio 43017-0702
(614) 764-6000

Fig. 6.2   Code of responsible use for OCLC participating libraries

(Reproduced by permission of OCLC)

234

It advocated exchange agreements with as few restrictions as possible, in line with the spirit of UBC, and included a recommended text for a bilateral agreement for the international exchange of MARC records via tape format. Receiving agencies were able to use and/or modify MARC records (i.e. make changes in order to achieve consistency with national cataloguing standards) within their own countries, and redistribute them to non-profit organizations. There was, however, one substantial proviso: that the records should not be used to produce the national bibliography of the originating agency in printed form or in machine-readable form.[21] Paradoxically, the recommended agreement was outdated by the time it was published, overtaken by advances in the technology of online access and networking; the formerly straightforward tape exchanges between two national agencies were now complicated by issues such as redistribution to commercial organizations and downloading of records in local systems.

A study made for IFLA in 1982 by McDonald, Rodger and Squires examined the adequacy of existing copyright laws for controlling international bibliographic data exchange.[22] Drawing on responses from national agencies in 21 countries, the report concluded that copyright law at the time did not provide a 'consistent and universal control mechanism' and recommended bilateral exchange agreements as a more effective method of controlling distribution, modification and redistribution of bibliographic records.[23] In the same year, Duchesne, Guenter and Tsai reviewed 22 agreements made by bibliographic centres and networks in Canada, including the agreements made by the National Library of Canada with five other national agencies.[24] Their study revealed a lack of standardization in layout, definition, wording and content, which they considered a barrier to effective nationwide networking. The adoption of standard guidelines for record exchanges at all levels, between and within countries, was recommended.

The burgeoning of MARC services in the 1980s and the experience gained by national libraries produced a second attempt to deal with the problem of international exchange agreements. In 1987 the International MARC Network Advisory Committee published *International transfers of national*

235

MARC records: guidelines for agreement, prepared by R. Duchesne.[25] 'National MARC records' are defined as those produced by or under the aegis of the national bibliographic agency of the country, including records relating to the national imprint or national bibliography of the country. There were two objectives: to achieve greater commonality and completeness in preparation of new agreements between national agencies, and to provide a framework for the modification of existing agreements. A single, standard agreement was believed to be unrealistic, given the diverse aims and circumstances of the national bibliographic agencies. Although exchange is assumed to be bilateral, the guidelines also support multilateral agreements and are effective with different kinds of services and products on different media (magnetic tape or optical disc) and in various MARC formats. Agreements based on the guidelines are legal documents, and close attention was accordingly paid to definition. The glossary includes many useful but hitherto loosely applied terms, e.g. 'adapted national MARC record', 'modified national MARC record', 'redistribution (of national MARC records)'; these are helpfully defined and exemplified.

The guidelines contain a specific warning on the need to guard against copying and redistribution of national records, stressing the need for any desired terms, conditions and prices to be fixed prior to record distribution.[26] As before, a receiving agency is prevented from using MARC records to publish the national bibliography of the country in which the records originated.

Faced with the inadequacies, or even inappropriateness, of copyright law, many countries have turned to exchange agreements and contracts, which stipulate precise conditions for use and distribution. Some national agencies, including France, Federal Republic of Germany, Sweden and Malaysia, have placed restrictions on the use of their national MARC records in an attempt to prevent unauthorized third-party usage (i.e. use by organizations other than the original recipient of the records).[27] In practice, this is hard to enforce, especially in respect of downloading (i.e. retrieval and storage of records from an online database). The situation is not without irony, since exchange formats, by their very nature, are intended to make interchange of data easy and flexible and for conversion to local internal formats. MARC records created by LC are in the public domain and thus freely usable within the United States, but subject to copyright elsewhere. UKMARC records may be used within the UK and EC countries only by licence. The Licence to Use British Library MARC Records, introduced in 1986, permits the reuse of records by third parties within the EC.[28] Three categories of Licence are involved: a User Licence, a Library Utility Licence (intended for library cooperatives) and a User(B) Licence (primarily for book trade and other organizations not maintaining a collection of library materials). For the period of the Licence, BL MARC records may be obtained from, and made available to, other organizations which are also Licence holders. Library utilities are also permitted to operate an online database containing BL MARC records. All records must display the British Library provenance flag. Use of BL MARC records outside the EC is determined by separately negotiated agreements, several of which have been made with other national libraries (e.g. National Libraries of Australia and Canada), with the Library of Congress and with library cooperatives (e.g. OCLC, UTLAS, RLG).[29]

Private sector competition

There is little information of general applicability on the true cost of creating comprehensive MARC records. At most, it can be said that they are time-consuming to produce, involve the use of highly trained staff, normally expert cataloguers, and are thus likely to be expensive. It is therefore understandable that record producers, especially national libraries and others in the public sector, should wish to protect themselves against loss of revenue and commercial exploitation of these costly products. At the IFLA Conference in Tokyo in 1986, the Conference of Directors of National Libraries (CDNL) approved two recommendations submitted by the International MARC Network Advisory Committee (IMNAC):

> 1 that national bibliographic agencies agree to inform and consult one another before entering into MARC distribution arrangements with other types of organizations, such as bibliographic utilities, to redistribute MARC records in other countries; and

2 that in cases where a national bibliographic agency finds
it advantageous to supply an organization other than a national
library in another country with records for redistribution, this
arrangement not be made exclusive.[30]

This expression of collective concern was a reaction to increased
competition from private-sector companies and library cooperatives, which particularly in the US, but increasingly also in
the UK and other countries, are involved in MARC-record
distribution. The distinction between commercial firms and library cooperatives has in recent years been blurred, with many
cooperatives becoming more market-oriented as they compete
for clients, sometimes across national boundaries.[31] National
libraries, as major producers with responsibility for creating
definitive national MARC records, may find themselves undercut by these potential rivals, and, as was noted in the case of the
copyrighting of the OCLC database, this may lead not only to
increased charges, but possibly also to lowering of standards.
The situation of many large-scale record producers is super-
ficially analogous to that of publishers and producers of audio
and video recordings, who feel threatened by organized photo-
copying and reproduction.

   Public-sector organizations maintain that, as they carry the
cost of producing the records, it is unfair for others, especially
commercial firms with capital backing, to profit from their
labours. Private-sector organizations counterclaim with reference to the substantial public subsidies underpinning national
libraries. Cuts in public-sector funding, however, and the need
for national libraries, along with other organizations, to be seen
to be offering value for money, have forced some agencies to
raise the price of their MARC products.[32] The altruism, albeit
subsidized, of former days has been largely replaced by more
commercial attitudes. Hall, observing that the British Library
has for many years set a relatively low price for its MARC-
record supply, wonders whether libraries accustomed to modest
prices will be prepared to pay more.[33] Increased competition has
certainly stimulated efforts to reach mutually beneficial agreements and in general to establish a relationship between public
and private sector which not only recognizes the rights of each
group, but also the economic realities of a changing market.

Standards

Machine formats

In Europe, North America and Australasia MARC has been a stable and acceptable standard for bibliographic data exchange and the availability of MARC records created by national agencies the major factor in the growth of large-scale catalogue databases. A switch to any other format as the basis for national networking appears improbable and would meet with considerable resistance. In the past, development of a national MARC format was seen as a natural first step towards participation in bibliographic data exchange; but this may no longer be the case. Simmons has pointed out that in some countries where library development is less extensive and well established, a new national MARC format, in the MARC/UNIMARC tradition, may not be the best choice as standard for external and internal bibliographic-record exchange; that the CCF, for example, with its independence of cataloguing rules and its ability to cope with records from both library and secondary-service communities, may have more to offer.[34] Other issues which might affect MARC at national level include further development and use of CD-ROM as a medium for storage and distribution of bibliographic data (discussed in Chapter 7); the linking of disparate systems based on ISO's Open Systems Interconnection protocols; and the development of standard machine formats for data exchange with the book trade.

The aim of OSI is the online connection, for a variety of purposes, of systems produced by different manufacturers. For systems to interconnect, there must be agreement on standards for communication of messages and data. The OSI Reference Model is a framework which makes it easier to see what standards are needed.[35] Many standards have already been developed, but there are still significant gaps in coverage. The OSI model comprises seven levels or 'layers', which correspond to defined stages of communication and at each layer standard procedures for data transfer, known as 'protocols', are required. Messages and data must pass through each of these layers, within each system, for communication to take place. The technical aspects of OSI are beyond our scope and are more than adequately discussed elsewhere.[36] Our particular interest is in the effect that the development of OSI and 'open systems' will have on MARC and other exchange formats and on the interchange of bibliographic records.

Most of the standard protocols defined for the lower layers of OSI can be readily accepted by MARC users, as they deal with the transfer of messages between computers, and the needs of the information community are no different in this respect from those of other groups. Representation of data passing between systems obviously involves character sets, which for bibliographic information are more extensive and specialized than for most other applications. The problems associated with character sets for use in open systems are nevertheless similar to those connected with data representation on magnetic tape, discussed in Chapter 2.

Areas of direct concern to MARC users occur at application layer and beyond: the interface between the application and the network. At application layer, many protocols are needed to support the wide range of operations required by the many and diverse users who will participate in the OSI environment. For successful interconnection of online systems within the library and information community, application-to-application communication standards are required to make possible the processing of data for particular tasks, such as catalogue updating, information retrieval and inter-library loans. Davison notes that in this area several application protocols are already being developed, each, unfortunately, incompatible with the others.[37] Bibliographic data are transferred between systems as part of data sections of network 'messages'; for this purpose an agreed standard communication format is required. MARC is utilized above the application layer, after system interconnection has been established.

At the time of writing there is no consensus about the effect of OSI developments on national MARC formats. Statements about the imminent demise of MARC and the capability of current OSI technology to achieve automatic transfer of bibliographic records in incompatible machine-readable formats must be treated with caution. Lynch is sceptical of many of the claims made for open-systems protocols, observing that those systems implemented to date all assume a common transfer format,

240

which, in the case of the Linked Systems Project in the United States, is the USMARC format for bibliographic data, or the USMARC format for authority data.[38] Thomas, while noting that MARC and its international variants owe more to the traditions and methods of library science than to techniques of data modelling from computer science, nevertheless admits that the latter are still inadequate for complete and effective handling of bibliographic data. He suggests the need, not for a new communication standard, but for a 'more complete formal specification language for bibliographic syntax and semantics'.[39] It appears, then, that MARC and other formats have a place in the open-systems environment, although specific issues, such as the capability of OSI implementations to handle local MARC variants and the future of the ISO 2709 record structure, remain unresolved. It is possible that record structures developed for data interchange on magnetic tape may be influenced, perhaps replaced, by other standards for electronic data interchange which will predominate internationally.

Book trade formats

Increased use of electronic information interchange in the book world creates a mixture of problems and possibilities for developing MARC networks. Bibliographic data created within the book trade are clearly an important part of national bibliographic resources and exchange of data between libraries and those involved with the book trade can bring only benefits. Allison sees a need for the establishment of publishers' databases containing records constructed according to accepted standards, which could be supplied by electronic means (perhaps via a data dissemination agency) to libraries, library suppliers and booksellers.[40] For exchanges of this nature agreement on common standards is needed. Current national MARC formats make little or no provision for the variety of non-bibliographic data required for book production and marketing, and suitable formats, not necessarily ISO 2709- or MARC-based, have been developed for these purposes. BEDIS (Book Trade Electronic Data Interchange Standards Committee) was established in the UK in 1986 to report on the existing standards for transfer of bibliographic and other data and to recommend common standards. Its discussion paper, published in 1988, recommends

241

the adoption of the MARC format for bibliographic data exchange and TRADACOMS and BISAC formats for other transactions.[41] The most powerful arguments in favour of MARC appear to be its widespread use by libraries and library suppliers in the UK and abroad, and its comprehensiveness (despite the lack of certain fields needed for use in the book trade). TRADACOMS (Trading Data Communications) standards are widely used in business and industry in the UK for the interchange of common commercial data (orders, invoices, delivery notes, etc.). The fixed-length format was developed by ANA (the Article Numbering Association) and can be used both for magnetic-tape exchanges and for direct telecommunications between computers via Tradanet, a nationally distributed network developed jointly by ANA and ICL.[42]

BISAC and SISAC are both committees of the Book Industry Study Group, Inc. BISAC (Book Industry Systems Advisory Committee) has developed standards for use in the book trade in North America and Australia for the electronic exchange of data by magnetic tape or telecommunications. There are several formats, including fixed- and variable-length Purchase order formats, an Invoice communications format and a Title status format, which is designed to give information about new book titles. Title status records contain bibliographic data, including title, author, publisher, date of publication and edition, as well as other data needed for trade purposes.[43] BISAC Purchase order formats are now recognized as a national standard: ANSI Z39.49–1985, *Computerized book ordering*. SISAC (Serials Industry Systems Advisory Committee) is concerned with standard serials formats, designed to facilitate computer-to-computer ordering and automation of serials procedures.[44] Its proposed standard, *Computerized serials orders, claims, cancellations and acknowledgements*, Z39.55, closely follows the BISAC variable-length format.[45] It conforms with ANSI Z39.2, with each record containing a leader, a directory with a tag for each data field and its starting character position, variable-length data fields separated by field terminators and a record terminator. Individual users can adapt the format, if required, to define a fixed-length format and minimal-level record.

Record content

A requirement of the UBC programme is that national agencies create authoritative and comprehensive records, according to internationally accepted standards, containing all data needed for a range of library-related activities, and including a full bibliographic description in line with ISBD principles. Ideally, a high-quality comprehensive record capable of fulfilling all external and internal requirements should be produced for every item immediately after publication. In practice, this is difficult if not impossible to achieve, even with the help of CIP programmes. Several potentially conflicting issues can affect the content of a national MARC record: the standards used, the currency (timeliness) of the record, its quality, suitability both for internal exchange and domestic use, its production cost, and the amount of cooperation possible between national agency and other organizations. The argument for comprehensiveness is strong. Receiving agencies can strip out unwanted data from full MARC records, but the reverse is not true; adding extra data locally involves effort and expense. No one disputes the right of individual libraries to use brief records; conversely, those libraries with a need for comprehensive records should not be disadvantaged. Comprehensiveness does not in itself guarantee quality; adherence to respected standards and rigorous quality control are needed. The argument for currency is equally cogent: a record is of little or no use if it arrives too late, and at a time when there is concern about the economics of record production the question must be asked whether it is preferable to produce briefer, but well-constructed, records more quickly. Moreover, it is often alleged that most local systems cannot in any case fully exploit comprehensive MARC records – a negative argument, which makes no allowance for development. The difficulty here, as Line has remarked, is that although there may be demand for brief records, there is no guarantee that everyone will be satisfied by the *same* brief record;[46] selection of data elements remains a contentious issue. A crucial problem is how to strike a balance between the varying demands made on national MARC records without impairing their quality and usefulness.

The content of MARC records is determined by external standards such as ISBD, AACR2 and other cataloguing codes, but in recent years there has been some questioning of the value to users of much of the descriptive data required for full ISBD/AACR2 cataloguing. That AACR2 allows three levels of description is sometimes overlooked, although its critics might claim that the choice of data elements at the first and briefest level was not based on any formal research into catalogue use. *ISBD(G)* also permits the selection of a subset of data elements, in all cases except the national definitive record. Work carried out at the Centre for Bibliographic Management (formerly Centre for Catalogue Research) indicates that users do not, in most circumstances, need or make use of full bibliographic descriptions and are better served by the inclusion of more subject information and by the provision of more access points to records.[47] Evidence from use of OPACs (Online Public-Access Catalogues) also points to the need for simpler records, with enhanced subject content and access.[48] A conflicting view is expressed by Naylor, who sees a divide between the desires of potential customers (of a nationwide database) and those of enthusiasts for catalogue reform.[49] Subject data in MARC records has been the topic of considerable discussion and research, especially in the US and UK, and the following comments are typical of many found in the literature: 'the [LC] MARC record does not provide adequate subject access to the material it has been used to catalogue';[50] 'subject access ... continues to be a problem ... partly because of the lack of subject data in the [UK]MARC record'.[51] The USMARC format now contains fields expressly for uncontrolled subject-index terms, for faceted topical-index terms and for terms reflecting occupations and functions treated as part of the subject content of an item. These were added to supplement the traditional fields for controlled subject headings (e.g. from LCSH, MESH and other recognized standards). UKMARC at present lacks fields for uncontrolled subject-index terms, but its field for PRECIS string (690) includes a highly specific statement of a document's subject content which can be used for postcoordinate online searching, using Boolean-type operators. UNIMARC also lacks fields for uncontrolled subject indexing, but includes several fields for controlled subject terms. All three formats have defined full contents-notes and summary-notes fields. Mitev, Venner and Walker have provided a list of

244

'subject-rich' fields in the MARC record, with suggestions for their exploitation in OPACs which were successfully implemented in their prototype online catalogue 'Okapi'.[52] The potential for subject data is thus present in the formats; the question is to what extent national agencies make use of these inherent facilities. This of course is related to other factors, such as cost and currency.

In a paper delivered in 1986 on the National Bibliographic Service and the UKMARC Resource (records created in the BL Bibliographic Services from books and serials received under legal deposit), it was admitted that constraint of costs had become a serious problem for the British Library, which intended significantly to reduce the quantity and specificity of the descriptive and analytic content of the UKMARC record, without change in the structural format.[53] This resulted, as described in Chapter 1, in the adoption of AACR2 level-one descriptive cataloguing for certain classes of material. In 1987 Joyce Butcher, then Head of Record Creation in British Library Bibliographic Services, highlighted the conflicting demands made on the national MARC record, which was intended to satisfy the needs of the national bibliographic reference service, to provide information for book selection and collection development and to act as a source of cataloguing data for libraries. She questioned whether the traditional record could adequately meet these varied demands, without sacrifice of timeliness, and called for a re-evaluation of its content.[54] This, logically, would involve a reappraisal of existing standards for record creation – a prospect guaranteed to arouse mixed feelings. There is agreement that standards, even if imperfect, are necessary to ensure accuracy and consistency and to facilitate data transfer between systems. Given the amount of time, money and effort which has been invested in current standards, their radical overhaul hardly seems imminent.

Cooperative input standards

CIP programmes have significantly improved the currency of national MARC records. Another contribution to national bibliographic control, and perhaps the first stage in building a national MARC network, is cooperation in the creation of records between national agency and other appropriate organizations. Cooperation is by definition an essential characteristic of any national MARC network and depends on the acceptance, by all participants, of common standards for record preparation.

In the UK the Cooperative Automation Group (CAG) has been responsible for drawing up a minimum exchange standard for bibliographic records in shared systems. The standard, which covers printed monographs, audiovisual materials, music, cartographic materials and serials, is related to AACR2 and to the UKMARC format, and in June 1986 was incorporated in the *UKMARC manual*, second edition, as *Appendix N: Recommended standards for bibliographic records exchanged in the UK national network*. This sets out fields for description, headings (main and added) and coded information of various types. Three categories of data are identified: M = mandatory if applicable, R = recommended if applicable, and O = optional. There is some differential treatment of materials, with certain data elements designated mandatory for certain classes of material, e.g. mathematical data in the case of cartographic materials. Notes are recommended for all items, but certain notes are mandatory for music and cartographic materials; statements of illustration are recommended for all items except serials, for which they are optional. The standard is 'intended for libraries in general', and was designed 'with regard for the current practices of UK libraries and with reference to the standards in use by UK library cooperatives'.[55]

National-level requirements are incorporated in USMARC format specifications for bibliographic and authority records. All machine-readable records contributed to a national database must adhere to these standards. Four national-level codes are specified:

M = Mandatory
A = Mandatory if applicable
O = Optional
U = Unused (i.e. undefined or not used because of the nature of the material, the nature of the content designator, the practices of the authorizing agency, etc.)

Minimal-level records are those for which data elements designated 'M' or 'A' are included.

Library cooperatives normally require members to adhere to a minimum standard for MARC record creation. OCLC, whose MARC format is an extension of USMARC, issues its own bibliographic input standards: AACR2 is required for author/ title and descriptive cataloguing.[56] BLCMP also requires use of AACR2. Its MARC format is similar to UKMARC, although differs in its treatment of analytical records and cross-references.[57]

United States

Interest in the possibility of networking on a national scale led to the formation in 1976 of what was to become LC's Network Advisory Committee (NAC), which has responsibility for advising the Library on the planning of a nationwide network. Its series of *Network planning papers* provide not only much useful information on significant networking issues, but also a valuable historical insight into the ideological and practical problems surrounding the concept of a national network. NAC's membership is drawn from a wide range of bodies, including the Council on Library Resources (CLR), the LC, the National Library of Medicine, the National Agricultural Library, major networks and professional and research organizations.[58] LC's Network Development and MARC Standards Office acts as coordinator and reports to NAC on progress made on projects under its direction. The Linked Systems Project (LSP), described briefly in Chapter 3, was conceived as the first stage – the bibliographic component – of a nationwide network. It began in 1980, funded primarily by CLR, with three participants (LC, RLIN, WLN; later joined by OCLC), its initial purpose to provide access for members of one network to the bibliographic resources of others. The NACO Project (formerly Name Authority Cooperative, now National Coordinated Cataloging Operations) was the first to benefit from LSP.[59] From its inception in 1977, NACO had operated in batch mode, with contributing organizations sending in authority data on worksheets, for checking at LC and conversion to machine-readable form. This inevitably caused a delay between the time of record creation and distribution. It was clearly desirable that NACO members have online access to LC's Name Authority File to enable them to verify headings against a full and current set of records. Furthermore, the most difficult and costly aspect of bibliographic record construction was believed to be the establishment of standard forms of headings, and the development of a nationwide authority file a prerequisite of an effective national bibliographic network. Speed of interchange of authority data is of vital importance in establishing standard forms of headings throughout a network. NACO, already well established, thus offered an obvious and suitable starting point. The Authorities Implementation was the first use of the LSP communication protocols, which were constructed within the framework of the ISO's Open Systems Interconnection (OSI) Reference Model.[60] The MARC format for authority data was revised and republished in anticipation of its use in the project. LSP, it must be noted, makes use of USMARC communications formats, although the open-systems protocols are format-independent, assuming only that communicating systems have agreed on a standard exchange format. By 1984, LC had completed the required telecommunications software (Standard Network Interconnection/SNI) and record-transfer software needed for distribution of online authority records to NACO participants. RLIN was the first to receive records in 1985, followed by OCLC in 1987; WLN has apparently been obliged to delay its LSP implementation for internal reasons. RLIN and OCLC now maintain a current copy of LC's Name Authority File, updated daily. Further improvements have enabled NACO participants who are also members of RLIN and OCLC to contribute data directly to LC: the data are transmitted via the LSP link, validated and immediately made available for online access to network users and distribution through the MARC Distribution Service to the library community in general.[61] The advantages are twofold: records are created with greater speed and, as a consequence, the possibility of duplication is vastly reduced. The system also permits staff at LC to review authority records online prior to their transfer to the Library.[62]

A further stage of LSP, currently under development, is the transmission of bibliographic records in USMARC format, the ultimate aim being the formation of a nationwide, decentralized database of MARC records, based on cooperative effort, with consistency and accuracy assured by adherence to common standards and online verification of headings. The National

Coordinated Cataloging Program (NCCP) Pilot Project, which involves LC and selected research libraries, is to explore the feasibility of sharing record creation in an attempt to increase currency, extend coverage, reduce duplication and ensure good-quality national-level records. Cooperating institutions follow agreed national-level standards for record creation, and conform to LC rule interpretations and procedures. The project is expected to provide valuable information for subsequent phases of LSP.[63] The existence of the USMARC communications formats obviously facilitated the establishment of the project, allowing effort to be concentrated on the development of other standards required. The resilience and adaptability of a data format originally designed for tape transfer must also be commended.

When fully operational, the linked systems network should enable users in one locality to search the catalogue or database of another network or local system using their own search commands and query language; the result of the search will be displayed in the user's familiar format. This function is sometimes described as 'information retrieval', 'intersystem search' or 'search/response'. Another important feature of LSP is record transfer. At present, data contributed by network users are drawn across the link to LC and then distributed by LC, along with its own records, to all LSP participants – a two-way process between LC and the utilities. Eventually LSP links will be established between other systems, e.g. between networks (inter-networking) and between local systems and networks, thus facilitating multi-directional record transfer and reinforcing the movement towards distributed processing. It is hoped that LSP will evolve into a linked nationwide network, capable of sustaining a range of library-related activities, as well as exchange of bibliographic data. Martin welcomes the success of LSP, but voices concern about the costs of development and maintenance, the problems of copyright and data ownership and the technical problems which may arise as local implementations of LSP are sought.[64] Avram, speculating on the future of LSP, considers that the technical and bibliographic problems are outweighed by the economic and political.[65]

United Kingdom

In the UK, proposals for a national bibliographic database were put forward in 1982 by the Cooperative Automation Group (CAG). This was founded in 1980, its membership derived from the British Library, the library cooperatives (BLCMP, LASER, SCOLCAP and SWALCAP), the Library Association, Aslib, SCONUL (Standing Conference of National and University Libraries) and COPOL (Council of Polytechnic Librarians), its aim to ensure 'the most effective articulation of the services provided by the British Library and the library automation cooperatives in the interests of the library community at large'.[66] The proposed United Kingdom Library Database System (UKLDS) was intended as a common database of cataloguing and location records, providing UK users with access to far more data than could be offered individually by either the BL or the cooperatives. The principal objectives of UKLDS were:

> 1   to obtain and provide access to an acceptable bibliographic record for items catalogued by a participating library
> 2   to obtain and provide access to information on UK library holdings, particularly those of libraries or library organizations which participate in the national interlending system, or whose collections constitute an important reference source.[67]

UKMARC was to be the communications format and the database was to consist of records in UKMARC format, initially drawn from the UKMARC and LC MARC records held by the BL, from the library cooperatives and from catalogues of the BL's Lending and Reference Divisions. Other libraries were to be encouraged to contribute records either in full UKMARC format or in a recommended simpler subset. Holdings data were also to be included, to facilitate access and interlending. From an early stage, careful attention was paid to the problem of bibliographic standards and related matters arising from the sharing of bibliographic data on such a large scale. Although precise details of the technical infrastructure of the system were left undecided, the database was to be held on a new online database facility administered by the British Library Bibliographic Services Division. The proposed system had been described at the 1982 ABACUS meeting as 'an extension of

BLAISE to accommodate bibliographic cooperatives operating in the UK, enabling all participants to share their resources through a centralized database from which selected records can be transferred to other systems',[68] but representatives of the BL and CAG particularly emphasized the flexible and pragmatic nature of the scheme. What was envisaged was not a 'national database' but a 'national data resource', fully compatible with developments in other countries, especially the United States and Canada, and allowing for local processing and the possible linking of local systems.[69] BL's role was to be managerial, not proprietorial. The database was to be accessible to all members of the library and information community, either by direct terminal access or by computer-to-computer link from local systems, and to operate on the principle of free exchange of records, with operating costs only to be recovered.

The attempt to draw the resources of the library cooperatives into a common framework, whether centralized or decentralized, was highly desirable, as they are the largest producers of MARC records outside the British Library. EMMA or Extra-MARC records, now restyled by the British Library 'external MARC records' are records for items for which BL MARC or LC MARC records are unavailable.[70] The vast majority are created by members of cooperatives, which maintain substantial files of these records; BLCMP, for example, currently holds around one million. Access to large numbers of external MARC records is a major reason for joining a cooperative, particularly for libraries whose collections are similar to those of other members. UKLDS was not initially seen as a threat to the continued existence of the library cooperatives; on the contrary, Hall, Director of BLCMP Library Services, observed that the proposed charging structure and mode of operation favoured the cooperatives.[71] The largest contributors of external MARC records were to attract the lowest charges, in itself an incentive to join or retain membership of a cooperative; moreover, members of cooperatives would have an assured connection, via their own network, to the database.

The initial response to UKLDS from the library community was favourable, although concern was expressed about coverage to be given to non-book materials, provision of subject access

251

and the nature of the database itself. There was considerable debate about the desirability of a centralized database and its acceptability in general terms and in connection with maintenance and updating of holdings and locations data.[72] This led to a review by CAG of all possible options, ranging from completely centralized to wholly distributed.[73] Another cause for concern was standardization and its associated costs. Cooperation in record creation and exchange requires acceptance of common standards, including an effective system for authority control. Would libraries be willing and/or able to meet recommended input standards? And would the financial resources needed to support UKLDS be better directed elsewhere?

By the end of 1983, there were serious problems, and in 1984 CAG issued a statement concluding that it was 'no longer a realistic objective to pursue the establishment of UKLDS in the way that was originally conceived'.[74] The reasons for the termination of the scheme appear to be economic and political, precisely those factors which Avram sees as major obstacles to national networking. CAG was faced with the immensely difficult task of providing a financial and marketing structure for UKLDS which would achieve a balance between the potentially conflicting interests of participants; in particular, of reconciling the willingness of the library cooperatives to become involved in the system, and their requirement to act competitively in the interests of their members. An appeal by CAG to the Office of Arts and Libraries (the government body which funds the British Library) for financial support for the cooperatives in implementing some of the technical aspects of the proposed system was rejected and no alternative sources were forthcoming. The situation contrasts with that in the US, where the Council on Library Resources has strongly supported the Linked Systems Project. A nationwide bibliographic network in the UK is now to be pursued in a decentralized way, possibly along North American lines, by encouraging links between different systems, using technology modelled on OSI, and by the exchange of records based on agreements which safeguard the interests of all parties. Despite the abandonment of UKLDS, much useful work resulted, including the CAG recommendations on standards for data in shared systems; the work on the Universal Standard Book Code (USBC) and its potential for eliminating duplicate records in merged files of MARC records from different sources; the progress on bibliographic standards for non-book materials; and the development of specifications for acronym keys that might be used in online record retrieval.[75]

UKLDS, as originally envisaged, would have brought the catalogues of many different libraries, especially those of universities, into one database, in effect creating a union catalogue. Improved access has subsequently resulted from the development of the Joint Academic Network (JANET) and the Consortium of University Research Libraries (CURL), a cooperative venture designed to facilitate common access to university library collections.[76] JANET is a multi-purpose network which embraces universities, polytechnics, national libraries and other institutions engaged in academic research and enables users, among other activities, to search the online databases and catalogues of participating institutions. Protocols for communication between network users are similar to, but predate, standards developed within the OSI framework. In time, transition to OSI protocols is expected. JANET is by no means a British version of the Linked Systems Project: there are no standards implemented at application level for bibliographic data processing and participation does not depend on the acceptance of any standard bibliographic data format, though many libraries in fact use MARC. No movements of bibliographic records between organizations have been reported and automatic transfer of searches is not yet possible. End-users must therefore conduct separate searches on each catalogue or database.[77]

In the years following the abandonment of UKLDS, the British Library has continued to establish links with other institutions, both inside and outside the UK, for the exchange of bibliographic data. Direct links with RLIN and NLM via a transatlantic telecommunications line were set up in 1985; the former is being used in connection with the Eighteenth-Century Short-Title Catalogue (ESTC) project, to provide a single database in California which can be accessed by teams working simultaneously in London and Louisiana.[78] The link with NLM not only provides access to the MEDLARS biomedical databases through BLAISE-LINK, but also enables direct entry of indexing data from the Library's Document Supply Centre to MEDLARS.[79] BLAISE Records, the record supply service initiated at the beginning of 1988, has been enhanced by an agreement between the British Library and OCLC for access to OCLC's database of more than 18 million records in USMARC format.[80] BLAISE Records subscribers may now search OCLC's database for records not obtained from the British Library's MARC files; all records retrieved will be converted by the Library into UKMARC format. In 1987, BLAISE was connected to JANET, thus offering network users access to its MARC files.[81]

A programme announced by the BL in 1988 involves the Library in a cooperative venture with the five other UK copyright deposit libraries (the Bodleian Library, Cambridge University Library, the National Library of Scotland, the National Library of Wales, the library of Trinity College Dublin).[82] The Copyright Libraries Shared Cataloguing Programme is designed to improve currency in record creation both for BL and other libraries and to reduce costs. It is intended that BL contributes the bulk of records (70%) and the other five libraries the remainder. Records will be sent to BL on magnetic tape for inclusion in the regular UKMARC exchange tapes and to the BNB MARC file on BLAISE-LINE.

The British Library's *Automation strategy*, published in 1988, outlining a five-year programme of development, affirms a continuing commitment to develop online network relationships both inside and outside the UK, and lists network capabilities for shared cataloguing among nine key areas for advance.[83]

The movement towards distributed systems, while in many ways beneficial, also carries a risk of fragmentation in record creation and supply, and the possibility of a breakdown in standards. At local level, this may in some ways be welcomed; but there are wider implications. Avram has lamented the 'negative impact of a lack of a nationwide focal point' in the history of nationwide networking in the US and of the need for firm coordination in the Linked Systems Project.[84] Similar apprehension has been expressed by the MARC Users' Group (MUG), an active organization which has monitored BL MARC services and coordinated pressure for improvement. It has also served as a forum for the exchange of information and

254

experience among UKMARC users and has carried out surveys on the use of MARC records, particularly in respect of subject access. MUG in 1988 convened a forum on the future of the national database, to consider in particular the means of supply and exchange of MARC records. It expressed concern about the proliferation of databases in the UK and the risk of fragmented effort, contrasting the situation unfavourably with that in the US, where cooperation had been enhanced by the Linked Systems Project. Its final statement recognized the two levels on which national bibliographic effort exists:

> 1 the creation of the national archival record for which the focus and responsibility lies with the British Library, as advised by the library community
> 2 the development of a network of databases from which users can be satisfied for various functions, the coordination of which may lie with the BL but the responsibility for which should be more widely shared.

Finally, it called for the consideration and planning of a national strategy for networking.[85]

Canada
The National Library of Canada is a pioneer in the application of new technology to networking. In 1981 it joined with other groups in the iNET Gateway Field Trial, a project initiated by the TransCanada Telephone System to test the feasibility of establishing an 'open' network for the exchange of a wide range of data among computer systems.[86] The iNET system used a set of protocol standards, based on the OSI Reference Model, designed to achieve cost-effective and 'user-friendly' access to systems as diverse as banking, library and information services, tourism and travel. Five other libraries joined the National Library in the Bibliographic Interest Group, and tested a variety of library-related applications, including database access and transfer of files of records between systems. Beckman notes that five quite different systems, four different computers and six different record formats were represented.[87] The report on the bibliographic component (the Bibliographic and Communications Network Pilot Project) confirmed the technical feasibility of a decentralized nationwide library and information network based on the OSI model and set out recommendations

255

for a nationwide network development programme, coordinated by the NLC.[88] Fundamental to the programme is a set of 'Principles of networking', which emphasize open access, adherence to common standards, voluntary but coordinated participation, decentralization where appropriate and the need for international network interfaces and liaison. Since the end of the iNET trials in 1983, several library applications protocols have been developed, including inter-library loans and file transfer to support bibliographic-record exchange.[89] File transfer is offered as an option in the NLC's MARC Record Distribution Service and the DOBIS Search Service.[90] Reporting to the Library's union catalogue database has been enhanced in a number of ways: MARA provides for MAchine-Readable Accession reporting; software has been developed to convert data between different formats; and a minimal-level CAN/MARC format has been published, which specifies the minimum mandatory data elements required for contribution to a shared database.[91] The NLC's own DOBIS database continues to be available via iNET. The NLC has published a series of *Canadian network papers*, which chart the development of the network and address significant matters, such as ownership of machine-readable data.

Australia

The Australian Bibliographic Network (ABN) is the principal network service of the National Library of Australia, delivering cataloguing data to member libraries and offering online access to the National Bibliographic Database.[92] ABN is the major focus in Australia for MARC-record exchanges. The network was initiated as a shared cataloguing service, with some expectation that it might develop into a national union catalogue. This is not yet the case, as some major libraries have remained apart, although there are over 800 members, almost half of whom contribute records to the database. Holdings and locations are included.

The National Bibliographic Database was built around a copy of the database of the Western Library Network (WLN), containing LC MARC records and records contributed by WLN members.[93] The National Library uses WLN software, under licence, to operate the network. These records have been augmented by records from the Australian MARC Distribution Service file (i.e. for books and serials listed in the *Australian national bibliography*) and by substantial numbers of records from the National Library itself. Exchange agreements bring in records from the United Kingdom, New Zealand, the United States and Canada, with the possibility of further additions from Malaysia, Singapore and Vietnam. Most records are received in USMARC format, and converted into AUSMARC. The total number of records in the database in 1988 was almost 5.7 million.[94] Duplicate records are identified and eliminated by a computer program which checks incoming records against those already in the file. The ABN Authority File provides authority control, automatically relinking records with invalid headings to preferred forms of heading. In 1988, two new services were introduced. The Authority MARC Service enables members to obtain machine-readable subject and name authority records either in USMARC or AUSMARC authority format. The Downline Loading Service allows users the option of receiving MARC records via electronic transmission, instead of magnetic tape.[95] All records are available either in USMARC or AUSMARC formats. The National Library is currently investigating OSI standards for incorporation as an option into its downloading facility.

If present trends continue, the national networks of the future are likely to be decentralized, cooperative arrangements, based on the linking of heterogeneous systems made possible by technological innovation and Open Systems Interconnection research and development. They will be coordinated, rather than dominated, by national libraries or national bibliographic agencies. In those countries where MARC formats are already established, these are likely to survive, adapted in response to technological progress, rather than completely replaced.

The ideal of one machine-readable record serving the needs of all users, from book trade to library, is far from being a reality, but may be attainable if cooperation between different sectors of the information community is maintained and encouraged.

Notes and references

1 *International guide to MARC databases and services: national magnetic tape and online services*, 2nd rev. ed., Frankfurt, Deutsche Bibliothek, for the International MARC Project, 1986.

2 *International cataloguing and bibliographic control*, published quarterly by the IFLA UBCIM Programme. Formerly *International cataloguing*, the title was changed in 1988.

3 *Network planning papers* are published by the Library of Congress, normally as proceedings of the Network Advisory Committee meetings. See especially Maruyama, L. S., *The Library of Congress Network Advisory Committee, its first decade*, 1985 Washington DC, LC, (Network planning paper no. 11).

4 *Guidelines for the national bibliographic agency and the national bibliography*, prepared by IFLA International Office for UBC, Paris, Unesco, 1979 (PG1/79/WS/18).

5 Anderson, D., *UBC: a survey of Universal Bibliographic Control*, London, IFLA International Office for UBC, 1982 (Occasional paper no. 10), 10.

6 Bell, B. L., 'Progress, problems and prospects in current national bibliographies: implementations of the ICNB recommendations', in *Proceedings of the National Bibliographies Seminar, Brighton, 18th August 1987, held under the auspices of the IFLA Division of Bibliographic Control*, London, IFLA UBCIM Programme, 1988, 29–37; Bell, B. L., *An annotated guide to current national bibliographies*, Alexandria, VA: Chadwyck-Healey, 1986.

7 Lewis, P., 'The future of the national bibliography', in *Proceedings of the National Bibliographies Seminar*, 59–62.

8 'Compact discs for national bibliography', *British Library Bibliographic Services newsletter*, **46**, June 1988, 1–3; British Library, *Gateway to knowledge: the British Library strategic plan, 1989–1994*, London, British Library Board, 1989, 11.

9 Maruyama, L. S., *op. cit.*, 11.

10 'National MARC records and international exchange', *British Library Bibliographic Services newsletter*, **42**, February 1987, 4–5.

11 Avram, H., 'Toward a nationwide library network', *Journal of library administration*, **8**, 1987, 97.

12 United Kingdom, *Copyright, Designs and Patents Act, 1988*, London, HMSO, 1988, Part I, Chapter 1, 1–8.

13 The legal issues in general are discussed in McDonald, D. D., Rodger, E. J. and Squires, J. L., *International study of copyright of bibliographic records in machine-readable form*, Munich, Saur, 1983 (IFLA publications 27), 25–39. See also Lahore, J., Dworkin, G.

and Smyth, Y. M., *Information technology: the challenge to copy right*, London, Sweet & Maxwell, 1984; *Intellectual property issues in the library network context: proceedings of the Library of Congress Network Advisory Committee Meeting, March 1988*, Washington DC, LC, 1988 (Network planning paper no. 17).

14 Duchesne, R., Guenter, D. A. and Tsai, S., *Ownership of machine-readable bibliographic data*, Ottawa, National Library of Canada, 1983 (Canadian network papers no. 5).

15 *US Code, Title 17, Copyright Revision Act, 1976*, PL 94–553 (S. 22), Sections 102–3. See also Laird, W. D., 'Current bibliographic database ownership issues and the protection of non-traditional formats', in *Intellectual property rights in an electronic age: proceedings of the Library of Congress Network Advisory Committee Meeting, 22–24 April 1987*, Washington DC, NDMSO, 1987 (Network planning paper no. 16), 35–43.

16 Avram, H., *op. cit.*, 109.

17 Martin, S. K., *Library networks, 1986–87: libraries in partnership*, White Plains, NY, Knowledge Industry, 1986, 147.

18 Mason, M. G., 'Copyright in context: the OCLC database', *Library journal*, **113**, (12), July 1988, 31–4.

19 Wells, A. J., *The International MARC Network: a study for an international bibliographic data network*, prepared for the International MARC Network Study Steering Committee, London, IFLA International Office for UBC, 1977 (Occasional paper no. 3), 19.

20 International MARC Network Study Steering Committee, *International access to MARC records: a summary report with recommended text for a bilateral agreement for the international exchange of MARC records*, London, IFLA International Office for UBC, 1980 (Occasional paper no. 7).

21 *Ibid.*, 6.

22 McDonald, D. D., Rodger, E. J. and Squires, J. L., *op. cit.*

23 *Ibid.*, 11.

24 Duchesne, R., Guenter, D. A. and Tsai, S., *op. cit.*

25 Conference of Directors of National Libraries, International MARC Network Advisory Committee, *International transfers of national MARC records: guidelines for agreement*, London, IFLA UBCIM Programme, 1987.

26 *Ibid.*, 8.

27 *International guide to MARC databases and services.*

28 The licensing system is operated by Marketing and Support, British Library Bibliographic Services, 2 Sheraton Street, London W1V 4BH, from whom details should be sought.

29 'Worldwide use of UKMARC', *British Library Bibliographic Services*

newsletter, **40**, June 1986, 5; 'National MARC records and international exchange', *British Library Bibliographic Services newsletter*, **42**, February 1987, 4–5.

30   *LCIB*, **46**, (17), 27 April 1987, 171.

31   Stubley, P., *BLCMP: a guide for librarians and systems managers*, Aldershot, Gower, 1988, 225–7, discusses the 'cooperative versus commercial' issue.

32   Avram, H., *op. cit.*, 105.

33   Hall, A. R., 'A view from the cooperatives', in *Bibliographic records in the book world: needs and capabilities: proceedings of a seminar held on 27–28 November 1987, at Newbury*, London, British Library, 1988 (British National Bibliography Research Fund report 33), 117–23.

34   Simmons, P., 'Using CCF: the Common Communication Format', *Information technology and libraries*, **5**, 1986, 285–94.

35   *Information processing systems – Open Systems Interconnection – basic reference model, ISO 7498/1*, Geneva, ISO, 1984.

36   See, for example, McCrum, W. J., 'What is OSI?', in *Open Systems Interconnection: the communications technology of the 1990s: papers from the pre-conference seminar held at London, August 12–14, 1987*, ed. by C. Smith, Munich, Saur, 1988 (IFLA publications 44), 24–33; Brown, T. P., 'Communication standards for online interchange of library information', *Library trends*, **31**, (2), Fall 1982, 251–63; Turtle, H., 'The Open Systems Interconnection (OSI) reference model', in *Telecommunications networks: issues and trends*, ed. by M. E. L. Jacob, White Plains, NY, Knowledge Industry, 1986, 41–65.

37   Davison, W., 'Application in the OSI environment', in *Open Systems Interconnection: the communications technology of the 1990s*, 54–68.

38   Lynch, C. A., 'Linked systems protocol: a practical perspective', in *Telecommunications networks: issues and trends*, 67–81.

39   Thomas, K. A., 'OSI and the evolution of library systems: prospects and challenges for the 1990s', in *Open Systems Interconnection: the communications technology of the 1990s*, 224–38.

40   Allison, J., 'Publishers' marketing databases: a source of bibliographic records for the book world', in *Bibliographic records in the book world: needs and capabilities*, 67–94.

41   Booktrade Electronic Data Interchange Standards Committee (BEDIS), Discussion paper, London, Whitaker on behalf of the MARC Users Group, 1988, 10–11.

42   Fenton, N., 'Standards and a network service for data exchange', *Computer bulletin*, June 1986, 32–4, (reprinted in *Electronic trans-*

mission standards for the book world: avoiding an electronic babel: report of a one-day seminar held on 15 October 1986, London, BNB Research Fund, 1986, 20–2). See also BEDIS, Discussion paper, 18–21.

43 Buckle, D., 'BISAC/SISAC', in *Electronic transmission standards for the book world*, 24–34; P. Holmes (Jordan & Sons Ltd), in an unpublished survey, has made detailed comparisons of TRADACOMS and BISAC formats.

44 Saxe, M. C., 'SISAC: the Serials Industry Systems Advisory Committee', in *The USMARC format for holdings and locations: development, implementation and use*, ed. by B. B. Baker, New York, Haworth Press, 1988, 215–27.

45 *Proposed American National Standard for Information Sciences – Computerized Serials Orders, Claims, Cancellations and Acknowledgements*, Z39.55, developed by the National Information Standards Organization, 1988. At the time of writing, a revised draft is being presented to NISO.

46 See *UK Library database system and union catalogues: proceedings of a seminar organised by the Cataloguing and Indexing Group* ed. by L. Favret and T. McSean, London, Library Association, 1983, Discussion session III, 91.

47 Seal, A., Bryant, P. and Hall, C., *Full and short entry catalogues: library needs and uses*, Bath, Centre for Catalogue Research, Bath University Library, 1982 (BLRD report 5669).

48 See, for example, Cochrane, P. A. and Markey, K., 'Catalog use studies – since the introduction of online interactive catalogs: impact on design for subject access', *Library and information science research*, **5**, 1983, 337–63; Walker, S., 'The free-language approach to online catalogues: the system', in *Keyword catalogues and the free-language approach*, ed. by P. Bryant, Bath University Library, 1985, 31–40.

49 Naylor, B., 'National cataloguing records: new proposals for a United Kingdom library database system', in *Databases for books: their uses for selling, acquiring and cataloguing: proceedings of the MARC Users' Group Seminar, 3 May 1983*, London, Library Association, 1983, 18–26.

50 Simonds, M. J., 'Database limitations and online catalogs', *Library journal*, **109**, (3), 15 February 1984, 329–30.

51 Congreve, J., 'Browsing through PRECIS: structured subject access in an online catalogue', in *Online public access to library files: second national conference*, ed. by J. Kinsella, Oxford, Elsevier International Bulletins, 1986, 67–77.

52 Mitev, N. N., Venner, G. M. and Walker, S., *Designing an online public-access catalogue*, London, British Library, 1985 (Library and

information research reports 39), Appendix I.

53   'The National Bibliographic Service and the UKMARC Resource', *British Library Bibliographic Services newsletter*, **42**, February 1987, 2–3.

54   Butcher, J., 'Suppliers' capabilities: BL Bibliographic Services', in *Bibliographic records in the book world: needs and capabilities*, 103–8.

55   *UKMARC manual*, 2nd ed., 1980–7, Appendix N, N/1.

56   *Bibliographic input standards*, 3rd ed., OCLC, 1988.

57   Stubley, P., *op. cit.*, 80–5 and Appendices C–D, explains essential differences between BLCMP and UKMARC.

58   Maruyama, L. S., *op. cit.*

59   McCallum, S. H., 'Linked Systems Project in the United States', *IFLA journal*, **11**, (4), 1985, 313–24; McCallum, S. H., 'Linked Systems Project, Part I: authorities implementation', *Library hi-tech*, **10**, 1985, 61–8.

60   *LCIB*, **45**, (10), 10 March 1986; *ibid.*, **47**, (4), 25 January 1988; Buckland, M. K. and Lynch, C. A., 'The Linked Systems Protocol and the future of bibliographic networks and systems', *Information technology and libraries*, **6**, 1987, 83–8; McCallum, S. II., 'USA – the Linked Systems Project', in *Open Systems Interconnection: the communications technology of the 1990s*, 108–18.

61   *LCIB*, **47**, (28), 11 July 1988.

62   *LCIB*, **46**, (41), 12 October 1987.

63   *LCIB*, **46**, (42), 19 October 1987; Avram, H. and Wiggins, B., 'The National Coordinated Cataloging Project', *Library resources and technical services*, **32**, 1988, 111–15.

64   Martin, S. K., *op. cit.*, 155–7.

65   Avram, H., *op. cit.*, 112.

66   Cooperative Automation Group, *Proposals for a UK library database system*, July 1982, 1 (also published in *BLBSD newsletter*, **27**, November 1982).

67   *Ibid.*, 2.

68   *British Library Bibliographic Services Division newsletter*, **28**, February 1983, 3–5.

69   *UK Library Database System and union catalogues*. See especially papers by P. Lewis, L. Brindley and D. Martin.

70   'MARC nomenclature', *British Library Bibliographic Services newsletter*', **44**, October 1987, 3–4.

71   Hall, A., 'UKLDS: implications for the cooperatives', in *UK Library Database System and union catalogues*, 52–5.

72   UK Library Database System: responses to the discussion paper', *British Library Bibliographic Services Division newsletter*, **29**, April 1983, 3–4.

73 'Progress towards UKLDS', *British Library Bibliographic Services Division newsletter*, **32**, February 1984, 1–2.

74 The statement was reprinted in *British Library Bibliographic Services Division newsletter*, **34**, October 1984, 2.

75 'Progress towards UKLDS', *loc. cit.*

76 Ratcliffe, F. W., 'The Consortium of University Research Libraries: a new cooperative venture in the UK', *Collection management*, **9**, 1987, 55–67.

77 Holligan, P. J., *Access to academic networks*, London, Taylor Graham for the Primary Communications Research Centre, 1986; Wells, M., 'The JANET Project', *University computing*, **6**, 1984, 56–62; Wells, M., 'A progress report on JANET', *University computing*, **8**, 1986, 146–53.

78 *British Library Bibliographic Services newsletter*, **39**, February 1986, 5.

79 *Ibid.*

80 Information from British Library Bibliographic Services factsheet on BLAISE Records, 1988.

81 *British Library Bibliographic Services newsletter*, **43**, June 1987.

82 'Bibliographic cooperation amongst the copyright libraries', Press release, British Library, 19 May 1988.

83 British Library, *Automation strategy*, London, British Library Board, 1988, 24.

84 Avram, H., *op. cit.*, 97.

85 MARC Users' Group/Library Association Forum on the Future of a National Database, January 1988, report.

86 *Linking: today's libraries, tomorrow's technologies*, Ottawa, National Library of Canada, 1984 (Canadian network papers no. 7).

87 Beckman, M., 'Linking systems and networks', in *Online public access to library files: conference proceedings: the proceedings of a conference held at the University of Bath, 3–5 September 1984*, ed. by J. Kinsella, Centre for Catalogue Research, Oxford, Elsevier International Bulletins, 1985, 75–82.

88 *Linking: today's libraries, tomorrow's technologies.*

89 Durance, C. J., *Linking: then and now: a status report on the networking program at the National Library of Canada*, Ottawa, NLC, 1987 (Canadian network papers no. 11).

90 Lunau, C. D., 'The National Library of Canada networking program: from protocol research to implementation', in *Open Systems Interconnection: the communications technology of the 1990s*, 119–31.

91 *Canadian MARC communication format: minimal level*, Ottawa, NLC, 1987.

92 National Library of Australia, *Annual report, 1987–88*, Canberra, NLA, 1988, 21–4. See also Horton, W., 'The Australian Bibliographic Network', *International cataloguing*, **16**, (1), January/March 1987, 8–10.

93 Cathro, W. S., 'The exchange of cataloguing data in the Australian Bibliographic Network', *International cataloguing and bibliographic control*, **17**, (2), April/June 1988, 19– –21.

94 National Library of Australia, *op. cit.*, 68.

95 *Ibid.*, 22.

7

Exchange formats and local systems

MARC networks have developed as a direct result of the acceptance of MARC standards in cooperatives. Libraries that wish to cooperate cannot ignore MARC. Format conversion, initially connected with international exchange and confined to conversion between different national formats, has more recently been encountered in local systems, many of which, though not designed with cooperation in mind, have considered joining MARC networks in order to assist with retrospective conversion projects or to take in MARC records for their current cataloguing. This chapter deals with exchange formats in local systems and includes sections on converting data to MARC.

MARC started off as a national standard in the US and UK and then with the development of UNIMARC became international. MARC is employed in local systems to a much greater extent in the United States than elsewhere, though it has been in national use for just as long in the UK as in the US.

Many national standards are discussed over periods of many years through official channels such as, in the UK, the British Standards Institution. UKMARC, however, was formulated by the British National Bibliography with little outside consultation. This was due to the necessity of cooperating with the Library of Congress. International compatibility could be said to have been achieved at the expense of national compatibility. However, there were no UK systems at the time which could have become a basis for any cooperative system. When the first cooperatives were set up, for example the Birmingham Libraries Cooperative Mechanization Project (now BLCMP), the Scottish Libraries Cooperative Automation Project (SCOLCAP)

and the South-West Academic Libraries Co-operative Automation Project (SWALCAP) (previously the South West
University Libraries Systems Co-operation Project), they
needed to follow the given standard in order to be able to take
records from the national database. Indeed, they were all
funded at the start by the Office for Scientific and Technical
Investigation, OSTI, and its successor, the British Library
Research and Development Department, and were obliged to
make the most of national standards, both official and
unofficial. There were in 1967 a number of automated systems
in the UK such as the London Borough of Camden's system.
The impetus for the development of this system, as indeed for
others, was local government reorganization in London which
had meant in many of the new boroughs the amalgamation of
two or three union catalogues. Automation had been used as a
tool to accomplish this. These systems often produced what were
little more than finding lists which could in no way be compared
with, say, the printed product from the British National
Bibliography, the major producer of bibliographic records in the
UK. They had been developed by individual library authorities
as systems purely for local use and were not intended to be
integrated with larger systems. Nor had these authorities
themselves made any use of standards beyond cataloguing codes
or even called for the development of standards.

MARC in different kinds of libraries
Public libraries generally put all their efforts into automated
loans systems, and the fullness of their cataloguing tended not
to increase as automation advanced. However, library authorities have come round to the view that it might be cheaper to
buy in records that have already been created instead of using
their staff time on generating original records.

The easiest way for academic and public libraries to obtain
records already created is to join a cooperative. The cooperatives work on the basis that most of the computer
processing is done on a central computer. This computer
produces catalogues in printout form or on fiche, and, more
recently, it has become possible as well to interrogate online the
computer database. Cooperatives usually charge libraries less if
they are contributors to the database as well as users of it.

266

However, contributions are usually accepted only in MARC format; otherwise the records cannot be used by other members and so are of no value to the cooperative system. Contributing MARC records can mean extra work in providing data which a library would not normally include; it also means providing and processing MARC coding including both content designators and information codes.

Alternatively, a library authority that has developed its own system can ignore MARC internally, but can still tap the large sources of records that have been built up by cooperatives or national agencies like the British Library and add them to its own database. The adoption by publishers of the ISBN as an identification number for books has helped here. This number is also used as the record number allocated to MARC records by the British National Bibliography, though, where an ISBN is not available or a publisher has used it wrongly, it is still necessary to use the BNB number. Records can be searched online, usually by any major access point, but more efficiently by standard numbers such as ISBN or BNB number. They can then be added to a file for inclusion in the library's catalogue. Alternatively, instead of an online search, forms can be filled in with record identifiers and local data such as branch location symbols or non-standard classification numbers. These records are then retrieved by staff at the cooperative rather than online from the library and the local data are keyed in at the cooperative.

The British Library established in 1974 the MARC Selective Record Service (SRS) for libraries that wanted to take records to add to their own system. Though the records were acquired in MARC, they could be converted into any format, most usually a simpler one, that the system required. Systems began to be described as MARC-compatible when all they could do was take in records in the MARC format and strip off the appropriate fields for adding to the database. This was ideal for large public library systems which took mainly new books that were catalogued by BNB and had little out-of-the-way material. Their only problem was that BNB often took so long to include the records they needed in the files from which the Selective Record Service drew that they had to catalogue a certain proportion themselves. In a system where cataloguing is not required to the MARC standard, these records are only of use internally and such an organization cannot reduce its costs by contributing records to a cooperative. This problem of lack of records when books were accessioned was vastly reduced when the Cataloguing-in-Publication (CIP) programmes were established both in the UK and North America. Since then, simple records, prepared before publication by cataloguers in national agencies, have been added to national MARC databases in the US and the UK and, latterly, elsewhere. These records contain enough data to satisfy local uses and, being created before the book is published, they are available as soon as libraries begin to acquire the book and demand the record for inclusion in their own catalogues. However, CIP is confined to books and does not cover non-book materials, so is of no assistance in the currency of those records.

Extra local fields in MARC systems

At this point, it is worth mentioning that since MARC and ISO 2709 formats in general are concerned with the exchange of data between institutions, local data fields have seldom been included; they have never been included as part of the UKMARC standard. Users of a MARC format are at liberty to add fields for their own purposes, but, if they are not to be exchanged, they do not need to conform to MARC; for instance, they do not need to have indicators or subfields. Nevertheless, it may be easier to write software that receives these extra-MARC fields in the same pattern as the MARC fields. Certainly, if the internal system format has a directory or tags, these additional fields will have to be treated in the same way. When a program is devised to convert data from the internal format to an exchange format, some of these fields may be disregarded, for example those fields that would be of interest to no one other than the original processing organization. Examples of the kind of field that systems need for internal purposes are name of cataloguer, date of cataloguing, number of copies, holding branch libraries. If a system is used for acquisition as well as cataloguing, then additional fields required would include date and name of vendor. A database used for loans would require borrower identifier and date.

So far, the only data in MARC which relate to an item in a particular library are for holdings and location. Obviously, a national library shelfmark is of use to people who intend to come from elsewhere to consult an item. Holdings information may be exchanged in the development and maintenance of union catalogues. Although there has never been very much pressure for MARC formats to include other kinds of fields for data which are primarily for internal use, there would be benefits if these data were included. It would assist in the transfer of data between systems, for example when an organization changes its software or if libraries are merged as may happen when institutions or local authorities are reorganized. Moreover, it might be of interest for one library to know which bookseller had supplied a particular book to another library if that kind of data were exchanged.

MARC in online systems

In the mid-1970s, online systems began to be developed in the world at large. Banks and airlines sent messages around the world and it seemed feasible and desirable to allow online access to bibliographic databases stored on computers at cooperatives. The British Library planned a large database system, to be known as MERLIN,[1] which was to be mounted on one of the most advanced British-made computers of the time, the ICL 2970. The idea behind this was that it would be open to any library to enter its records on the database. Records were to be stored on a database following the relational model and a format christened MERMARC was developed which could act as a bridge between MARC and the relational database. Records would have been contributed to the system in either the UKMARC or MERMARC formats. The system was never completed. The development of EURONET meant that the UK government had to hasten to get an online database host.[2] The British Library became the European host for MEDLINE, the database of the US National Library of Medicine (NLM). They purchased the NLM software, the Elhill software package, and ran it on an IBM, the computer for which the software was written. They then added other databases which were derived from the MARC databases that hitherto had been stored only on tape and named the system BLAISE. The Elhill software was not written for MARC processing, and it was a year before the MARC editor was designed. This enabled an external user of the database to view records in MARC format and copy them to files on the BLAISE computer in which it was possible to make alterations to the records which were subsequently used in the production of the catalogue for that user.

More recently, with the advent of readily available micro-computers, downloading has become a possibility. It became feasible to interrogate databases and copy records retrieved from them into intelligent terminals or microcomputers. Using an intelligent terminal or a microcomputer with a modem attach-ment or a direct line to a computer, a searcher can save all the data appearing on the screen into a file. This may be edited later to provide printouts for users. Alternatively, these records can form small databases stored on the microcomputers or can be uploaded to mainframe or minicomputer systems. Software has been developed for the purpose, but usually the records are copied in a format which does not have the ISO 2709 directory common to all MARC records on tape. The formats used for this type of interchange may be purely the formats used for display. In those instances, it may be difficult to analyse the data and transfer them into the appropriate fields in a database. Alternatively, data may be downloaded in formats that resemble those used in cataloguers' diagnostic (Figure 7.1), the output from the computer, on printout, being arranged in a way that is convenient for checking by the cataloguer. This kind of output avoids any arrangement which is not helpful for the cataloguer, such as that of the ISO 2709 format. But each field is delineated in such a way that a program can be written that can analyse the data and channel them into the appropriate fields in the receiving database.

The British Library developed a system for taking records from BLAISE and manipulating them in a microcomputer. This way, there was no need to have files on the BLAISE main-frame computer and thereby incur storage charges. This was marketed as CORTEX and ran firstly on a Zentec and later on a Sirius microcomputer.[3] Having taken data from BLAISE and manipulated them to suit their needs, users could send the data back via the telephone line or on a diskette to the British Library for incorporation in their catalogues. Data were not downloaded implementation codes: nam0

001	11699
100	$a19891104d1988 ¦¦¦y 0ENGy0103
101 0	$aENG
200 1	$aNormal professionalism and the early project process
	$eproblems and solutions
	$fRobert Chambers
210	$aBrighton
	$cInstitute of Development Studies
	$d1988
215	$ai, 19 p.
225 0	$aDiscussion paper
	$fInstitute of Development Studies
	$x0308-5864
	$v247
410 0	$12001 $aIDS discussion paper$v247
	171002aInstitute of Development Studies
	$cBrighton, England
700 1	$aChambers
	$bRobert
712 02	$aInstitute of Development Studies
	$cBrighton, England

Fig. 7.1   Example of diagnostic-type display format

in ISO 2709 format but in a diagnostic-type display format. There is now a system which can be used on IBM-compatible personal computers called BLAISE recorder.[4]

Unfortunately, there has never evolved a standard format for records which can serve as a suitable arrangement for presentation to the user (so that the appropriate records can be verified as being of interest), and can also facilitate the adding of those records to databases.

If it is necessary to obtain records in the ISO 2709 format to add to a database, the records are usually obtained on tape in ISO 2709 format by means of an extra request, rather than by being downloaded. This request may be made by creating a file of record identifiers of the records retrieved which can then be sent online to the database host.

In the 1970s, MARC systems were mounted on mini-computers and, from the early 1980s onwards, library automation packages were developed for microcomputers. Few of these were designed round ISO 2709, but requests from users have ensured that ISO 2709 interfaces were built into some of them. In many cases, these, like systems running on larger computers, could take in MARC records but could not provide them.

Retrospective conversion

Retrospective conversion means adding to automated catalogues records of items that were originally catalogued manually. The ideal way of converting existing card or other printed catalogues would be to put them through a machine that could read them and convert them into the MARC format. As yet no such machine has been built. The main problem is that the old cards or printed catalogues were never intended to be converted in this way but were designed for human use, and, in many cases, expert human use. With many catalogues, only an expert librarian could analyse what the particular codes and typefaces meant. In the early 1980s, an attempt was made to convert the British Library Department of Printed Books printed catalogue to machine-readable form using a machine known as the Kurzweil Data Entry machine which was a very sophisticated CIM (Computer Input Microfilm) machine. This had been used by the UK Department of Health and Social Security in Newcastle for reading handwritten forms where boxes had been filled in. However, in the British Library project, the resulting machine-readable records were not supplied in any format approaching MARC because it was felt at the time that it would be too difficult to add tags, indicators and subfield identifiers automatically. The project was eventually discontinued because, even without MARC, the amount of editing work required indicated that it would be more efficient to keyboard the data from scratch and eventually that course of action was, in fact, taken. Data were then produced in the MARC format, though it appeared as a very rudimentary MARC format when viewed on BLAISE in the British Library Catalogue Preview file, without indicators, and with only elementary subfielding.

Most retrospective conversion activities that have resulted in the production of new MARC records have involved the upgrading of records by cataloguers who may have seen only a catalogue record and not the original document. This is happening with the British Library project mentioned above, though access to the original document is available if absolutely necessary. The earliest documented example of retrospective conversion in the UK leading to MARC records was the EMMA project run by LASER (London and South East Regional Library Cooperative).[5] EMMA stood for Extra-MARC material, a use of MARC in the sense of the set of records available in the MARC format. The British Library also created in the early 1970s a file of records taken from BNB from its inception in 1950 until 1968 when MARC production began. These had been produced prior to the adoption of the first edition of *AACR* and so conformed to a different cataloguing standard.

The way that retrospective conversion is usually undertaken now is to approach a cooperative to see what proportion of the records that need converting is available in their database and then, if necessary, convert the rest oneself or have them converted by the agency. This is possible because a large core of records has been produced over the years by other organizations in their retrospective conversion activities and these can be made available more widely. These records can usually be supplied in any required format including different ISO 2709-based formats. The use of records from American-based cooperatives such as OCLC has made the use of USMARC in local systems in the UK widespread.

Walt Crawford's book *MARC for library use*[6] has a very useful chapter entitled 'Using MARC in the library' where he discusses retrospective conversion and its problems from a very practical viewpoint. Though aimed at the North American audience, the lessons to be learned apply equally to the UK. Indeed, as time goes on, UK libraries are turning more and more to transatlantic cooperatives such as OCLC, so UK experience becomes more and more like that of the US.

Stand-alone ISO 2709-based systems on large computers
Every national library that developed a MARC format needed computer software to process the data. Before the 1980s, they invariably developed their own software until commercial software became available. However, already by 1967, about the same time as the development of MARC, the International Labour Office in Geneva had developed a software package for an IBM mainframe for information retrieval known as ISIS. This was in turn given to other members of the UN family and to organizations in developing countries. The software was eventually provided with a module which converted data to the ISO 2709 format. It was in use in national institutions in certain developing countries, but it does not appear to have been used by any national libraries, probably because it would have needed substantial adaptation to implement MARC, such as the possibility of using three-digit tags; only two-digit tags were permitted.

The International Development Research Centre (IDRC) in Ottawa developed a system based on the concept of ISIS (but running on the Hewlett Packard 3000 series of minicomputers) which they completed in 1977 and named MINISIS. ILO Library quickly decided to replace their ISIS package by MINISIS as it was advantageous for them to have their own minicomputer rather than share the resources of the organization's mainframe with other users. As a result, ILO no longer needed the ISIS system and maintenance of it passed to Unesco which had one of the larger ISIS installations.

John Woolston, Director of Information Systems at IDRC, was very keen to see MINISIS proving as valuable a tool to secondary services as MARC systems had been and were proving to the national-library networks. He therefore modelled the system on the format that had been developed by and for them, the UNISIST Reference manual format. The package was designed to use mixed alphabetic and numeric tags (A01 to Z99). Interfaces were developed to systems that exchanged data via the ISO 2709 format including AGRIS and the Commonwealth Agricultural Bureau system. Data could be exported from MINISIS into ISO 2709 three-digit tags. Having been based on the *Reference manual*, it had up to nine subfields (numbered 1 to 9; 0 was used for fields with only one subfield).

However, none of these could be repeated in a field and they had to appear in numerical order.

In 1983, the IFLA General Conference met in Singapore. MINISIS was being planned for a number of libraries in the region including the library of the Universiti of Sains in Malaysia. It was spreading quickly because of the policy of IDRC to distribute it free-of-charge to organizations in developing countries. A number of influential delegates were concerned that MINISIS did not appear to support MARC to the same extent as tailor-made MARC-compatible systems. The outcome of this concern was that a study was made on behalf of IFLA and funded jointly by the British Library, Library of Congress and the National Library of Canada. The aim of the project was to see what was required to make the package MARC-compatible to the extent that it would enable data entry and output to conform to what were the usual practices in organizations that used MARC. The enhancements required are outlined in a report.[7]

The result of the study was that IDRC extended the package to enable data to be entered using MARC subfield identifiers which could be repeated if required. Additions were made to enable these identifiers to be converted to the punctuation required by ISBD. The package was tested on UKMARC at the Universiti Sains in Malaysia, on a format based on USMARC at the National Library of Mexico and on UNIMARC at the library of the Institute of Development Studies at the University of Sussex in the UK. It was finally released in the basic MINISIS package (though still available as an add-on rather than as an integral part of the package) in version G of the software distributed towards the end of 1988.

Over the last few years, systems like GEAC and LIBERTAS have been provided with integral MARC interfaces. LIBERTAS, developed by the SWALCAP cooperative used MARC from the outset. GEAC, on the other hand, went in that direction because users wanted it. The National Libraries of France and Portugal both have GEAC systems which use formats based very closely on UNIMARC.

Microcomputer systems
With the advent in the mid-1980s of microcomputers large

275

enough to host library databases, many packages came onto the market for information retrieval. These were mostly intended as stand-alone packages and rarely incorporated an ISO 2709 interface.

One exception to this was the CDS/ISIS software package for microcomputers and certain minicomputers. This is a package that has been developed for MS/DOS machines (IBM compatibles). The development of the first version was completed by Unesco in 1985.

As long ago as 1980, Unesco had been advised by the UNISIST International Centre for Bibliographic Descriptions (UNIBID) that it was becoming feasible to develop an automated library system on a microcomputer. At first, the idea was to develop a data-entry system which would promote the use of the UNISIST Reference manual format, but as time went on it appeared that a full bibliographic information system could be mounted. Unesco negotiated with the Institut für Maschinelle Dokumentation in Graz, Austria, to install a software system they had developed in a number of sites in developing countries. Unfortunately, work on the software package floundered and the package was rather difficult to use, especially in organizations in developing countries remote from technical help.

Unesco then decided to develop its own microcomputer system and based it on the mainframe ISIS which it was well able to do as it was then, as mentioned above, maintaining that package. Because Unesco was then – and still is – a promoter of standards, it was necessary to bring the CDS/ISIS package in line with standards. Its records are stored with directories analogous to those of ISO 2709. It also accepts data in ISO 2709; indeed that is the only way the package permits the entry of records in batch. Otherwise, online data entry is the norm. Since it has a very sophisticated print formatter, it is much more flexible in its forms of output than in the formats it accepts for data entry. Consequently, data can be output for transfer into many different systems as well as ISO 2709-based systems.

The mainframe version originally supported only two-digit tags and the microcomputer version, being modelled on it, was intended to be the same. Again, pressure from the people involved in standards promotion in Unesco prevailed and tags were expanded to three digits. The history of this is encap-

276

sulated in version 1 of the software which has an automatically generated default print format which has only two digits and does not display the hundreds digit. This feature was clearly not upgraded at the same time as the possible tag-length was extended. CDS/ISIS is an ideal tool for organizations that need to contribute records to a database via ISO 2709. The National Library of Portugal has circulated the software to libraries in a network it is building up, using as an exchange format the national MARC format which is based very closely on UNI-MARC. Records can be entered into the CDS/ISIS database and then exported on diskettes to the National Library's GEAC system.

Very few other microcomputer systems support MARC to the full, although some have interfaces to enable them to take in MARC records. Many of the suppliers of software packages, when asked at exhibitions, claim unfamiliarity with MARC or play down its value. They all say that they could include conversion modules if required and there is no reason to doubt this; but as the cost of writing an interface would probably fall heavily on the requester, it is in many instances not likely to be realized.

Most commercially-produced systems that support MARC have been developed in the United States. Colglazier describes how a book catalogue was produced from USMARC records obtained from MARCIVE, one of the many US distributors of MARC records.[8] These were input into Bibliofile for the production of cards and labels and Per-Cite for the production of a catalogue. This was a catalogue of about 500 records which listed the holdings of a number of church libraries. It was all accomplished on a microcomputer.

The MITINET/MARC package which runs on MS/DOS was developed in the United States. It has been reviewed in *Information technology and libraries* by David Badertscher.[9] The system is geared to USMARC and prompts for the entry of the main heading and the different ISBD areas and includes fields for subject headings and classification and other local data. In the title area, title, other title information and statement of responsibility (subfields a, b, and c of field 245) are prompted. The system provides the correct ISBD punctuation. As the system is specific to one format, USMARC, it has built into it

277

defaults for the indicators in each field which have to be changed if different values are required. According to information accompanying the package, each record created by the system is saved in the MARC format, including label and directory. As this is a microcomputer-based package, these records are created on hard or floppy disk.

This is clearly a package that has set out to keep as close to the MARC standard as possible. There is nothing similar produced in the UK.

ISO 2709 in CD-ROM

ISO 2709 is essentially a tape standard though it can be used for other transfer media. CD-ROM disks are not transfer media as such since they are an integral part of the system on which they are run and so the format on the disks amounts to an internal system format. A CD-ROM system supplier who provided an ISO 2709 interface for exchange would be promoting the downloading of data from the CD-ROM; indeed, there would be no other reason for providing data in that format, and, for commercial reasons, many CD-ROM suppliers would not want their data to be incorporated in other information-retrieval systems. There are exceptions to this. A project has been set up to provide articles on medicine on CD-ROM for the Pan-American Health Organization. The project has been conducted at BIREME in São Paulo, Brazil, and uses the CDS/ISIS software package. Various modules of the CDS/ISIS package including ISO 2709 conversion are located on the CD-ROM disk along with the bibliographic records and are loaded into the microcomputer to be used in searching the data on the CD-ROM. Since records on CDS/ISIS have a directory like ISO 2709 there is no reason to suppose that ISO 2709 could not be used as a CD-ROM format.

CD-ROM databases usually exist in another medium before being converted to CD-ROM. Many CD-ROM producers can receive data in a variety of formats, only one of which is ISO 2709. Indeed, MITINET/MARC advertizing literature states that records in ISO 2709 format can be loaded from the system into CD-ROM catalogues. So, ISO 2709 can be used in the generation of CD-ROM, though CD-ROM packages do not themselves usually output ISO 2709 data.

278

Conversion between formats

The reader who has reached thus far will have learned that there is a large number of formats which can be classified under the MARC umbrella and a few that are on the periphery of the family. When there is a need for systems to interact with each other, conversions are obviously going to be required. Some formats have been designed as bridging formats and are intended for conversion of data between different formats. The two most outstanding examples are UNIMARC and the Unesco Common Communication Format. UNIMARC was intended to be a format for the receipt of data from a multiplicity of national formats. The CCF was intended to take data from UNIMARC and the UNISIST *Reference manual*. How much conversion is done between formats? It is difficult to say. The earliest conversions were from LC MARC to UKMARC. The British Library took Library of Congress tapes and converted them from LC MARC to UKMARC. The Library of Congress never wrote conversion programs to reciprocate this until 1985; the only data imported into their system were from the National Library of Canada which used a closer variant of the LC format.

OCLC, the cooperative operating internationally based at Columbus, Ohio, offers data conversion as part of its service. It started out using LC MARC but having expanded into other countries recognized the need to convert data for its customers into other national formats.

Developers of exchange formats feel the necessity to demonstrate that they can act as such. The UNIMARC Test (see Chapter 4) was designed to show how data could be converted into UNIMARC from national formats. The *Reference manual* was not published before a test had taken place at the University of Sheffield in 1974. Both these tests were undertaken using manual data entry on to worksheets. Unfortunately, this kind of activity is of limited value. It gives very little indication of how easy or difficult it would be to write conversion programs between formats. The use of this method was justified probably because, in those days, data processing was an expensive or difficult business to undertake for experimental purposes as it would have needed a full-blown conversion program to be developed on a mainframe computer.

Conversions cannot usually be made sufficiently generalized

to work on all possible occasions. Because exchange formats depend on underlying cataloguing rules, conversions between formats entail conversions between cataloguing rules. Conversion programs have been written to enable the transfer of data between the Library of Congress and the British Library. However, minor changes of practice by those entering data in Washington can cause conversion programs to be thrown awry in London. This is especially true of fields that have no exact equivalent in each database.

When an exchange format such as the CCF is developed and divorces itself completely from cataloguing rules, data converted into it will be easily distinguishable from data that have originated from a different format. Whether this matters depends on the use that is to be made of it. Records formulated according to different cataloguing codes will not sit happily side-by-side in a printed bibliography of national bibliography quality. On the other hand, they will be useful as finding lists or even as loan records in union catalogues, the chief problem being detection of duplicates.

The CCF has sparked off a number of activities in data conversion. At the IBICT in Brazil, Unesco supported a project to develop a conversion language, a notation to enable the easy specification of data conversion required between formats. In Yugoslavia, exercises are under way to test the feasibility of conversion between the UNIMARC format which is used by most of the state libraries and the CCF which is being developed as a bridging format.[10] In Colombia, the CCF has been the model for the national switching format (FCCC) and conversions have been made between each local format and the FCCC and between the FCCC and the CCF.[11] In 1988, UTLAS, a Canadian cooperative, developed a conversion program for converting data from one of their internal formats into the CCF. The conversion parameters were developed from tables prepared by Peter Simmons, one of the editors of the CCF, and a database was prepared consisting of bibliographic records relating to francophone developing countries. This was done on behalf of the Banque Internationale d'Information sur les Etats Francophones (BIEF).[12] Simmons also prepared a similar set of tables for conversion between UNIMARC and the CCF and with the help of a programmer at the University of

British Columbia developed a program for microcomputers which would enable a file of ISO 2709 records in one format to be converted to another by means of a table which could be prepared in a user-friendly controlled language.[13] This program, though capable of being generalized, is so far being tested only on the UNIMARC to CCF conversion.

Software facilitating conversion

Certain software systems facilitate conversion. As mentioned above, ISIS and MINISIS support ISO 2709 conversion. Both software systems include a program that converts the data structure of a record into that of ISO 2709 and can take an ISO 2709 record and add it to a database. Extra facilities to convert data structure, useful if converting from one format to another, are dealt with differently between the packages.

a) *CDS/ISIS*

CDS/ISIS requires a parameter table to be drawn up for each conversion. This is called in to operate each individual conversion, as required. A table has to be written for each direction. If one's system has data elements defined according to UKMARC and one wishes to produce a file of UNIMARC records structured according to ISO 2709, a table must be prepared (called an FST or Field Select Table). This table will have each UNIMARC tag in the left-hand column and the corresponding UKMARC subfields that are to be converted to it on the right, with the new subfield identifiers that UNIMARC requires stored as literals. In effect, the conversion table is set up like a print format, converting codes into printed characters. Here is an example.

A personal author with primary intellectual responsibility entered under surname is represented in UKMARC as 10$aSmith$hJohn in field 100. The same in UNIMARC is stored in field 700 as __1$aSmith$bJohn. To convert from UKMARC to UNIMARC, the conversion table would have the following entry (note that the subfield identifier in CDS/ISIS has to be represented by ^).

700 0 '__1'(|^a|v100^a,|^b|v100^h + | % |)

This means that a field 700 is to be generated. There is no way of generating the indicators, if variable. Indicators represented by a space followed by '1' mean in UNIMARC that the personal name is one that is entered under surname, and in this conversion table it is assumed that all personal names would be formulated in this way. '__1' in the conversion table indicates that the field must start with __1 (__ here indicates space.). The parentheses () indicate that a potentially repeating field should be transferred as a repeating field: the subfields should be kept together within fields. Otherwise the system would take each subfield a and place them all next to each other, then each subfield h, with the result that joint authors $aBrown$hJohn and $aSmith$hMary would be converted as ^aBrownSmith^b JohnMary. The 'logical not' symbols '¦' are used as parentheses to indicate that the data within them are literals (data produced by the computer under certain conditions and not entered as data) and should occur repeating before each occurrence of the data in the following subfield. Each time subfield a of field 100 occurs, the data will be placed next preceded by ^a. Each time subfield h occurs in UKMARC, it will be preceded by ^b. Each repeat, other than the last will be followed by % which indicates a repeat of the field.

b) *MINISIS*

MINISIS works in a different way. Conversion between formats has to go via a MINISIS database with its distinctive MINISIS tags (A01 to Z99). Special programs can be written to process any individual field. Within the general framework of the package, data from fields in the source format can be broken at distinctive characters such as $a or at the first instance of a particular punctuation mark such as a comma and sent to different destination fields. Prefixes and suffixes up to four characters long can be added to data. If necessary, data could be put through the MINISIS conversion program more than once with different conversion parameters.

c) *TINMAN*

TINMAN was developed by IME (Information Made Easy), principally by Peter Noerr, who had worked on the development and maintenance of MARC-based systems, including MERLIN, in the British Library. The software is a relational information-retrieval system and has been adapted for libraries as the TINLIB package. The package includes a module called the Converter which includes an interface for ISO 2709 which was developed for a client who wanted to process records from a scientific information service. Again by customer demand, it has incorporated tools to facilitate format conversion. These are basically database import and export tools: anyone who uses the package for conversion from one format to another specifies a database and then develops import and export functions to accomplish the format conversion. The conversion facilities of many systems allow for little more than the conversion of field tags and possibly subfield identifiers. TINMAN is much more sophisticated and allows conversion of text within a field to different text within another; subfields may be converted to fields and vice versa. A profile language is used in making the conversion specification. This is so powerful that all foreseeable requirements in conversion can be handled by the language.

Conversion and compatibility

The mechanical aspects of conversion may or may not be easy. The difficulty is always going to lie mainly in the logical compatibility between fields in the different formats which are subject to conversion. If one format, such as UNIMARC, has a large variety of notes fields categorizing its notes and another has only a general notes field, it will be possible to convert from the format with the more specific fields to the one with the less specific fields, but not in the other direction. Conversion in one direction may be possible but conversion back to the original will never be possible. In many cases, discussions in this area have been clouded by the terminology used. Claims made by systems designers that their systems are compatible with accepted standards are all too frequently based on an ill-conceived and imprecise conception of compatibility.

Lancaster made for Unesco a study entitled *Compatibility issues affecting information systems and services.*[14] This was commissioned by those responsible for Unesco's General Information Programme because they had put and were continuing to put a great deal of effort into promoting compatibility (for example the development of the CCF) and wanted an opinion on whether this was the right way to go.

Lancaster cites a number of different explanations and definitions of compatibility. He quotes from Henderson: 'Systems are considered to be compatible when the results of processing in one system are directly usable by other organizations having similar but not necessarily identical systems.'[15] Lancaster himself states that compatibility can be achieved without standardization;[16] some procedure or device can be used to reconcile different practices as when one record format can be transformed, by computer program, into another. Standardization, though, does help. Even if everyone does not adopt the same standard format, it will help if only a few are adopted rather than everyone developing their own format.

Preferable to compatibility is convertibility used both in Henderson and in the UNISIST feasibility study where convertibility is defined as 'a quality of systems whose products can be made interchangeable through conversion programmes'.[17]

What would a test of convertibility between formats consist of? If any data from format A could be converted into format B and those data taken and converted back to A and the result were identical to the original data, then the formats could be said to be convertible.

It is very likely that such convertibility between formats could exist only when both formats had been devised to hold data formulated according to the same cataloguing code and, indeed, when use of the code was a mandatory feature of that format.

Is format conversion which cannot pass this test of convertibility in any way invalidated? Is it all a waste of time and effort? The answer must be in the negative. Many organizations taking data created elsewhere are not as stringent in their requirements as are the producers of the source data. National bibliography records in UNIMARC could be of use to a secondary service using the CCF to merge files of records from different sources. At the other extreme, a national bibliography may never be able to use any records produced externally even by another national agency without manual inspection and editing.

Since there is a need to merge data from different sources formulated according to different codes, exchange formats have attempted to assist in the transfer of data between systems. However, exchange formats are only as good as the data which are being converted. If an exchange format can accommodate many other formats, it usually means that the exchange format has been devised to have a place easily identifiable for data from the source formats. This would also suggest that it would not be easy to export data from the exchange format into any of the source formats.

A frequently expressed view about any particular format is that one day there will come a time when it will be used in a consistent way by all users. Unfortunately, the reverse is probably more likely to be true; formats will be more likely to diverge with time though this may be counteracted by publications such as the *UNIMARC handbook* which aimed to standardize the use of a format. Formats are seldom if ever used in a completely consistent way except within one system, be it a cooperative or a single database. As soon as different systems begin to use one format, practices are likely to diverge. Since the early days of MARC in the UK, BLCMP practice has differed from that of the British National Bibliography, later the British Library Bibliographic Services. Even within the British Library itself, there have been some differences in practice between the Department of Printed Books and Bibliographic Services which both parties have learned to live with.

The content of the records may differ even more than the formats, for individual data elements often require different treatment in different contexts. Many of the actual and potential conflicts in application of formats were mentioned in Chapter 1, where the diverse nature and purpose of bibliographic records was illustrated. There are differences not only between various sectors of the information community but even among libraries whose needs on the surface appear similar. Corporate body headings, for example, are often preferred for local use in a form differing from that adopted by a national library for national exchange records or the national bibliography; names of government bodies in catalogues in government libraries may be formulated in a different way from that offered in public-library catalogues. Subject headings are a prime example of data elements where responsiveness to local need is a priority.

Organizations also change their use of a format over a period of time. The changes made in the USMARC format during the 1980s caused problems in processing for recipient agencies such as the British Library.

Using other people's records is always a compromise. The exchange format is part of the compromise. The ideal exchange format is just as elusive as the ideal classification scheme.

Notes and references

1 Hopkinson, A., 'MERLIN for the cataloguer', *Aslib proceedings*, **29**, 1977, 284–94.
2 Robinson, S., 'Sleeping Beauty: MERLIN, a state-of-the-art report', *Program*, **14**, 1980, 1–13.
3 Chapman, P. and Noerr, P., 'BLAISE CORTEX: a microprocessor system for libraries', *Information processing and management*, **19**, 1983, 77–81.
4 Moore, C., 'BLAISE recorder: communication software for information retrieval and record supply', *Vine*, **71**, 1988, 25–30.
5 Yeates, A. R., 'EMMA project progress report', *Vine*, **25**, October 1978, 10.
6 Crawford, W., *MARC for library use: understanding the USMARC formats*, White Plains, NY, Knowledge Industry, 1984, Chapter 12.
7 Woods, E., *The MINISIS/UNIMARC Project: final report*, London, IFLA UBCIM Programme, 1988 (UBCIM occasional paper 12).
8 Colglazier, M. L., 'A book catalog produced from USMARC records using Bibliofile, Per-Cite, Biblio-link and Word Perfect', *Information technology and libraries*, **7**, 1988, 417–29.
9 Badertscher, D. A., '[Review of] MITINET/MARC', *Information technology and libraries*, **7**, 1988, 326–30.
10 Willer, M. and Pantelic, S., 'The use of the Common Communication Format in Yugoslavia', *Program*, **23**, April 1989, 163–73.
11 Simmons, P., 'Using CCF: the Common Communication Format', *Information technology and libraries*, **5**, 1986, 285–94.
12 Newman, R. W., *The Unesco/UTLAS Common Communication Format conversion project*, Toronto, Utlas, 1988 (to be published in *Proceedings of CCF Users' Meeting*).
13 Simmons, P., *A computer program for bibliographic record conversion* (to be published in *Proceedings of CCF Users' Meeting*).
14 Lancaster, F. W. and Smith, L. C., *Compatibility issues affecting information systems and services*, Paris, Unesco, 1983.
15 Henderson, M. M. and others, *Cooperation, convertibility and compatibility among information systems: a literature review*, Washington, DC, National Bureau of Standards, 1966.

16 Lancaster, F. W., *op. cit.*, 3.
17 UNISIST, *Study report on the feasibility of a world science information system*, Paris, Unesco, 1971, 147.

General note: information on computer software packages, where no citation is given, was taken from suppliers' publicity literature or system manuals.

Conclusion: Exchange formats: the future

During the last 25 years, a radical change has occurred in the mechanisms for the transfer of bibliographic data. Paradoxically, the current situation can be judged both success and failure; success in that millions of records structured according to ISO 2709 are now available for exchange; failure in that there is a multiplicity of implementations of ISO 2709 and that the full potential of computing has not been harnessed to make the necessary conversions between each.

Amid a proliferation of national formats is UNIMARC, a serious contender for the role of international format, but accepted only by the library community. National MARC formats act also as intranational exchange vehicles, and some national formats, for example USMARC, have become virtually international. The question must be asked whether the simplest solution is for everyone to adopt USMARC, undoubtedly the most widely used format, or family of formats, as holdings and authorities formats may be included here. Hospitality to a wide range of bibliographic data within a single communication format was, after all, the philosophy underlying the original LC MARC II format. National pride and political considerations would undoubtedly prevent this, although the influence of USMARC is pervasive. Nor would acceptance of the USMARC format for bibliographic data in its present form meet the needs of sectors of the information community outside the libraries, for example the abstracting and indexing services and the book trade. The CCF has been heralded as a suitable bridging format between the libraries and the secondary services, but is insufficiently detailed to provide all the requirements of national bibliographies, and, except in its

288

extension in FORMEX, has never had any consideration by the book trade.

Gatenby, arguing for the retention of AUSMARC in the face of competition from UK and USMARC, offers theoretical and pragmatic reasons in favour of the national format.[1] The theoretical issues, concerning the essential qualities of the format, are perhaps less cogent than the pragmatic: the fact that most systems in the country have developed around the national format and that change would present serious problems. Were the cost and effort of maintaining national formats to become prohibitive, there might be a move towards more established formats such as US or UKMARC, or to UNIMARC or even CCF. Indeed, this is happening as new national formats are developed which are based very closely on the international and early national formats. Adapting an international format, especially one such as CCF, may involve some compromise and abandonment of tradition. The history of bibliography and cataloguing has shown that public expressions of readiness to cooperate in standardization of bibliographic data are often tempered by an unexpressed desire to cling to practices believed to be essential for the fulfilment of national and local needs.

ISO 2709 owes its position as a universally recognized standard to the success of MARC. It is, however, a tape standard and the use of tape for bibliographic data exchange will no doubt decrease as time goes by. Although the conversion of data to another standard (should one be accepted) would not be too difficult, corporate inertia, coupled with economic restraints, may tie many organizations to ISO 2709. Acceptance of an exchange format involves the receiving agencies in the production of conversion software. Although the cost of this may be low in comparison with the benefits gained, it is by no means negligible. Moreover, many bibliographic agencies face severe organizational problems in having programs written or changed. Substantial investment, both in finance and computing expertise, has been made in programs geared to ISO 2709, and it seems doubtful that this commitment would be lightly abandoned. Possible incentives for a departure from the standard are a switch from one medium to another and obsolescence of the computer systems which drive existing conversion programs. If new technology forces a change in record structures, ISO 2709–1973 may be inadequate; yet a mark of the inertia may be seen in the fact that though ISO 2709 was revised in 1981, very few implementations of it have made use of the extended directory or other features within the revision.

Confidence in the longevity of MARC is shared by Derek Law who, in a paper summing up the 13th Annual Seminar of the MARC Users' Group, remarked that libraries had tens of millions of pounds invested in MARC. He felt that cooperation was likely to grow rather than decline and it would be 'fundamentally underpinned by the MARC record structure'.[2]

Stephen Massil in a study on data formats for machine-readable media for the British Library Research and Development Department states, in his conclusion, that the role of ISO 2709 is circumscribed, perhaps on the verge of elimination, by CD-ROM.[3] He is not, however, forecasting the demise of MARC in all its aspects, only the ISO 2709 record structure.

Even if the record structures change, it seems unlikely that the ISO-style tags and identifiers will disappear, especially as their precise specification is seen as a function of implementation formats. They will be seen more often, perhaps, in a diagnostic-type format. The experimental CD-ROM produced jointly by Bibliothèque Nationale and the British Library can display records of French origin in UNIMARC and those of British origin in UKMARC. The displays are formatted so that data are shown alongside appropriate tags and not structured according to ISO 2709, though a separate ISO 2709 interface is provided. The ease with which online systems can import or export complete MARC records, while restructuring them for display to the user in a variety of other formats, has removed many of the arguments against the suitability of MARC structure and content designation in online catalogues and databases. Thus, the role of ISO 2709, but not that of the tags and identifiers, becomes much more limited.

In the final analysis, end-users need bibliographic items, not bibliographic records. Exchange formats are only one of many bibliographic tools. UBC – Universal Bibliographic Control – is not an end in itself but a tool for achieving UAP – Universal Availability of Publications. Hope Clement looks to the future in concluding her paper on the International MARC Network and national libraries.[4] Audiovisual and new electronic materials are costly and difficult to catalogue and in many countries this kind of material is not covered in any bibliography. Despite CIP and the use of minimal standards in cataloguing, bibliographic records are too slow in appearing to prevent other agencies, which are the customers of the national agencies, from having to catalogue their own acquisitions. The two cornerstones of UBC, completeness of coverage and speed of record delivery, are goals not always realized. MARC formats were developed in the early days of library automation and before the cheap dissemination of large databases on media like CD-ROM was possible. Yet cataloguing rules and formats have not essentially changed. Cataloguers have in many ways used automation to produce products that resemble those of the pre-automation age. Clement wonders if the solution lies in 'a whole new concept of bibliographic control using technology in a totally different way to take advantage of the power of computers or telecommunications'.[5]

Whatever these solutions might be, the future is likely to see more exchanges, not only of secondary material in the form of bibliographic records, but also of full-text data. The standard formats developed for these may well become the formats of the future with formats for bibliographic citations as a subset. Nevertheless, such formats could still, as is FORMEX, be based on ISO 2709. Bibliographic data elements will always need identifiers and those currently used in MARC formats are probably as good as any other. The only reason for them to change would be if technology required changes in the record structure; for example, the influence of the CCF could lead to the use of tags extended to, say, five digits.

Finally, there is the record content, determined by standards external to the formats. Despite the impressive achievements in standardizing bibliographic records inspired by IFLA and implemented by national libraries and bibliographic agencies, uniformity in cataloguing practice is far from being realized. Radical changes would be required to effect complete harmony within the library community, let alone between that community and the secondary services. Fundamental changes in cataloguing rules would of course have an impact on exchange formats. UNIMARC and CCF are themselves a recognition and reminder of the persistence of national and local cataloguing rules.

Any changes which may come about in the record structure will undoubtedly be felt by systems analysts who write programs to convert records from an exchange format into a system's internal format, but will be of little concern to the average MARC user who thinks of MARC as a set of codes defining the data elements of a record in automated systems or on worksheets and diagnostic printout.

Our estimate, then, is that MARC and other exchange formats will continue for some time. As long as organizations wish to exchange records or derive bibliographic data from central agencies, and until computer technologists devise cost-effective and relatively simple ways of transferring between systems bibliographic data in different formats, exchange formats remain necessary. Of their character and orientation, it seems fitting to echo the sentiments of Henriette Avram in stressing the need to 'promote efficient interchange while learning to accommodate those differences that it is not possible to resolve'.[6]

Notes and references

1　Gatenby, J., 'What is the future of AUSMARC?', *LASIE*, **18**, (1), July/August 1987, 4–12.

2　Law, D., 'Cooperation and the future of national networks', in Horsnell, V., ed., *Mechanisms for library cooperation: getting our act together: proceedings of the 13th Annual Seminar of the MARC Users' Group*, Aldershot, Gower, 1988, 133–52.

3　Massil, S. W., *Study on data formats for machine-readable media: 1: report on ISO 2709*, Boston Spa, British Library, 1987 (BLR&D report 5930).

4　Clement, H., 'The International MARC Network and national libraries', *Alexandria*, **1**, (1), 1989, 23–34.

5　*Ibid.*, 33.

6　Avram, H. D., 'International standards for the interchange of bibliographic records in machine-readable form', *Library resources and technical services*, **20**, 1976, 25–35.

Glossary

These definitions reflect the usage of terms in the text. Acronyms and abbreviations are included.

A & I services
    Abstracting and indexing services, also called 'secondary services'.

AACR2
    Anglo-American cataloguing rules, 2nd edition.

ABN
    Australian Bibliographic Network.

Access point
    Any name or term used for searching, retrieval and identification of a bibliographic item.

Added entry
    An entry in a catalogue or bibliography which is additional or secondary to the main entry. Added entries are often presented in brief form, with less descriptive detail than main entries.

AGRIS
    International Information System for the Agricultural Sciences and Technology of the UN Food and Agriculture Organization.

ALA
    American Library Association.

Analytical entry
    An entry in a catalogue or bibliography for part of a larger item, e.g. for a chapter from a book. There is normally also an entry made for the larger (host) item. *See also* Component part, Host item.

ANSI
    American National Standards Institute.

Application layer

In OSI (q.v.) the name of the functional level that enables the programs running on a system to interact with programs and/or data on other systems.

Architecture

The design or internal arrangement of a computer or computerized system.

ASCII

American Standard Code for Information Interchange. The character set adopted by the majority of computer systems and the one on which the international standard reference character set (ISO 646) and corresponding national standards are modelled.

AUSMARC

The Australian national MARC format.

Authority record

Record containing data representing a preferred or established form of heading (author, title or subject). Normally also contains information on variant forms from which references are required. Also, a record of a rejected form of heading, with reference to the preferred term.

Batch processing

Data processing method in which a sequence of computer activities prepared in advance acts on data without human intervention or interaction. Contrasted with Online (q.v.).

BEDIS

Book Trade Electronic Data Interchange Standards Committee.

Bibliographic description

An assemblage of bibliographic details, sufficient to identify and describe an item, normally placed beneath, or following, a heading in a catalogue or bibliography.

Bibliographic hierarchy

Related bibliographic items ranked in an order which indicates the whole/part relationships existing between them.

Bibliographic information interchange format

See Exchange format.

Bibliographic item

Any document, publication or other record of human communication; any group of documents, or part of a

294

document, treated as an entity.

Bibliographic level

The position of an item in a bibliographic hierarchy. Examples of levels commonly recognized include analytical, monographic, series, collection.

Bibliographic record

A collection of data elements, organized in a logical way, which represents a bibliographic item; in machine systems, a collection of fields describing one or more bibliographic units treated as an entity.

Bibliographic utility

See Library cooperative.

Bibliography

A list of books or other items. Refers both to printed and computer-held forms.

BIREME

Biblioteca Regional de Medicina (São Paolo, Brazil).

BISAC

Book Industry Systems Advisory Committee.

BL

British Library.

BLAISE

British Library Automated Information Service. BLAISE-LINE is the BL's own service, offering bibliographic records in MARC format; BLAISE-LINK is operated in collaboration with the US National Library of Medicine and offers access to biomedical and toxological information.

Blank

See Space.

BLBS

British Library Bibliographic Services (now the National Bibliographic Service).

BLCMP

BLCMP Library Services Ltd. Formerly known as Birmingham Libraries Cooperative Mechanization Project.

BLD MARC record

Bibliographic record in UKMARC format produced by or for a department of the British Library.

BL MARC record

Bibliographic record in UKMARC format produced within

the British Library, either a BNB MARC or BLD MARC record.

BNB

British National Bibliography. The name of both the printed bibliography listing UK publications, and the organization set up to produce this in 1950. Absorbed by the British Library as its Bibliographic Services Division in 1973.

BNB MARC record

Bibliographic record in the UKMARC format produced by BL Bibliographic Services for the BNB and related databases and services.

Boolean operators

AND, OR and NOT; used in online information retrieval for combining separate concepts at the search stage.

Bridging format

An exchange format designed to transfer data between exchange formats rather than between internal formats.

CAG

Cooperative Automation Group.

CANMARC

Canadian National MARC format.

Catalogue

A list of items held in one or more collections.

Cataloguing code

A set of rules for preparing bibliographic records for use in catalogues and bibliographies. Normally excludes rules for subject data, concentrating on bibliographic description and choice and form of (author/title) access points.

CCF

Common Communication Format.

CD-ROM

Compact disc – read only memory.

Character

Any symbol representing a letter of the alphabet, a digit or a sign, including punctuation and diacritical marks. In machine systems, each character is represented by a number of bits (binary digits) which are present in the computer, or on magnetic tape, diskette or other storage device, as electrical charges or magnetic blips. A space is also a character.

Character set

A group of machine (binary) equivalents of the total number of characters that can be exactly represented within a given computer system.

CIP

Cataloguing-in-Publication. Normally refers to programmes, coordinated by national bibliographic agencies, whereby cataloguing data are made available in advance of publication in national bibliographies and machine-readable records and printed in books, usually on the verso of the title page.

CLR

Council on Library Resources, Inc.

Coded data

Data elements held in coded form, as opposed to free-text or natural-language form.

CODEN

Six-character alphanumeric code assigned to serials and other publications to provide unambiguous identification of their titles.

COM

Computer Output Microform. May be microfilm or microfiche.

Command language

A set of codes used for interrogating a database or other information-storage and retrieval system. Includes codes for functions such as search, print, finish, and codes for data elements such as author, title, etc.

Communications format

See Exchange format.

Component part

A part of a document or other material, e.g. a chapter in a book, an article in a journal, an individual sound track on a recording. Depends for its bibliographic identity on details of the containing item.

Content designators

The codes and conventions used to identify and distinguish data elements in a machine-readable record, i.e. tags, indicators and subfield identifiers.

Control character

A character code in a character set reserved for systems

purposes and not for a character with a graphic representation, e.g. ASCII character 31, the first character of the subfield identifier.

Control fields
Fields containing data needed for processing the record.

Control number
See Record identifier.

CURL
Consortium of University Research Libraries.

Data element
A defined unit of information.

Data-element identifier
A one-character code used to identify a data element within a variable field.

Database
Any organized collection of data. Normally used of data in machine-readable form.

DBMS
Database Management System. Set of programs designed to maintain data held in a database and to facilitate access by different users for a variety of applications.

Delimiter
Character used as initiator, separator or terminator of data elements within fields.

Diacritical mark
A mark or sign used to distinguish different values or sounds of the same letter or character, e.g. ö ō.

Diagnostic
Computer printout for checking.

Directory
An index or table giving the location of fields in a machine-readable record. In ISO 2709 each directory contains a variable number of 'entries' each representing a field in the record and giving the tag, length and starting character position of the field.

Disc/disk
Flat, circular storage device, in which data are stored in tracks. 'Disc' is used for 'compact disc', the first application of which was in music recording; 'disk' is the normal term for magnetic disks used in computer systems.

Diskette
   A magnetic disk used in a microcomputer. Also called 'floppy
   disk' because of its flexible material.
DOBIS
   Dortmunder Bibliothekssystem or Dortmund Online Library
   System developed at Dortmund University Library. Offered
   by IBM as DOBIS/LIBIS (Dortmund and Leuven Library
   System).
Downloading
   Transferring data via telecommunications or direct line from
   a remote database, usually on a mainframe or large mini-
   computer, to a local computer.
Duplicate checking
   Activity carried out within a system intended to find multiple
   instances of records relating to the same bibliographic item.
EBCDIC
   Extended Binary Coded Decimal Interchange Code.
   Character set developed by IBM which has largely been
   superseded by character sets based on national and inter-
   national standards.
EMMA
   Extra-MARC Material. Used in the UK to mean records
   created in MARC format by agencies other than the British
   Library. BL now prefers the term 'External MARC record'.
End-user
   The person who will actually use the information retrieved,
   as opposed to any intermediary or professional who under-
   takes the searching on the end-user's behalf.
Entry
   Selected bibliographic data relating to a bibliographic item,
   listed or entered in a catalogue or bibliography under one
   possible access point or heading. The data are drawn from
   the master bibliographic record and more than one entry may
   be made for each item.
Escape sequences
   Series of characters in computer-readable form which signal
   that the following character(s) are to be regarded as belonging
   to a different character set.
Exchange format
   An arrangement of data according to predefined rules

(usually in machine-readable form) intended to facilitate the transfer of data between systems, and using tags or set positions in the record for the identification of data elements. Contrasted with 'Internal processing format'.

Field
A defined character string, identified by a tag or by position within the record. A field contains one or more subfields.

Field separator/terminator
Character used to mark the end of each variable field within a machine-readable record.

File
A collection of related records.

Fill character
Special character used to indicate that the record creator has chosen not to or is unable to supply information normally expected.

Fixed field
A field whose length is predetermined and remains constant between records.

Flag
Character, bit or other device in a record used to indicate a specified condition.

Floppy disk
See Diskette

Format
A predetermined and formalized order or arrangement of data. In machine systems comprises physical structure, content designation and data content.

Free-text
'Natural' language, i.e. words and phrases occurring in documents or freely selected by cataloguers and indexers, as opposed to 'controlled' language, i.e. terms chosen from subject headings lists or thesauri. Used with slightly different meanings in different contexts.

Hard copy
Eye-readable print; printed output from a computer.

Hardware
The electronic and physical components of a computer system.

Heading
A name, term or phrase situated at the head of an entry in a catalogue or bibliography. Used to provide access. Normally formulated according to agreed rules.

Holdings record
Record designed to carry details of items held in a particular collection.

Host item
Item containing component parts (q.v.), e.g. an issue of a journal containing separate articles, a book containing separate contributions.

ICSU/AB
International Council of Scientific Unions Abstracting Board.

IFLA
International Federation of Library Associations and Institutions.

IMNC
International MARC Network Committee (formerly IMNAC, International MARC Network Advisory Committee).

Indicators
Numeric or alphabetic characters associated with a field which supply information about the content of the field and/or about the relationship of the field with others in the record. Indicators can also be used to show how the field may be manipulated for catalogue production and other applications. In ISO 2709-based formats, indicators precede the data in the field.

Information codes
Coded data elements in a record giving information about certain aspects of the item represented which may or may not be found in data fields elsewhere in the record. The purpose of information codes is to provide easy and fast access to data useful for information retrieval.

INIS
International Nuclear Information System, of the International Atomic Energy Agency.

Interchange format
See Exchange format.

Internal processing format
  Format designed for use internally, within a particular system.
Inverted file
  An index to key parts of a database of bibliographic records providing fast access to record content. Called 'inverted' because the hidden, inner parts of the records are 'turned inside out' and come to the surface in the index.
ISBD
  International Standard Bibliographic Description.
ISBD(G)
  General International Standard Bibliographic Description.
ISBN
  International Standard Book Number.
ISDS
  International Serials Data System.
ISO
  International Organization for Standardization.
ISO 2709
  International standard: *Documentation: format for bibliographic information interchange on magnetic tape.*
ISSN
  International Standard Serial Number.
JANET
  Joint Academic Network.
LASER
  London and South Eastern Library Region.
LC
  Library of Congress.
LCIB
  Library of Congress information bulletin.
LCSH
  Library of Congress Subject Headings.
Leader
  See Record label.
Library cooperative
  Term favoured in the UK for large-scale cooperative organizations offering a range of automated library services based on resource-sharing. Described in North American usage as 'bibliographic utilities' or 'bibliographic service

networks'. Examples include OCLC, RLIN, WLN, UTLAS, BLCMP, SWALCAP.

Library housekeeping

Processes in a library related to all functions except information retrieval, e.g. issuing, reservations.

Linked Systems Project (LSP)

Project conducted by the Library of Congress and major US library cooperatives which uses Open Systems Interconnection standards in order to communicate information and exchange records.

Linking

Used to refer to techniques developed for showing relationships between bibliographic records, e.g. to link a record for a superseded serial with the record for its successor. Also applied to the linking of fields within the same record.

Local data

Data not normally intended for exchange purposes; may be local to one or a group of users.

Local format

See Internal processing format.

LOCAS

(British Library) Local Catalogue Service.

Machine-readable record

A record in a form readable by a computer (in certain contexts readable also by other machines).

Main entry

An entry in a catalogue or bibliography containing full details of an item. The main-entry heading is determined in accordance with appropriate rules and is normally the heading to be used for the uniform citation and identification of the item.

MARC

Machine-readable cataloguing.

MINISIS

Generalized information-management and retrieval system based on ISIS (Integrated Set of Information Systems).

Modem

'Modulator-demodulator'. Device for converting signals from a computer into a form suitable for conveyance over the telephone network.

Monograph

A non-serial publication. A book.

MUG

MARC Users' Group.

NAC

Network Advisory Committee (of the Library of Congress).

National bibliographic agency

The agency primarily responsible for creating records in the national exchange format and for producing the national bibliography. Usually the national library.

National MARC record

Record in the national MARC format produced by the national bibliographic agency.

Network

Any system of interconnecting individuals or organizations, whether computer-based or not. Normally qualified to indicate more precise character, e.g. Bibliographic network, intended for cooperative creation, exchange and use of bibliographic records; Local area network (LAN), computer network operating over a limited distance, often within one building or group of buildings (e.g. university campus).

NLA

National Library of Australia.

NLC

National Library of Canada.

OCLC

Online Computer Library Center, Inc.

OCLC Europe

Supplies OCLC systems and services throughout the UK, Ireland and continental Europe.

Online

Direct access to a computer, allowing immediate and inter-active processing of data.

OPAC

Online public-access catalogue. Library catalogue held in a computer and accessible via a terminal. Usable by members of the public with little or no instruction.

Open network

Network in which disparate systems are linked and interchange of data among participants is made possible by acceptance of common standards and procedures (protocols) for data transfer. *See also* OSI.

OSI

Open Systems Interconnection. A concept established by ISO with a Reference Model which forms the basis for the development of protocols to enable the linking of heterogeneous computer systems. Communication can take place regardless of the source or manufacturer of hardware and software components in each system.

Package

A piece of software or set of programs which, from the user's point of view, fulfils a number of related functions.

Postcoordinate/Precoordinate

Two contrasting indexing systems for treatment of compound subjects. In postcoordinate systems subject terms are assigned separately and combined at the time of searching; in precoordinate systems terms are combined at the time of indexing and presented to users as predetermined, 'ready-made' subject headings or statements.

Printout

Data produced directly from a computer printer.

Program

A set of instructions which when entered into a computer performs a function by manipulating data.

Protocol, Communications

Mutually agreed procedures for the communication of information between computer systems.

Record

In general, something recorded for future use. In machine systems, the full set of data concerning a particular item or entity in a database or computer system. *See also* Bibliographic record.

Record identifier

String of characters assigned by the agency creating the record, to act as unique identifier.

Record label

A fixed field at the beginning of an ISO 2709-based record which gives information needed for processing. Known as 'leader' in USMARC.

Record separator/terminator
Character used to mark the end of a record. Follows the field separator of the last field in the record. Also known as 'Record mark'.

Record structure
The arrangement of the fields of a record; often equated with 'format'.

Reference
A statement in a catalogue or bibliography directing the user from one heading or entry to another. References between headings may be used to direct users from rejected to preferred forms of heading (*See* references) or to alert users to other, related heading (*See also* references). Is also used to mean a bibliographic citation.

Retrospective conversion (RECON)
The conversion to machine-readable form of records which predate the automation of a library's catalogue. 'RECON' projects are usually undertaken at a later date, frequently with the assistance of files of machine-readable records for older material created by national libraries and other organizations.

RLG/RLIN
Research Libraries Group/Research Libraries Information Network.

Romanization
The conversion into the Roman alphabet (used in most modern European languages) of text in non-Roman scripts.

SCOLCAP
Scottish Libraries Cooperative Automation Project.

Secondary service
An organization providing abstracts of, and/or indexes to, publications, especially periodicals, conference proceedings, reports, etc.

Serial
A publication issued in successive parts, intended to continue for an indefinite period. Examples include periodicals, newspapers, annuals and monographic series. Normally carries some kind of numbering or chronological designation.

SISAC
Serials Industry Systems Advisory Committee.

Software
A computer program or collection of programs.

Space
An empty place between characters in printed or written material, which in computer systems must be held as a character of equivalent status to characters for letters, digits, etc. Also known as 'blank'.

Structure
See Record Structure.

Subfield
Part of a field requiring individual treatment; a separately identifiable part of a field.

Subfield identifier
Also called 'subfield code', 'subfield mark'. One or more characters preceding and identifying a subfield.

Subrecord
A group of fields within a record treated as a distinct entity. Often made for parts of items, e.g. analytical records.

SWALCAP
SWALCAP Library Services Ltd. (SLS). Formerly known as South West Academic Libraries Cooperative Automation Project.

Tag
A string of characters used to identify a field. Three-character tags are prescribed in ISO 2709.

Terminal
A device for sending input to and receiving output from a computer.

Tracings
A list (usually found on the main catalogue entry) of all the headings under which entries have been made for an item in a catalogue.

Transliteration
The conversion of one alphabetic script to another, the individual characters normally being converted on a one-to-one basis (cf. Romanization).

UAP
Universal Availability of Publications.

UBC
Universal Bibliographic Control.

307

UBCIM

Universal Bibliographic Control and International MARC Programme.

UDC

Universal Decimal Classification.

UKLDS

United Kingdom Library Database System.

UKMARC

The British national MARC format.

UN

United Nations.

Unesco

United Nations Educational, Scientific and Cultural Organization.

UNIBID

UNISIST International Centre for Bibliographic Descriptions.

Uniform title

Title by which a work with more than one title is to be consistently identified in a catalogue or bibliography.

UNIMARC

Universal MARC format.

UNISIST

Refers to Unesco's Intergovernmental Programme for Cooperation in Scientific and Technological Information.

Uploading

Transferring records, usually from a smaller to a larger computer.

USMARC

The three MARC communications formats which are the official national formats of the United States.

Utilities

See Library cooperative.

UTLAS

UTLAS International Canada (formerly University of Toronto Library Automation Systems).

Variable-length field

Field whose length (in terms of characters stored in the computer) varies to suit the data intended for that field; particularly appropriate for bibliographic records in which data elements vary from item to item.

VDU

Visual Display Unit, normally a computer terminal with TV-style screen for display of data.

Vernacular data

Data held in the language or dialect of a particular country or place.

WLN

Western Library Network, both cooperative and supplier of software to other organizations.

Appendix

Sample printouts supplied by courtesy of
The Library of Congress

```
Leader      _____cz___22_____n__4500
001 __   sh 85029534
005 __   19890317152956.7
008 __   860211¦¦_anannbab¦_____¦b_ana_¦¦¦__
040 __   $a DLC $c DLC $d DLC
053 __   $a QA76.755
150 _0   $a Computer software
360 __   $i subdivisions $a Software $i and $a Juvenile software
         $i under subjects for actual software items
450 _0   $a Software, Computer
550 _0   $a Computer software industry
550 _0   $a Computers
550 _0   $a Programming (Electronic computers)
680 __   $i Here are entered general works on computer programs
         along with documentation such as manuals, diagrams and
         operating instructions, etc. Works limited to computer
         programs are entered under $a Computer programs.
681 __   $i Note under $a Computer programs
```

THESAURUS RECORD FROM CDMARC SUBJECTS

```
    Computer software
        [QA76.755]
        Here are entered general works on computer programs along
    with documentation such as manuals, diagrams and operating
    instructions, etc. Works limited to computer programs are
    entered under Computer programs.
        SA subdivisions Software and Juvenile software under
            subjects for actual software items
        UF Software, Computer
        RT Computer software industry
           Computers
           Programming (Electronic computers)
        NT Computer programs
           Computer viruses
           Electronic data processing documentation
           Free computer software
           Integrated software
           Systems software
```

Search Browse Format Action Database Quit   CDMARC Subjects

```
┌─ Subject Terms ─────────────────────────────┐
│ ┌─ Computers ───────────────────────────┐   ┌──────────────────────────────┐
│ │  BT  Computer industry                │   │ Record(s) Selected :       1 │
│ │      Cybernetics                      │   │            Viewing :       1 │
│ │   ┌──────────────Thesaurus Image Format──────────────────────────────┐
│ │   │      Computer software                                            │
│ │   │          [QA76.755]                                               │
│ │   │          Here are entered general works on computer programs along│
│ │   │      with documentation such as manuals, diagrams and operating  │
│ │   │      instructions, etc. Works limited to computer programs are    │
│ │   │      entered under Computer programs.                             │
│ │   │          SA subdivisions Software and Juvenile software under     │
│ │   │              subjects for actual software items                   │
│ │   │          UF Software, Computer                                    │
│ └───┤          RT Computer software industry                           │
│     │             Computers                                            │
│     │             Programming (Electronic computers)                  │
│     └──────────────────────────────────────────────────────────────┘
```

ESC ->Back F1 ->Help F4 ->Save F5 ->Print F6 ->Format Toggle
Top of Record

```
Leader    *****nz___22*****n__4500
001       n  78087607
005       19840322000000.0
008       781129n¦_acannaab¦_____¦a_aaa_¦¦¦__
040   __  $a DLC $c DLC
100   10  $a Dickens, Charles, $d 1812-1870.
400   10  $a Boz, $d 1812-1870
400   10  $a Dickens, Karol, $d 1812-1870
400   10  $a Dikens, Charlz, $d 1812-1870
400   10  $a Dikkens, Charl'z, $d 1812-1870
400   10  $a Sparks, Timothy, $d 1812-1870
400   10  $a Ti-keng-ssu, $d 1812-1870
670   __  $a His Kuai jou yu sheng chi, 1978: $b t.p.
          (Ti-keng-ssu) p. 2 (Charles Huffham Dickens)
```

BRIEF CARD IMAGE FROM CDMARC NAMES

```
Dickens, Charles, 1812-1870.
        Found:
        His Kuai jou yu sheng chi, 1978: t.p. (Ti-keng-ssu) p.
2 (Charles Huffham Dickens)

Boz, 1812-1870
Dickens, Karol, 1812-1870
Dikens, Charlz, 1812-1870
Dikkens, Charl'z, 1812-1870
Sparks, Timothy, 1812-1870
Ti-keng-ssu, 1812-1870

AACR 2  EVAL
Entrd.: DLC 781129                        n 78-87607
840322
```

THESAURUS IMAGE FROM CDMARC NAMES

```
        Dickens, Charles, 1812-1870.
           UF Boz, 1812-1870
              Dickens, Karol, 1812-1870
              Dikens, Charlz, 1812-1870
              Dikkens, Charl'z, 1812-1870
              Sparks, Timothy, 1812-1870
              Ti-keng-ssu, 1812-1870
```

Search Browse Format Action Database Quit   CDMARC Names

```
┌ Name Headings ─────────────────
│  *Dickens, Bernard Morris              ┌─────────────────────────────
│   Dickens, Brian.                      │ Record(s) Selected :      1
│  *Dickens, Carolus, 1719-1793          │        Viewing :          1
│               ┌───────────Tagged Record Format─────────────────
│     Leader    *****nz___22*****n__4500
│     001       n  78087607
│     005       19840322000000.0
│     008       781129n¦_acannaab¦_____¦a_aaa_¦¦¦__
│     040   __  $a DLC $c DLC
│     100   10  $a Dickens, Charles, $d 1812-1870.
│     400   10  $a Boz, $d 1812-1870
└──  400   10  $a Dickens, Karol, $d 1812-1870
      400   10  $a Dikens, Charlz, $d 1812-1870
      400   10  $a Dikkens, Charl'z, $d 1812-1870
      400   10  $a Sparks, Timothy, $d 1812-1870
      400   10  $a Ti-keng-ssu, $d 1812-1870                       |
```

ESC ->Back F1 ->Help F4 ->Save F5 ->Print F6 ->Format Toggle

312

```
Leader    *****cam__22*****_a_4500
001          82006436 /AC/r852
008          820412r19821864ohu_____s00011_eng__
020    __   $a 0821406310
050    0_   $a PR4883.L4 $b C5 1982
082    0_   $a 823/.8 $a Fic $2 19
100    10   $a Leith, Disney, $c Mrs.
245    14   $a The children of the chapel / $c Mary Gordon and
             Algernon Charles Swinburne ; edited, with an introduction
             by Robert E. Lougy.
260    0_   $a Athens : $b Ohio University Press, $c [1982]
300    __   $a xlix, 185 p. ; $c 22 cm.
500    __   $a Originally published: 1864.
520    __   $a In the year 1559, ten-year-old Arthur Savile is
             impressed into the service of the Chapel Royal, where he
             is brutally mistreated but learns to survive by means of
             his wit and ingenuity.
610    20   $a England and Wales. $b Chapel Royal $x Fiction.
651    _0   $a Great Britain $x History $y Elizabeth, 1558-1603 $x
             Fiction.
651    _1   $a Great Britain $x History $y Elizabeth, 1558-1603 $x
             Fiction.
700    10   $a Swinburne, Algernon Charles, $d 1837-1909.
700    10   $a Lougy, Robert E.
```

CARD IMAGE FROM CDMARC BIBLIOGRAPHIC
(will change after prototype)

PR4883.L4 C5 1982

    Leith, Disney, Mrs.
      The children of the chapel / Mary Gordon and Algernon
Charles Swinburne ; edited, with an introduction by Robert
E. Lougy. -- Athens : Ohio University Press, [1982]
      xlix, 185 p. ; 22 cm.

      Originally published: 1864.
      In the year 1559, ten-year-old Arthur Savile is
impressed into the service of the Chapel Royal, where he is
brutally mistreated but learns to survive by means of his
wit and ingenuity.

      ISBN 0821406310

      1. England and Wales. Chapel Royal--Fiction.   2. Great
Britain--History--Elizabeth, 1558-1603--Fiction.   3. Great
Britain--History--Elizabeth, 1558-1603--Fiction.   I.
Swinburne, Algernon Charles, 1837-1909.   II. Lougy, Robert
E.   III. Title.

Control number: 82-6436 /AC/r852

```
          LC CALL NO.:  PR4883.L4 C5 1982
     FORM OF MATERIAL:  Book
                 LCCN:  82-6436 /AC/r852
                TITLE:  The children of the chapel /
            PUBLISHED:  Athens : Ohio University Press, [1982]
          DESCRIPTION:  xlix, 185 p. ; 22 cm.
                NAMES:  Leith, Disney, Mrs. (MAIN ENTRY)
                        Swinburne, Algernon Charles, 1837-1909. (ADDED
                          ENTRY)
                        Lougy, Robert E. (ADDED ENTRY)
              SUBJECT:  England and Wales. Chapel Royal--Fiction.
                        Great Britain--History--Elizabeth,
                          1558-1603--Fiction.
                        Great Britain--History--Elizabeth,
                          1558-1603--Fiction.
          STANDARD NO:  ISBN: 0821406310
      DEWEY CLASS NO.:  823/.8 Fic  ED: 19
                NOTES:  Originally published: 1864.
                        SUMMARY: In the year 1559, ten-year-old Arthur
                          Savile is impressed into the service of the
                          Chapel Royal, where he is brutally mistreated
                          but learns to survive by means of his wit and
                          ingenuity.
```

PROCESSING INFORMATION

```
          RECORD STATUS:  Changed Record
         TYPE OF RECORD:  Language material
              BIB LEVEL:  Monograph/item
              ENC LEVEL:  Full level
         DESC CAT FORM:  AACR 2
           DATE ENTERED:  820412
      CATALOGING SOURCE:  Library of Congress
        MODIFIED RECORD:  Not modified
```

```
Search  Browse  Format  Action  Database  Quit            CDMARC Bib
┌─ Subject Heading──────────────────────────────────────────────┐
│┌─ Search Results────                                           │
││  bk   1982  Leith, Disney,  The children of ┌──────────────────────────┐
││                                             │ Record(s) Selected :   1 │
││                                             │        Viewing :       1 │
││                                             └──────────────────────────┘
│┌───────────────────Tagged Record Format──────────────────────┐
│ Leader   *****cam__22*****_a_4500                              │
│ 001       82006436 /AC/r852                                   │
│ 008       820412r19821864ohu_____s00011_eng__            │
│ 020    _  $a 0821406310                                       │
│ 050   0_  $a PR4883.L4 $b C5 1982                             │
│ 082   0_  $a 823/.8 $a Fic $2 19                              │
│ 100  10   $a Leith, Disney, $c Mrs.                           │
│ 245  14   $a The children of the chapel / $c Mary Gordon and  │
│           Algernon Charles Swinburne ; edited, with an introduction │
│           by Robert E. Lougy.                                 │
│ 260   0_  $a Athens : $b Ohio University Press, $c [1982]     │
│ 300    _  $a xlix, 185 p. ; $c 22 cm.                         │
└───────────────────────────────────────────────────────────────┘
```

ESC ->Back F1 ->Help F4 ->Save F5 ->Print F6 ->Format Toggle

```
  cs = 3 and cs = 4
  mp    1776                    An Accurate map of the present seat of war b
  vm m 1913                     Anne de Boleyn = Anne Boleyn / Eclipse ; dir
  bk    1972  Bradshaw, Kenn    Parliament & Congress [by] Kenneth Bradshaw
  bk    1972  Bradshaw, Kenn    Parliament & Congress [by] Kenneth Bradshaw
  bk    1981  Bradshaw, Kenn    Parliament and Congress / Kenneth Bradshaw &
  vm m 1919                     British Canadian Pathe News. No. 83A / Briti
  bk    1972  Building Resea    Proceedings.
  bk    1987  Cain, Bruce E.    The personal vote : constituency service and
  bk    1945  Ceylon Indian     Memorandum of the Ceylon Indian Congress to
  bk    1985                    Change in the Amazon basin / edited by John
  bk    ¦¦¦¦  Chaput, Rollan    Disarmament in British foreign policy, by Ro
```

ENTER ->Sel   Del ->Del   F2 ->Start Again   ESC ->Back
F1 ->Help   F10 ->View Record

Index

Italicized page references imply substantial or important explanatory material. References are made to the glossary only when substantial information is contained there. No reference is made to the glossary for spelled out acronyms.

Level, Bibliographic *see* Bibliographic level
LIBERTAS 27
Libraries
bibliographic records for 29–30
use of MARC 266–8
Library Association (UK) 250
Library cooperative *glossary*
bibliographic records for 27–8
commitment to MARC 82
ownership of records 174, 231–2
UK 265–6
UKLDS 250–2
see also National MARC networks; Networks
Library of Congress 65, 75, 94, 100, 177, 179, 228, 247, 257, 275, 280
Card Number 78, 92
early history of MARC 75–82
MARC Distribution Service 82–3, 95
MARC Office 180, 247
see also LC Classification; LCSH; MARC II format
Licence to copy records 237
Linford, John 113
Linked Systems Project (LSP) 94–5, 101, 176, 241, 247–9, *glossary*
Linking techniques 59–60, *glossary*
UKMARC 145
UNIMARC 186
USMARC 156–8
USMARC holdings 161
Local data 144, 217, 268–9, *glossary*
Local format *see* Internal processing formats
Local government reorganization 266
LOCAS 65, *glossary*
see also BLAISE
Locations record *see* Holdings and locations record

London, University of 96
London Borough of Camden 266

MAB1 109, 180
Machine-readable data file *see* File
MADOK 109
Magnetic tape 45, 50, 62, 289
Mahidol University 118
MAHIDOLMARC 118
Main entry 10, 13, 194, *glossary*
Malaysia 118, 236, 257
see also Universiti Sains Malaysia
MALMARC 118
MARBI 83, 99–100, 102–3
MARC xv, 27–8, 54, 57, 61, 65, 67, 68–9, 70–119
criticisms of 106–7
different usages of the term 71–3
relationship with ISO 2709 52, 70–2
see also specific MARC formats, e.g. UKMARC, MALMARC
MARC I format 76
MARC II 56, 58, *76–82*, 85–6, 114, 167–8, 223, 273, 279
acceptance as international standard 91
MARC-compatibility 283–6
MARC Formats for Bibliographic Data (MFBD) 98
MARC-like formats 74
MARC Pilot Project 75–6
MARC Users' Group (MUG) 105, 254–5
13th Annual Seminar 290
MARCAL 114
MARCIVE 277
Massil, Stephen 117
Master bibliographic record 29
MEDLARS 253
MEDLINE 269
MEKOF 114, 210
MERLIN 113, 269
MERMARC 113, 269
Mexico 115, 275

Microcomputer 66, 108, 183–4, 216, 270–1, 275–7
Minimum exchange records standard 246, 291
Minimum specifications 29, 256
MINISIS 22, 55, 67, 116, 204, 274–5, 282, *glossary*
MITINET/MARC 277–8
Mnemonic tag 55
MONOCLE 108
MOSTEMARC 118
MS/DOS *see* IBM microcomputers
Multilevel description 18, 103, 114, 145
Multilingual records 108–10
Multiple access catalogues 23
Multipart items 145

NACO 84, 102, 247–8
NAL *see* National Agricultural Library (US)
Name access point *see* Access point
Name Authority Cooperative *see* NACO
Names, recording of 158
National Agricultural Library (US) 102, 247
National bibliographic agency xii, 24, 227–30, 291, glossary
National bibliographic records, production and content 24
National bibliography 227–8
National Coordinated Cataloging Operations *see* NACO
National Information System for Science and Technology (India) 117
National level bibliographic record 85, 246
National libraries xii, 47
National Library of . . . *see* under the name of the country for national libraries
National Library of Medicine (US) 90, 102, 247, 253, 269
National MARC networks 229–30 and bibliographic control 226–8

machine formats for 239
National MARC records *glossary*
comprehensiveness 243–5
international distribution agreements 232, 235–7
National MARC services 119
National Science Foundation (US) 203
Nationalism 111
NATIS 168
Network 93, 176, 226–57, *glossary*
see also Open Systems Interconnection
Network Advisory Committee (NAC) 247
New Zealand 257
NFAIS 203, *glossary*
Non-book materials 91, 95, 100, 103, 145, 153, 170, 174, 231, 246, 291
see also Audiovisual materials
Non-Roman scripts 19, 22, 65, 158
Norway 110
Notes field 157

OCLC
bibliographic records 27–8
copyright of database 232
input standards 247
LSP, involvement in 247–8
use of records in Europe 96–7, 111, 254
OECD Development Centre 216
Office for Scientific and Technical Information (OSTI) 76, 202, 266
Office of Arts and Libraries (UK) 252
Okapi 245
Online information retrieval systems, bibliographic records for 30–1
Online public access catalogue *see* OPAC
Online systems, use of MARC 269–72

325

Visual materials format,
   USMARC   100

Wales, National Library of   254
Weisbrod, David   85
WLN   95, 247, 256, *glossary*
Woolston, John   274

Work *vs* book   4–5
Worksheets   59
World Information System for
   the Sciences   168, 201

Yugoslavia   111, 181, 280